THE QUIET REVOLUTIONARIES

THE QUIET
REVOLUTIONARIES

Seeking Justice in Guatemala

FRANK M. AFFLITTO
AND PAUL JESILOW

UNIVERSITY OF TEXAS PRESS, AUSTIN

COPYRIGHT © 2007 BY THE UNIVERSITY OF TEXAS PRESS

All rights reserved

Printed in the United States of America

First edition, 2007

Requests for permission to reproduce material from this work should be sent to: Permissions, University of Texas Press, P.O. Box 7819, Austin, TX 78713-7819.
www.utexas.edu/utpress/about/bpermission.html

⊗ The paper used in this book meets the minimum requirements of ANSI/NISO Z39.48-1992 (R1997) (Permanence of Paper).

LIBRARY OF CONGRESS CATALOGING-IN-PUBLICATION DATA

Afflitto, Frank M., 1960–
  The quiet revolutionaries : seeking justice in Guatemala / Frank M. Afflitto and Paul Jesilow.
    p.   cm.
  Includes bibliographical references and index.
  ISBN 978-0-292-71676-6 (cloth : alk. paper) — ISBN 978-0-292-71677-3 (pbk. : alk. paper)
    1. Disappeared persons—Guatemala.   2. State-sponsored terrorism—Guatemala.   3. Disappeared persons' families—Guatemala.   4. Disappeared persons' families—Guatemala—Political activity.   5. Human rights movements—Guatemala.   6. Guatemala—History—Civil War, 1960–1996.
I. Jesilow, Paul, 1950–   . II. Title.
  HV6322.3.G9A34   2007
  972.8105'3—dc22

                                              2007012436

For our families, and in particular, Frank's beloved children—
Khalil, who is the Angel of his life, and Jamileh, who will always
be his "One Love." And . . .

to the woman under the tree in that town; to the woman who
slaughtered the rooster for Frank; to the woman who provided
him with enough blankets while he slept in that cold mountain
home; to all the children who touched his life during fieldwork,
and, hopefully, he theirs; to the man who said they were "not
dogs"; to the frail woman, stronger than we, who traveled many
bus routes and wanted her son's bones; to the woman who sobbed
uncontrollably in Frank's arms; to the young woman and her
boyfriend in front of whom Frank sobbed uncontrollably; to the
campesino *who shared a beer with Frank as they tried to discuss*
some hopeful topics while teaching him how to tell the ficheras
"no thank you" without offending them; to she who watched up
the road for the two; to her with the little notebook; to the grand-
mother; to the elderly woman who danced the son *with Frank that*
Christmas; and to so many others—none of you know how deeply
we carry you all inside of us each day, even a decade and a half
later.

CONTENTS

ACKNOWLEDGMENTS

The most important person or persons to whom we owe a profound debt of gratitude in this endeavor have been the many Guatemalans who, often at great risk and always through great effort, cared for Frank, guided him, poured their wounded hearts out to him, and shared with him their hopes for a better world.

Many individuals in academia have greatly contributed to our understanding of the processes we describe in this book. Kitty Calavita spent untold hours reading, commenting, and providing direction. We have benefited from her profound professional and human concern for the world's women. John Dombrink and Norma Stoltz Chinchilla provided lasting and formative impacts on this work. Leo R. Chávez provided Frank with compassionate mentoring and uniquely wise guidance during graduate school. Thomas J. Crawford and Roxane C. Silver provided invaluable initial methodological and conceptual guidance during Frank's first years at the University of California, Irvine, later augmented by the help of Richard McCleary. Myrdene Anderson and Jeffrey A. Sluka provided their communication, guidance, mentoring, and instruction over the years, as well as the patient stances they have held, which are models to be emulated. Valerie Jenness, as always, was responsible for helping us get things right by pointing out what we had missed. We thank Alison Brysk for help and thoughts; at many points, we stand on her shoulders. We thank Julianne Ohlander for her immense patience and Dianne Christianson, Patty Edwards, and Areum Kim for their production help.

We are indebted to Francisca González and Bertha López, research assistants and coders in the early stages of data conceptualization and categorization, for their hard work, insight, and genuine, heartfelt concern for the sufferings of oppressed peoples. Frank is particularly appreciative of Bertha's daughter Rubi, who must now be reaching adulthood. He is grateful for every ray of sunshine her young presence in his life brought him, and we wish her multitudinous blessings and good health.

Organizations that provided financial and/or professional recognition include the Society for the Psychological Study of Social Issues (SPSSI), the School of Social Ecology at the University of California, Irvine, and its Department of Criminology, Law, and Society, the University of Memphis, the Association for Criminal Justice Research (California), and the Pacific Coast Council on Latin American Studies, along with grassroots Guatemalan support organizations in the United States.

We are thankful to the anonymous reviewers of this book while in manuscript form, as well as those of previously published or submitted peer-reviewed articles and book chapters, who have provided insights that we had overlooked. And we appreciate the help of Theresa May and the staff at the University of Texas Press.

Finally, we are very grateful to all the anonymous Latin Americans who have contributed to and influenced this book, among them those in the Salvadoran and Guatemalan communities of Southern California who at great pains assisted Frank in pilot testing and gaining contacts and, of course, the hundreds of Guatemalans in that nation and their mass organizations, all of whom shall remain anonymous.

THE QUIET REVOLUTIONARIES

Introduction

Regional, national, and international armed conflicts and more localized episodes of civil unrest have been common features of life for millions of people during the past decade. Despite the much-acclaimed end of the Cold War, ongoing military occupations, violent interethnic conflicts, and desperate living conditions are seemingly more common features of international reality than are lasting features of peace. Violence and social protest have continued in countries that have achieved increased democratic control, such as Indonesia, Rwanda, the Palestinian Authority, the Democratic Republic of Congo, and Iraq. In all of these areas, issues of justice play some role in stimulating the violence.

In this book we focus on Guatemalans, who have suffered violence and intimidation as a result of civil unrest in their country. We examine their perceptions of justice and its counterpart, injustice, and how those impressions came to be formed through their experiences with state-sanctioned terrorism. We do not center our attention on the perpetrators of the violence or the atrocities they committed or on the people they slaughtered. Rather, we focus on intimates of those who were murdered or "disappeared," that is, kidnapped, never to return; we focus on these survivors, whom we call "the quiet revolutionaries." They would probably not agree with their characterization as revolutionaries, primarily because they associate the term with their country's former armed Marxist rebels. Few of these individuals were radical before their loved ones disappeared. The actions they told us about, from their perspectives, were simply efforts to obtain justice with respect to their husbands, children, or other blood ties. But in seeking justice, many of them went through a transformation from indigent, powerless victims who turned to God for justice to radical workers who sought justice in the name of the disappeared. In this role, they were important tools in the efforts to change the actions of the Guatemalan government because it was through them that the image and memory of the disappeared were invoked as a rallying point for demonstrations. It was they who caused the world to turn its attention to Guatemala. This is true whether we are talking about our anonymous informants, whose stories appear here, or Nobel Peace laureate Rigoberta Menchú, who wrote about the slaughter of Mayan Indians at the hands of state-controlled forces,[1] or American lawyer Jennifer Harbury,[2] who staged a one-person hunger strike outside the White House after her husband, a guerrilla commander in Guatemala, was murdered.[3]

If asked, the survivors would probably deny that they were revolutionaries. They did not attempt to bring down the government. Rather, they demonstrated against state-sanctioned terrorism and the impunity granted its perpetrators. But their stories are what caught the interest of the world audience as they told tales of the disappeared and murdered. In that regard, the acts of the death squads and other paramilitary groups served as an impetus for bringing together many Guatemalans, blurring ethnic, geographic, and even class lines to form a popular movement;[4] it was these acts of violence against the quiet revolutionaries' loved ones that drove individuals toward political action and the creation of a social movement to end impunity. We call these survivors "the quiet revolutionaries" because their goal required a revolutionary transformation of Guatemalan society—from one based on fragmentation and discrimination to a pluralistic one based on shared values.

The perceptions our respondents held about justice in Guatemala were largely shaped by a thirty-six-year civil war that ended in 1996 and that, according to Guatemala's Supreme Court, conservatively left more than 100,000 civilians dead, 35,000 widows, and 200,000 orphans and destroyed more than 440 villages.[5] Most of those killed during the latter half of the war, the period represented by our data, were in many cases poor farmers or agriculturalists slaughtered because the army blurred their rural identity with guerrilla membership. In many areas of the country, from the military's perspective, a farmer was a guerrilla or at least so likely to be a guerrilla that he or she might as well be killed. In the countryside, the army almost randomly slaughtered people, figuring that killing enough agriculturalists—most of them Mayan Indians—would terrorize people to dissuade them from supporting guerrillas and would get rid of a few guerrilla sympathizers who might be mixed in with the pool of victims. Just the fact that one was poor was often enough to make one targetable in the counter-insurgency-terror logic practiced in many areas of Guatemala.

Most of those killed by the army and its agents during the civil war were not rebels. The survivors of the state violence whose stories we report here deny that their missing loved ones were guerrilla fighters. They may have been unaware of their relatives' political and social involvement. But it is more likely that their family members had not been rebels. They were simply disappeared or slaughtered because someone, through envy or whatever motive, pointed them out as "guerrillas" or because guerrillas operated nearby and the Mayan farmers, being the poorest, most deprived sector of the national population, were most likely to be the social base of the revolutionaries; thus they were the most likely candidates for armed struggle due to their very poverty and necessity.

Guatemala has a history of oppression toward its Mayan population and a lack of democratic ideals. Indigenous peoples throughout much of the world have long been oppressed by European invaders. In Guatemala the Spanish invasion undermined the indigenous population's way of life and eventually led to the devastation of the people and their cultures. During the twentieth century, economic development encroached on previously isolated Indian areas.[6] Conflict over democracy and social development cultivated guerrilla movements, the members of which found Indian lands to be ideal sanctuaries from which to prepare their assaults. Drug traffickers also found the isolated lands favorable for their activities. On the other side were official and paramilitary armed forces that hunted the guerrillas and drug traffickers in the jungles and highlands and that routinely murdered and otherwise brutalized innocent Maya.[7] In Chapter One we describe this history to establish a context for understanding the state-supported violence to which the survivors were responding. We are interested in giving the reader a general knowledge of the country's history and some themes that we will discuss as the book progresses.

This research required not only traditional academic strategies and study but additionally perseverance, investigatory stealth, and ongoing deprivation of Western middle-class comforts. It often required Frank Afflitto, who did all of the Guatemalan interviews, to place himself in physical danger, to "walk" alongside informants in their daily lives, withstanding common violent occurrences and surveillance as well as the heat, cold, and hunger associated with everyday living among rural Guatemalans. In many ways the data collection more closely resembled an adventure tale than it did traditional academic undertakings, including smuggling the data out of the country. Chapter Two describes the hardships Frank endured and the strategies he used while he conducted eighty lengthy interviews in two separate field trips during 1990 and 1992. He returned to Guatemala during parts of 1993, 1995, 1996, and 1999 to conduct additional interviews and gain other information.

The Guatemalans interviewed for this book experienced much more emotional and physical pain than you or we would care to endure. Some of them as well as their family members were raped, held against their will, and tortured, and they endured knowing that loved ones were disappeared and murdered. One of the military state's goals was to intimidate them and other Guatemalans into submission, to render them too frightened to act against the terrorist apparatus.

The violence certainly created silence among segments of the population. The immunity afforded death squad members by criminal justice system agents was probably, in large part, an intended outcome of the violence. But the tactics used by the state-sanctioned terrorists had unintended effects. Most notably, they were the impetus for bringing together Guatemalans who demanded an end to impunity and the implementation of justice.

From initial chance encounters at morgues, police stations, and army barracks, as they searched for the missing or while trying to establish responsibility for the murders of those found dead, there grew a common sense of purpose among a diverse group of people. They included, to name but a few, a *ladino* plantation worker from Escuintla;[8] a *ladina* lower-middle-class housewife from the capital city; a preliterate, predominantly monolingual, rural Kaqchikel Indian woman; an urban *ladino* trade unionist; and a K'iché Mayan university instructor. As the survivors sought information about their missing loved ones, they formed organizations designed to address their concerns and the concerns of constituencies that had survived similar atrocities.

The development of these communities of resistance countered the intended disruptive effects of state-sanctioned terrorism and was a first step toward building a pluralist society. The fundamental, unifying belief of these communities was that impartial law did not exist in Guatemala. From their perspective, law and justice in their country were not blind but rather served the interests of a powerful elite. Individual activities of everyday citizens were subordinate to the narrow concerns of a ruling clique. Individual freedom, prized and necessary in democratic societies, was absent from the world of individuals interviewed for this book. The law could be used in a discriminatory fashion to justify a wide variety of limitations on individual freedom. The labeling of anti-state activity as "terrorism" or "subversion," for example, allowed state-sanctioned forces to use violence against peaceful citizens.

Communities of survivors of the counterinsurgent civil war and death-squad terror arose in response to the violent repression and the cloak of impunity that shrouded the perpetrators. The communities were made up of a variety of organizations.[9] But it is the members of these groups and not the groups themselves that are the subject of this book. We do not dwell on the particulars of the varying organizations. Our interest is in the mechanisms that led people to participate, the link between individual motivation and eventual social action.

Our focus in this book is on the empirical story of how the quiet revolutionaries experienced, managed, and responded to the fact that those closest to them were murdered or disappeared. There is also an analytic story to recount, which most importantly involves linkages among the psychological mechanisms the quiet revolutionaries implemented to deal with ongoing ambiguous situations; the formation, evolution, and manifestation of a broadly defined social movement; and the development of a collective identity. All of these elements emerge in the book, but we note them here to make clear our intention to tie together these matters.

We begin both the empirical and analytic telling of the quiet revolutionaries' accounts with the psychological mechanisms they employed to deal with their losses. It is, in many ways, the ambiguous nature of disappearances that started the quiet revolutionaries on their journeys to activism. They were unsure whether their loved ones were alive or dead, and this created a psychological quandary for them. The chronic ambiguity may even have been worse than the initial loss. They desperately sought in vain to alleviate their anxiety. In Chapter Three we argue that their search for their disappeared loved ones and their eventual pursuit of justice for the murdered and disappeared, including their participation in the popular movement, were means to alleviate their daily pain and that these steps were consistent with their culture.

In Chapter Four we are specifically interested in the formation of the quiet revolutionaries' perceptions of justice and how these judgments pushed them toward activism. Generally, perceptions of justice occupy a central role in our social and psychological life from early on. We probably all remember incidents from our childhood that we perceived as unjust. "That's not fair" seems to be a common complaint of children. While we may view much of what happens to us as inequitable, life must somehow deliver a measure of justice. We depend upon, or expect, certain levels of fairness for our own mental well-being. In general, we expect people to behave in a certain fashion, and when they do not, it threatens the most intimate areas of our psychosocial selves.[10]

During our lives, each of us develops a mental system of justice through which we view the world.[11] This view may be altered from time to time, depending on circumstances. Illustrative is the change in political parties that people make as they move up or down the economic ladder. What was correct and just when they were poor, for example, seems unfair now that they have money.

Justice is not a concrete ideology. Perceptions of justice may differ from one culture to another and between individuals within any society. We see this in many of the earliest known written works, both secular and religious. It can be argued, for example, that in the story of Jesus' crucifixion, his execution came about as the result of the Roman Empire's state terror apparatus exercising its authority over what it perceived as a political threat in its occupied territories. According to accounts, Jesus was accused of and tried for crimes against the state and executed alongside common criminals. The public exhibition and mutilation of the bodies were prominent components of the sentencing. From the Roman view, Jesus' execution was just punishment for his behavior. Later interpretations obviously differ from the Roman view.

Our own perceptions of justice probably affect us each day more than we realize. In some fashion, we use them to determine for us a vast array of conceptual items: whether our acts and those of others should be categorized as impartial and rational, the nature and limits of our rights and those of others, the duties we owe to others and others owe to us, and the benefits and entitlements we expect from society for ourselves and others, to name a few.[12] Our perceptions of justice act as a filter through which we view the world. Courage, for example, is a virtue, but not when we perceive its practitioners as using it to support injustice.[13]

In Guatemala, perceptions of justice were largely affected by state-sanctioned terrorism. The victims of the violence were primarily innocents; most were guilty of simply living in an area the army categorized as being under guerrilla control. Few of the thousands who were killed were actually rebels. They had committed no crimes under Guatemalan law. Their executions were carried out without a legal mandate. Rather, they were extrajudicially executed by government-associated forces. Moreover, prior to the signing of the 1996 peace accords, the sponsors of the violence and its perpetrators were almost never brought before a court. State agents explained the horrific deeds as the actions of common criminals, but with a handful of rare exceptions for generally high-profile assassinations such as that of anthropologist Myrna Mack Chang, no one was arrested for or charged with the crimes.

The quiet revolutionaries felt they had a right to know the whereabouts of missing loved ones and to know the identities of those who had exercised the violence. Furthermore, they wanted, as one of their number noted, "trials and castigation for the assassins of the people." They felt that they were right in pursuing legal accountability for the sequesters. Their missing loved ones had been denied, from their perspective, the protection of the law, as extralegal assassinations and disappearances bypassed legal procedures. Justice could be resurrected if those same legal procedures were put to use to uncover and punish the guilty. It was important to the quiet revolutionaries to use the legal system, as opposed to vigilante activities or armed rebellion. The use of legal procedures would have allowed the written law to operate in its intended fashion and defeat impunity. The survivors' experiences with state authorities, however, only increased their sense of injustice. Their pursuits became aborted attempts, so prolonged that the legal system eventually was seen by them as anything but a tool for achieving their goals. Their pursuits were met by a string of injustices that impeded them in their searches. They argued that procedural justice did not exist in Guatemala and that the justice system was ineffective. For them, the executions and disappearances kindled a desire for legal justice, a small flame that was fanned into a blaze by the further injuries they faced as they sought information about loved ones.

Justice, for the surviving family members of the disappeared, would entail finding their relatives (or their bodies) and empowering civilian legal institutions over armed security forces. Such goals, however, were beyond the efforts of individuals and required a social movement, which we describe in Chapter Five. The quiet revolutionaries came to identify themselves as Guatemalans, due in part to their membership in the heterogeneous social movement. They saw that their interests were the same as other members of the group and in fact the same as the majority of Guatemalans. Their activities as members of the social movement and the state security forces' efforts to repress them strengthened this identity and allowed the quiet revolutionaries to claim the moral high ground. They were not armed revolutionaries. Nor were they enemies of the people. They were Guatemalans acting for the national community. Their nationalism was used to legitimate their actions for themselves and their supporters. It was an ideology that helped mobilize political action against the ruling elites and increased the solidarity of the group.

The strength of the communities to which our informants belonged lay in the empowerment of the disenfranchised through socially acceptable resistance. Such empowerment took the form of more democratic, grass-roots participation in political mobilization, something that had been lacking during Guatemala's military-dominated political history. The political participation involved societal sectors that had traditionally been peripheral in governing Guatemala: rural Maya, women, urban poor, youth, the uneducated, and orphans. Many of these members, who came from once differing social spheres, found themselves in the similar situation of belonging to groups whose members had experienced terrorizing counterinsurgency repression and the impunity of death-squad institutions. During demonstrations, they demanded to know the whereabouts of their disappeared loved ones and other missing community members and for official recognition of the state's role in the formation and propagation of the death-squad apparatus. Their actions and the terrorist apparatus' responses to them solidified the ties they had to each other.

The emergence of communities of resistance defied the intended disruptive effects of state-sanctioned terrorism through unification. An essential aspect of the emergent communities' importance rests on such unification as a step toward nation building. As these disparate individuals came together and saw each other as survivors of the same suffering by the same hand, they formed communities. When they looked past their sufferings to a positive, altered vision of society, they became Guatemalans and participants in nation building. They were no longer simply women or students or union members or Maya. They now had a broader, emotional connection to a collective identity as Guatemalan. They donned the identity that the army and oligopoly had denied them. They created a pluralist national unity based on the common experiences of broad sectors of Guatemalan society as a community of survivors of state-sanctioned violence that symbolically and organizationally undermined the goal of the state terror apparatus and created an opportunity for change.[14]

During the same period as the social movement expanded, major players in the Guatemalan civil war were discussing an end to the hostilities. The quiet revolutionaries likewise desired peace, but it was not their first goal. Ending impunity and establishing justice for the disappeared and murdered were their aims. To achieve their aspirations, they wanted the police and judiciary to be free to act in the equal interest of all Guatemalans and not merely in favor of the political oligopoly and army. They opposed efforts that undermined accountability for murder and torture. At the moment, it was unlikely that anyone in the movement would have foreseen that the peace accord discussions would result in undermining the movement to end impunity. But that is exactly what occurred. During this period, to counter the system of impunity and judicial ineffectiveness, the resistance community created a quasilegal system that involved gathering evidence of the existence and violence of death squads and security forces. Testimonies, such as the 6,000 compiled during a Catholic Church project, gave community members the opportunity to pass judgment on state-sanctioned authorities as being those guilty of the vast majority of the horrific deeds. In doing this, the community performed duties that the Guatemalan criminal justice system had traditionally been too cowardly and corrupt to perform. Survivor-based justice claims in Guatemala contributed to the establishment of an alternative, popular justice system, counterpoised to the reign of armed impunity.

However, continued impunity had dark consequences in post–civil war Guatemala. Most notable at the time was the murder of Guatemalan Bishop Juan José Gerardi, who had been the driving force behind the Church report. And although his murderers were eventually tried and convicted, the outcome was likely associated with idiosyncratic matters such as the international visibility of the case. Lacking such scrutiny, as was the situation for trials involving less celebrated victims, the Guatemalan judicial system remained impotent.

At the turn of the twenty-first century, the Guatemalan criminal justice system lacked the ability and motivation to do much about crime. The system during the civil war was emasculated by the military in order to maintain impunity. The legal institutions were unable to reestablish themselves as effective units after the war ended. A partial result was rapidly escalating crime rates. Vigilante justice became somewhat commonplace in Guatemala as a result of the pervasive view that legal officials would do nothing about criminal behavior, and lynching became a common tool used by individuals to control the increased crime. Moreover, Guatemala seemed to remain in the same hands as it had been for decades. The ruling party was conservative, and its political leader, former dictator and the progenitor of the scorched earth policy, Efraín Ríos Montt, was the elected leader of Congress until early 2004. In Chapter Six we describe how the peace accords affected the social movement and the continuation of impunity in Guatemala, as well as the public's responses to growing lawlessness.

In our concluding chapter we tie perceptions of justice to the practice of rule of law and how these matters are associated with democracy. Democracy is not necessarily about elections or majority rule. It may be more about having one's interests considered than it is about other matters. Rule of law is the means by which people can come to see their interests considered. The law is a powerful thing. Laws can be used to establish rights and duties and to define differing social phenomena as legal or illegal. One perspective regarding the enactment of law sees the process as involving all members of society. It is a consensual process in which the outcome reflects the needs and desires of all society members. But law also can be seen as a political tool used by the powerful to support their own interests. From this perspective, law serves as an instrument of power in the processing of competing group claims. Those who control it are able to get their way.[15]

In Guatemala the law was the tool of a powerful elite. Individual activities of everyday citizens were subordinate to the narrow concerns of a ruling clique. Individual freedom, prized and necessary in democratic societies, was absent from the world of individuals interviewed for this book. The law could be used in a discriminatory fashion to justify a wide variety of limitations on individual freedom.

The lessons from Guatemala should not be lost on those attempting to implement democracy and its ideals in various corners of the world. The success or failure of new postwar government efforts to implement democracy in Guatemala, Iraq, Palestine, and elsewhere may very well depend on citizens' perceptions of how well they provide justice. Without justice, individuals are unlikely to establish a pluralistic, collective identity as citizens of the nation. Rather, they will identify themselves as members of the disenfranchised groups, whether they be the Maya of Guatemala or women or prisoners of the coalition forces in Iraq. Under such circumstances, democracy is unlikely to flourish.

CHAPTER ONE

Some Background

At a glance, Guatemala appears to be a paradise. It is a lush country, and the nearly year-round vegetation in most of its regions makes it a rich habitat for wildlife and ecotourists, who are also attracted by the opportunity to view the physical remnants of a once-dominant Mayan civilization and to meet the living offspring of that culture in the marketplaces. Guatemala's population is nearly 50 percent Mayan Indian,[1] and it includes more than twenty linguistic groups.[2] Writers whose work appears in conservation publications gush about the area. One in *Audubon* observed that it was "especially amenable to tourists, offering unparalleled scenic beauty and a leisurely pace of life not found elsewhere."[3] That is faint praise, however, when compared to the amour of an ornithologist. "Bird-watching is wonderful," he proclaims. "The park includes over 4,000 Mayan structures, many still buried, and includes pyramids from which birders can view bat falcons and other birds."[4]

The world that the tourist likely sees is far removed from the reality of most of Guatemala's 12 million residents. Their daily living conditions are improving but still reflect some of the most appalling social and health indicators in the Western Hemisphere, if not the world. Per capita income during the 1990s barely surpassed $100 per month. More than a third of the adult population were officially unemployed; about two-thirds were literate;[5] most individuals never made it past the sixth grade.[6] The situation was probably far worse among the indigenous population; 1989 data indicated that 91 percent lived in extreme poverty (compared to 45 percent of the nonindigenous population). There were more than 1,000 citizens for every licensed doctor practicing in the country. About 50 of every 1,000 infants died before completing their first year of life; almost 6 children out of every 100 born never saw their fifth birthdays. More children were left without mothers to raise them; more than 1 of every 100 women died as a result of pregnancy complications.[7] And many of these motherless youngsters were orphaned because their fathers were lost either to the killing or social disorganization the war fostered. It is hardly surprising to learn that Guatemalan children then were and now are among the world's most malnourished.[8] The situation remains worse in rural areas, where comprehensive emergency obstetric care has been virtually unavailable,[9] and there has been limited access to water, sanitation, and electricity.[10]

Water is illustrative of some of Guatemala's problems. Bacteria in water are a substantial cause of diarrhea, which in turn is a major killer of children in Guatemala.[11] Only 80 percent of the nation's population has access to running water.[12] Personal experience has taught us that "running water," in both rural and urban areas, is often untreated or undertreated so that the presence of fecal matter is substantially above what is considered safe. Monies have been allotted for drinking-water chlorination, but subsequent water treatment has been insufficient or nonexistent, allegedly because officials in some municipalities diverted the funds into their own pockets. And asking people to boil water before using it to make it safe means requesting the utilization of scarce resources. Most families have no access to electricity or natural gas for use in a stove. For them, such a seemingly benign request as boiling water signifies more work for family firewood gatherers, who must locate and carry, often over long distances, hefty loads of this steadily depleting natural fuel. Such are the everyday difficulties that many face in Guatemala.

Recently, Guatemala's manufacturing industry has become the most developed in Central America, and Guatemala has played a key role in the clothing-assembly industry in the past decade.[13] But it is not surprising that the country relies on its land to produce its most profitable exports: coffee, bananas, and sugar products.[14]

Guatemala's economy has been based on agriculture throughout its colonial and more recent history. Wealth depends upon ownership of or access to land.[15] Land in any rural country such as Guatemala is the base from which one acquires the ability to produce marketable goods for domestic consumption as well as for export. Arable land is the key component to economic productivity and prosperity. The more one has, the better off one is. As a result, efforts to acquire land have played an important role in Guatemalan history. For the most part, the effect of these efforts has been to transfer former communal Mayan lands to private ownership.[16] In this regard, the history of Guatemala differs little from that of other countries of the Americas.

There are, however, a few points that should be noted here, as they are important precursors to Guatemala's recent civil war and the concomitant slaughter of Indians. In particular, we want to highlight three themes: the privatization of former Mayan communal lands; the forced labor of Maya; and, racism against the Maya. Our description of these matters is meant to acquaint the reader with a historical understanding of more recent events. It is far from a detailed account, and some readers may have wanted us to dig deeper into matters upon which we only touch. There are numerous well-written articles and books that provide a more in-depth understanding of the history of Guatemala that we recommend to the interested reader.[17]

THE FIRST EIGHTY YEARS

Guatemala's independence in 1821 is a good place to begin a brief discussion of land transfer. At the time, there were a few urban Spanish centers and an abundance of rural Mayan communities. Early efforts to privatize the Indian lands were couched in the accepted economic language of the time; communal lands were identified as feudal barriers to economic development by members of the government. Private ownership, the argument went, meant that land would be put to its most appropriate ("best") use, and so the Mayan lands became the prime target of land reforms. A major tool to accomplish the task was a decree initiated in 1877 that authorized the privatization of communal lands.[18] There is some disagreement among Guatemalan historians as to the success of this and other measures. One view is that they were very efficient and that by the early 1900s maybe half of the Mayan communal lands had been appropriated.[19] The rural Indians are said to have fought against the theft of their native land but to have been defeated by government forces.[20] Events of the period, from this perspective, are portrayed as a moral play in which the indigenous population was "exploited by cruel, ruthless 'white' landowners eagerly assisted by *ladino* (mixed-race) politicians and military officers."[21]

A more recent view is that the Mayan communities were not always hurt by land privatization and that the process of privatization was neither fast nor complete. The author of a review piece on the topic noted that "merely issuing a decree promoting land privatization or 'abolishing' indigenous communities in no way guaranteed that such things would actually happen."[22]

Despite this proviso, overall the extent of Mayan communal land diminished during the last decades of the 1800s in favor of large, privately owned plantations, many of them for farming coffee.[23]

The issue of coffee production is related to the Maya's land loss and to their subjugation as a people. Here again, the historians disagree about some of the details. There is no debate, however, about the preeminence of coffee. From the 1880s onward, coffee has been Guatemala's principal export crop.[24] A portion of the land used for coffee production was appropriated from Mayan communal grounds during the last decades of the nineteenth century. One perspective holds that as a result, "a huge population of disenfranchised Indians" was made available to work on the plantations.[25] Without land, the Maya had to work on plantations for cash—or starve.

An alternative view is that the extent of the Mayan land loss was smaller than the normal assumptions about it. Purveyors of this perspective hold that the decline never threatened the community's existence, primarily because coffee did not occupy a great portion of the arable land; most cultivated soils were being used for other crops. Marketable coffee grows in different ecological conditions than do many food crops, and so it rarely clashed directly with food production.[26] From this perspective, the indigenous population maintained their ability to make a living off the land they still held and were unwilling to work for the meager wages offered by the plantation owners. As a result, the argument goes, the Guatemalan government needed to take action in order to secure the necessary workers for the plantations. Laws were enacted in 1877 and 1878 that legally required indigenous people to toil on the coffee plantations that had been established near the Pacific coast. During the 1880s more than 100,000 highland Maya were forced to labor for extended periods under the dictums.[27]

The forced labor laws of the 1880s illustrate that the government's capitalist argument—used to seize Maya communal lands—was likely self-serving and not based on a strong belief in the tenets of Adam Smith. Historically, it was nearly impossible to attract free labor to work on plantations, a major reason the southern U.S. states opposed the ending of slavery and the coming of capitalist conceptions such as free labor. Capitalist ideology favors free labor and presupposes that individuals in a society will be allowed to seek any occupation they choose without being hampered by duties or obligations that might arise from their birth.[28] Factors other than capitalist ideology were at work with respect to the Maya.

The privatization and transfer of communal Mayan lands to other purposes as well as the forced labor of the highland Indians are linked to racism among the elites of Guatemala, whose beliefs were used as rationalizations for oppressing the indigenous people.[29] But before we condemn the Guatemalan oligopoly for its attitudes, let it be noted that much deadlier ones existed at the same moment among U.S. citizens toward their native population, and it is only in recent history that U.S. racial minorities have had more than minimal participation in government life. Indeed, the indigenous populations of all the Americas have been subjugated by Europeans and their offspring. In Guatemala this meant that the Maya were marginalized within society and denied any "meaningful participation" in the government.[30]

SETTING THE TABLE

In reality, few people in Guatemala's history have had the opportunity to involve themselves in government matters. Guatemala has had more than its fair share of authoritarian regimes and was ruled by dictators or authoritarian governments through most of the first half of the twentieth century.[31] Manuel Estrada Cabrera (1898–1920) had the greatest longevity, perhaps because he established a secret police of spies and assassins to help keep him in office. He is also credited with looting the treasury and jailing or exiling anybody who did not like the way he ran things.[32] Years later, he was used by Nobel laureate Miguel Angel Asturias as the model for the main character in the novel *El señor presidente*.[33]

Cabrera, however, was not the only "bad boy" in Guatemalan history. Following him was Jorge Ubico (1931–1944), who some claim was even worse.[34] The tendency, however, to see Ubico as an evil individual or as a great man is illustrative of the tendency to cast Guatemala's civil and governmental leaders as characters in a moral tale. Ubico was likely a reflection of the times. He came to power in 1931, following the worldwide economic crash in 1929. During the 1920s Guatemala had experienced "limited political democracy." A chronicler of the period notes that

> the Congress and the press were relatively free. Repression remained, but less than in the past, at least in the cities. The urban population demanded economic concessions and dared to stage strikes . . . wages did increase and several unions were legalized.[35]

The Depression put an end to these changes. As elsewhere in the world, Guatemala's elites felt that the times required a strong-handed leader. In particular, they feared the communist call for a redistribution of the land. Ubico loathed communists, and his opposition to the ideology resulted in a favored status for landowners. He was opposed to industrialization because he thought that factory workers, as members of the proletariat, would eventually become communists. His opposition to industrialization safely kept the landowners in positions of power and likely prevented an expansion of the middle class that normally accompanies the decline of feudal socioeconomic patterns.[36]

Guatemala did well economically under Ubico; he balanced the budget and built up the infrastructure. But he ruled with an iron fist; he had strike leaders arrested, and those who spoke out against him faced repression. An expert on Jorge Ubico's regime concludes,

> Economic development and a national transportation and communication system inextricably changed the nation, creating new social sectors and affecting other previously marginal groups . . . Eventually, the social changes resulting from Ubico's programs rendered his methods obsolete, and [he] proved unable to change his policies to deal with these new elements and the resulting national circumstances.[37]

In 1944, following the fall of Ubico, Guatemala elected a new president and began what has come to be known as the "Ten Years of Spring."[38] During the decade of democratically elected presidents, Guatemala experienced a capitalistic revolution as its leaders attempted to end feudalism in the country. At the same time, the government was constantly criticized by landowners, the military, and the church.[39] There were, however, forces outside of Guatemala that also helped shape matters in the country and were to have a continuing influence.

UNITED FRUIT

Part of the blame for Guatemala's string of dictators is heaped on the Boston-based United Fruit Company. It became the largest North American banana importer during the first half of the twentieth century.[40] Early in the century, the company established operations throughout Central America by employing methods already well established among U.S. industries. Pouring money into the pockets of the region's politicians helped the company in gaining favorable legislation and in winning contracts under which it could acquire land for next to nothing and pay its employees even less.[41] The company became known as *el pulpo*—the octopus—to the people of the region,[42] and the Central American countries became known as "banana republics" in the U.S. press—both signs of the company's impact on the region.[43]

In Guatemala, by the mid-1920s United Fruit had more than 5,000 banana workers, making it the country's largest employer.[44] More important to our story, the company was the largest U.S. presence in Central America. To a certain extent, U.S. interests in the region were the same as the interests of the United Fruit Company. In 1900, when a United Fruit Company–controlled enterprise negotiated a contract with the Guatemalan dictator Estrada Cabrera to operate the country's most important railroad line, the *New York Times* reported it on the front page under the heading "Americans Win in Guatemala."[45] To put it another way, for some U.S. politicians, defending United Fruit in Central America was the same as protecting the interests of the United States, and the company could, on occasion, count on U.S. diplomatic efforts and if necessary military might to aid it.[46]

United Fruit's presence in Guatemala played a role in the events that kindled the country's long civil war. Between 1944 and 1954, two democratically elected presidents took actions that irked the banana monolith. Under President Arévalo (1945–1950), several laws were passed that benefited employees, including a social security system and a labor code that authorized workers to form unions and strike.[47] By 1949 the country had more than ninety legally incorporated unions.[48] President Jacobo Arbenz (1951–1954) also irritated United Fruit. In 1953, as part of a land reform law passed the previous year, he seized more than 400,000 uncultivated acres from the banana producer and passed the land along to 100,000 peasant families.[49] At the time, agricultural land in Guatemala was controlled by a minute portion of the population—2 percent of the farming units controlled 72 percent of the usable land—and land reform seemed like a good idea to the nation's legislators.[50] Guatemala paid United Fruit for the expropriated acreage, but not a fair market value. Rather, Arbenz determined the price of the land to be the same as United Fruit's evaluation of the acreage for tax purposes and paid the company in long-term bonds.[51]

For some commentators, the expropriation was just. "He took from the company that which it had acquired from corrupt dictators."[52] But United Fruit officials did not feel that way. Apparently, neither did Guatemala's Supreme Court, which declared the confiscatory land law unconstitutional. President Arbenz, who was not above using some of the antidemocratic tactics of the dictators, had the opponents to the law removed from the high court.[53] United Fruit, for its part, had had enough of elected presidents and put its efforts into getting rid of Arbenz by promulgating propaganda against him and by supporting a coup sponsored by the U.S. Central Intelligence Agency (CIA).[54]

THE COLD WAR

It was not specifically United Fruit interests that sparked CIA concern. Rather, it was the anti-communist zeal so prevalent in the United States of the 1950s that most influenced the agency's activities.[55] By 1954 the CIA had organized a small military force in Honduras, Guatemala's eastern neighbor. The agency likely had some interest in what was happening to United Fruit. Secretary of State John Foster Dulles and his brother, CIA Director Allen Dulles, as well as numerous others within the Eisenhower administration, were either shareholders of the company or had been high-ranking company officials.[56]

The Communist Party had gained a strong presence in Guatemala following World War II. The 1952 Agrarian Reform Act, the terms of which allowed the seizing of United Fruit's land, is an indication of the leftists' clout.[57] But there were also strong interests within Guatemala opposed to communism, most notably within the Catholic Church.

Anti-communist thinking within the Church had begun in the 1930s as a reaction to the spread of the atheistic doctrine. By the 1950s such thinking was pervasive and had become "a second dogma in the applied theology of much of the church hierarchy."[58] For many Guatemalans of the time, it may have been difficult if not impossible to separate the Church's religious teachings from its anti-communist agenda. In 1953 Guatemala's archbishop, for example, organized a national pilgrimage in which a replica of Jesus moved "from village to village to lead the crusade against communism."[59] One year later, he called upon Guatemalan Catholics "to fight and defeat the efforts of communism."[60] That President Arbenz had communists within his government and was seen as the darling of the Communist Party made him a political enemy of the Catholic Church. It was within this fertile soil that the United States and the CIA cultivated the overthrow of Arbenz.

The CIA had not been happy with political developments in Guatemala for some time and had begun covert operations within the country in 1951, placing one of its agents in an unlikely (and, as it turned out, unproductive) position within the Institute of Anthropology and History in Guatemala City.[61] By the next year, the CIA was fishing for a military force that could overthrow the leftist Arbenz administration. There was, however, a major obstacle facing the CIA plotters, and they knew it. According to a

September 11, 1953, top-secret CIA memorandum, Guatemala lacked "internal conditions that could be developed into a vital threat to the present Arbenz Administration."[62] The CIA and U.S. government might have been unhappy with the situation in the Central American democracy, but the Guatemalan people were not opposed to their leader's actions. Absent internal strife, there was little hope for a successful coup. CIA officials decided to create conditions within Guatemala that would nurture revolt. As a first step, U.S. President Dwight Eisenhower authorized $2.7 million for psychological warfare, political action, and subversion, among other activities.[63]

The CIA, with the aid of other U.S. agencies, first gathered support from Guatemala's Central American neighbors by providing them with military and development aid. In exchange, the United States got political support for its anti-communist position and allowances from the neighbors for the U.S.-supported Guatemalan "rebels" to operate from within their countries. The most visible result of the political bribery was passage of an anti-communist resolution aimed at Guatemala at the March 1954 meeting of the Organization of American States (OAS).[64] Also during 1954, the CIA established airfields in Guatemala's neighbors and manned them with pilots who were ready to back the coup in exchange for money. By May 1954 the CIA was operating a radio station, broadcasting from transmitters hidden in the jungles outside Guatemala's borders, and attacking Arbenz, at times with fabricated news stories.[65]

During June 1954, CIA officials stepped up their activities in anticipation of an imminent coup attempt. Another internal agency memo suggests that officials and operatives of the CIA may have faked Guatemalan aggression toward Honduras to stir up animosity from the Central American neighbor. Within Guatemala the CIA was also active, taking actions including defiling churches with communist slogans in order to create resentment.

The military coup, led by U.S.-funded Carlos Castillo Armas from his base in Honduras, began on June 17, 1954. Castillo Armas and his small military force did not get very far. It was not necessary. The U.S.-controlled radio station in Honduras broadcast tales of exaggerated victories while operatives in Guatemala did what they could to make the armed rebellion appear threatening. But, of more importance, Guatemala's military high command approached President Arbenz and demanded his resignation. The strongly anti-communist army leaders were unwilling to defend a president who they perceived as having granted too much leverage to leftists.[66]

On June 27, 1954, Arbenz resigned, bowing to the political and psychological terrorism that was directed at him by the United States and his own army. He and his aides fled the country, and in his place stood Colonel Carlos

Enrique Díaz of the Guatemalan military. He did not hold power long. Díaz banned the Communist Party, but when the U.S. ambassador purportedly provided him with a list of communists to be executed, from a total roster of 50,000, to his credit he balked.[67] "It would be better," he is quoted as saying, "that you actually sit on the presidential chair and that the Stars and Stripes fly over the Palace."[68]

In the end, it was the CIA-favored Carlos Castillo Armas who took the reins of government.[69] In October 1954 Guatemalans were given the opportunity to "elect" Castillo. He was the only name allowed on the ballot, and voters had the option of voting yes or no. Once in office, he required literacy as a prerequisite for voting (which disenfranchised 72 percent of the population), banned political parties, censored the press, attacked the labor movement (removing the legal status of more than 500 trade unions), ended land reform, and gave back the expropriated land to its former owners.[70]

One cannot look at the CIA's role as the only culpable one in the military coup and change of government. Eastern *ladino* Guatemalans were to lose status as European descendants due to the land reform that benefited the majority indigenous population in the western highlands and coastal areas. A racist dimension to *ladino* dissatisfaction cannot be ignored nor downplayed. In addition, as we have alluded above, in a predominantly agricultural nation, land is the foundation of all wealth. The large plantation owners on the southwestern coastal plains were to be economically hurt with the land reform, even if only symbolically at first. Their labor base, for example, might be compromised if the Indian population was given enough land to become self-sufficient and more so if the Indians' ability to sell their surplus farm goods for cash was strengthened. Many Guatemala City urbanites as well as military officers were (and still are) large landholders dependent upon Mayan labor for their economic viability at harvest time. Any efforts via land or other reforms that threatened the economic or social power base of the military elite through diminished control of the highland Indians or through heightened power of the trade unions was simply not to be tolerated. Thus, for a number of reasons, CIA planning found allied sectors in the Guatemalan nation.

THE TERROR BEGINS

The anti-communist sentiment held by the Catholic Church, the landed interests of Guatemala, and its military probably played the major role in inaugurating the slaughters that became commonplace in the decades after 1954. But it has become conventional practice to blame the United States.[71]

The United States may not be wholly to blame; earlier Guatemalan leaders had occasionally eliminated opposition by assassination. But the CIA may have galvanized widespread use of the violent tactics that later Guatemalan leaders would use against their countrymen. Evidence from CIA records revealed that the agency's plan for a successful coup in Guatemala in 1954 called for the roundup of communists and collaborators as well as the assassination of members of the Arbenz government and military.[72] An agency document, *Study of Assassination*, explained the best methods for carrying out the executions, including tips on accidents, drugs, edged and blunt weapons, and firearms.[73] Within days following Arbenz' sudden departure, CIA officials were in Guatemala uncovering information on Guatemalans who belonged to pro-Arbenz political groups, labor and student organizations, and farming cooperatives. The CIA left the material for the new Guatemalan security forces to apply.[74] For many commentators, the paper trail is more than sufficient evidence to finger the U.S. agency as the culprit that ignited the decades of terror.[75]

New legislation following the 1954 coup grossly restricted political participation by outlawing varied social movements and by severely limiting suffrage.[76] Radical politicians and labor leaders bolted from the country, state institutions were closed, and leftists were fired from their government jobs.[77] Communist organizations were banned, and existing labor groups were disbanded by law. About 17,000 alleged communists and communist sympathizers were arrested and imprisoned, and a reported 300 people, mostly popular leaders and activists, were killed.[78] The new leaders also returned to the original owners about 80 percent of the land that had been distributed to peasants under the previous administrations.[79]

The goal of the laws and decrees following the coup was to minimize opposition, particularly from communists. But the actions also minimized opportunities for any legitimate opposition to the government and further restricted access to Guatemala's political system and any chances for a democratic society. Members of Guatemala's political center disappeared in fear, leaving the military and oligopoly in charge.[80] The two groups struck a deal. The old, landed elites had neither the ability nor desire to govern. Rather, they clung to making money. It was left to the military to govern.[81] Under such an arrangement, democratic solutions to Guatemala's social problems were unlikely.

During the remainder of the 1950s, opposition to the ruling government was mostly from military officers who vied with each other for political power.[82] As 1960 ended, things had not changed much. It is then, on November 13, that the thirty-six-year civil war is said to have begun with an insurrection from within Guatemala's military elite. The military rebels captured a base and issued a leftist statement, calling for "installation of a regime of social justice in which riches pertain to those who work and not to the exploiters, those who starve the people, and the gringo imperialists."[83] But left untouched was the hegemony of the military. The colonels who led the revolt prefaced their manifesto by claiming that "only the army can cooperate effectively with the people."[84] The revolt was unsuccessful, mainly because the rank-and-file members of the army failed to join the insurrection. It was nearly three years before the revolution would rise again, this time as an armed guerrilla movement manned with former university students and military men.

THE GUERRILLA MOVEMENT BEGINS

The difficulties facing Guatemala were prevalent in other countries of the region, most notably for our story Cuba, where in 1959 Fidel Castro successfully led a communist overthrow of the government. The Cuban insurgency was a blueprint for revolutionaries in other countries such as Guatemala, where access to political solutions was unavailable to the vast majority of the population. The Cuban revolution also gave communists a foothold in the Americas and frightened conservative U.S. politicians.

There was a direct, prior relationship between Castro and Guatemala. He and Ché Guevara had there acquired ingredients of their political indoctrination during the leftist presidency of Arbenz.[85] Guevara, in fact, took refuge in the Venezuelan embassy in Guatemala during the 1954 coup, as he had been in the country at the time working with trade unions and a cadre of the Communist Party, studying their seemingly successful electoral influence. That Castro would aid Guatemala's guerrilla organizations, according to one commentator, amounted to "repayment of an ideological debt."[86]

Castro offered guerrilla training to the Guatemalan insurgents, and in January 1962 a small group of Guatemalan military men arrived in Cuba. Also in Cuba were a group of twenty Guatemalan students on university scholarships. But they soon traded their academic studies for military training as guerrillas.[87] During the coming years, these individuals and others returned to Guatemala and attempted to duplicate Castro's military success. Their efforts frightened the country's staunch anticommunists, who stepped up military action to quell the unrest. For its part, the United States increased its support for training the Guatemalan army in counterinsurgency tactics and for bolstering the national intelligence machinery,[88] factors that, according to a United Nations report, contributed to the violations of human rights that followed.[89]

COUNTERINSURGENCY: JUSTIFIED TERRORISM

Counterinsurgency efforts, from the viewpoint of government forces in Guatemala and their U.S. allies, were aimed at undermining guerrilla support in rural areas.[90] The anti-communist rhetoric justified a vast array of state-sanctioned terrorist acts against the Guatemalan people, including the elimination of key leaders and militants, in order to create fear and suppress the will for change.[91] The system of terror was necessary, according to some commentators, because the military governments had never held legitimacy in the estimation of a vast majority of the civilian public.[92] Guatemala's rulers, from this viewpoint, sought a passive consensus by which they could rule by default. In this scenario, the general population was too frightened to rebel against the terror-wielding powers.

State terror tends to target a sociodemographic range of specific social groups for extermination and terror.[93] The violence is distributed among often varying and disparate social sectors in order to generate fear in particular populations according to specific state demands of the moment, always keeping in mind that the state wishes to maintain and further consolidate its power. Urban police forces, for example, can be used to sequester and "disappear" trade union leaders during a period of labor struggle. Later, however, the police can become a target group as the state assassinates its members so as to leave few witnesses to its terror policies.[94] In either case, the apparatus and policies of terror for state consolidation remain in place. What may change, according to historical demands, is the intensity of the violence, the authors of the terror, the method of application, and the targeted groups of violence. In Guatemala the varying waves of state-sanctioned terror have been aimed at intimidating or annihilating distinct social sectors.

Throughout its four-decade history, state-sanctioned terrorism in Guatemala manifested itself in different stages or waves of terror, although others might disagree with the parameters of the periods we identify.[95] Each wave involved varying tactics and levels of violence. The violence also affected differing social ranges, groups, or identities, depending upon the time period and historical circumstances. A wave of terror could be directed at common, petty criminals or at potential bases of political opposition such as non-unionized factory workers who were considering unionization.

The first wave of terror began with the CIA-sponsored coup of 1954 and extended through another military coup in March 1963 headed by army Colonel Peralta Azurdia. It was in the second stage (1963–1970) that military-dominated consolidation of political, economic, and social power began on a previously unrealized scale. This period of state terrorism saw the propagation of counterinsurgency tactics by the military and police that included sequesters, torture, public exhibition of mutilated corpses, and the phenomenon of enforced disappearance for which Guatemala is infamous.

State-sanctioned terrorism is theatrical or dramatic in nature, "spectacle" terror, according to one expert.[96] Corpses are left in visible, public places for a reason. The more horrific and spectacular the death and subsequent public display of annihilated political opponents, it is arithmetically argued, the more pronounced the deterrent effect for opposition activities. The sensationalistic nature of the violence maximizes the terrorist actor's message of apparent omnipotence, invincibility, and surety of victory. The public display of a corpse demonstrates the results of horrible punishments in a way that forces the victim to wear his or her "sentence."[97] The heinous nature of these deaths and the "thousand little deaths" that led to them are inscribed on the corpses. Budding opponents of the sociopolitical system are symbolically notified that if they choose political involvement, they will likely die in a slow, excruciating, and mutilating manner. This aspect of state terrorism indicates an intense hatred of political opposition, a hatred so great that those who even threaten its use must be punished horrifically and often unimaginably so.

The third stage of state-sanctioned terror (1970–1978) followed the near-annihilation of the guerrilla movement and the consolidation of military rule. It was sparked by the 1970 rise to presidential power of military candidate Carlos Arana Osorio, who had been chief of the counterinsurgency campaign. There were remnants of possible guerrilla support bases, and state-supported terror was used to eradicate them, but it was also directed toward urban petty criminals.[98] There simply were few active political opponents to the military government. And those who were around were cautious in what they said and did, choosing to express their opposition to the government through nonviolent protest and resistance.

The fourth wave of terror was initiated in 1978 with the army-perpetrated massacre of approximately one hundred Kekchí Indians at the town of Panzós,[99] and it lasted until the end of military government in 1986. It is from this period that most of the individuals interviewed for this book drew their experiences. During this period of open military rule, the terror machine achieved unbridled visibility. This fourth terror wave was in reaction to a decade of intensifying unarmed protests during the 1970s,[100] as well as to the impending armed revolutionary victory of the Sandinistas in Nicaragua and the rise of a well-rooted revolutionary guerrilla movement in neighboring El Salvador. Guatemalan government leaders portrayed the state's violent actions as being necessitated by these national and regional events. President Jorge Serrano Elías (1990–1994), for example, in a *New York Times* article published during the first year of his administration, blamed Guatemala's legacy of violence on the country's then-thirty-year civil war. For him, the existence of the insurgency was cause for all human rights abuses.[101] "I can assure you that once we sign a peace agreement [with the insurgents], all these abuses will cease," declared the president. He cited a pervasive "culture of death" and the propensity for all parties in Guatemala to "work outside the law." The exercise of terror "is the history of this society, not just of the military," stated the president.[102]

Widely accepted documentation indicates that the fourth stage of state-sanctioned terror produced the majority of dead and disappeared victims in modern Guatemalan history.[103] On March 23, 1982, Efraín Ríos Montt seized power and initiated a scorched-earth policy. Traditional Indian patterns of subsistence were largely disrupted and distorted in many areas due to the actions.[104] More than 400 (nearly 700 in some reports) indigenous communities—villages and hamlets—were eradicated by the policy, which is widely recognized to have emulated U.S. counterinsurgency programs previously utilized in the Vietnam conflict. More than 100,000 people fled the country, and additional thousands took shelter in the mountains to escape the slaughter.[105]

The Guatemalan violence was designed to disperse and interrupt the guerrillas' social base while also killing enough people to ensure that at least some guerrillas would be among the slaughtered. Commonly employed was a 10 percent counterinsurgency formula. It held that for ten persons killed, at least one subversive would be among them. The intensity with which this formula was put into practice depended upon army intelligence defining a particular village as red, pink, yellow, or green.[106]

"Green" communities were thought to be free from guerrillas. They were watched but for the most part not bothered. At the other end of the spectrum were "red" villages, which were assumed to be under communist control. Here, the army might kill all in a community, including the children, making no distinction between rebel and resident. Presumably in the minds of the state terrorists, the more red the village, the fewer the number of "innocents" who were slaughtered. Such an analysis allowed the assassins to transform the victims into individuals who probably deserved the punishment. The slaughtered were not Guatemalans or Maya. Rather, they were collectively identified as rebels who were enemies of the state.

Between the red and green extremes were "yellow" and "pink" villages. The terror in these communities was much more selective and tended to be employed to frighten guerrilla sympathizers into inaction or flight.[107]

CIVILIAN GOVERNMENTS

The advent of civilian government in 1986 with the administration of President Cerezo Arévalo (1986–1991), symbolized a change in Guatemala. Elections were held, and an expert on the topic commented that they "were considered 'free and fair' (nonfraudulent) as well as competitive."[108] But elections do not, on their own, equal democracy. In Guatemala, outspoken criticism of the government remained a dangerous pursuit, and large portions of the rural population were still under military control.[109] The elected government was civilian in nature, but the military remained in charge, maintaining its political and economic hold on society.[110] Violence was more selective, though no less barbaric.

In part, the change in Guatemala was probably due to a lessening of hostilities between the revolutionaries, who had united in 1982 as the Unidad Revolucionaria Nacional Guatemalteca (URNG, Guatemalan National Revolutionary Unity), and the government. The URNG, prior to the elections, rightly recognized that a military victory was not possible, and the revolutionaries initiated efforts to establish political negotiations with the new government following its election in 1986.[111] By 1990 both sides realized that a military solution was improbable, and newly elected civilian President Jorge Serrano Elías began negotiations with the URNG in early 1991.[112]

As the peace talks with the insurgent front were under way, the state used more sophisticated and less publicly identifiable means to eliminate and neutralize political opponents and common delinquents. The change in state-sanctioned violence was accompanied by a partial loosening of the army's institutional worldview and strict "us versus them" counterinsurgency model. The period was characterized by the widespread use of psychological as well as physical torture and less open military involvement in repression. Violent, intimidating, but not always life-threatening, warnings were given to victims. The use of plain-clothed attackers was a prominent mechanism to frighten opponents. Trade unionists reported that they were openly followed as an intimidating tactic. But more violent means were also aimed at them, including attempts on their lives by drivers of unmarked cars with lights off at dusk.

DEALERS OF DOOM

The vast majority of those who carried out the violence during the decades-long civil war were members of Guatemala's security forces and their organized proxy allies, commonly referred to as "death squads." The dealers of doom included forces from the Guatemalan army, the National Police, the Guardia de Hacienda (Treasury Guard), and the Policía Militar Ambulante (Mobile Military Police). It was primarily the Guatemalan army, however, that committed the terrorism.

The army effectively controlled national political life in Guatemala since the military coup of 1963.[113] Those in command of the military were able to control all security forces in the country by use of the army's intelligence division.[114] The two principal coordinated intelligence services—the G-2 and the Archivo, the intelligence division of the Presidential General Staff—reputedly organized and controlled all other intelligence branches. The G-2 alone had at least 2,000 operatives nationwide.[115] But other security forces were involved, including the Mobile Military Police and a special unit of the National Police.[116]

Beginning in 1981, Civil Self-Defense Patrols (PACs) became a part of the military intelligence group. Most males in indigenous communities were forced to join the patrols. Intimidation of one type or another was used to pressure community members to take up arms on the side of the army. Failure to join resulted in punishment including execution. These patrols were a cheap way for the army to extend its hold into rural communities, since the units' members were unpaid. The patrols drew civilians into the civil war and extended the violence. PAC members were bullied by military leaders to carry out their wishes. But when needed, the government publicly identified the patrols as the culprits who carried out the mass killings. The exact number of individuals who were active in the civilian patrols is not known; no official records were kept. However, the number was large, perhaps 900,000 peasants in the early 1980s. In 1995, when they were dissolved, an estimated 375,000 rural Guatemalans were members of the "volunteer" patrols.[117]

Much of the actual dirty work of assassination was carried out by death squads. They first widely appeared in 1966 with the purpose of threatening, torturing, and executing political opponents, and their existence created terror among the general population. The units were not an official part of the government, but they were funded by the army and were often composed of off-duty security-force operatives or persons formerly in public service who relied on their contacts in official circles to obtain weaponry, intelligence information, or clandestine orders to eliminate political or perceived political opponents.[118] Moreover, the death squads could not have organized, performed sequesters and assassinations, and imprisoned their victims in secret prisons without being discovered if not for some form of governmental assistance or collusion.[119] Their former members have even now largely remained untouched, and there have been virtually no prosecutions or arrests of their members, a situation that the government has done little to change since the war ended in 1996.

IMPUNITY

In a very real sense, Guatemalans were twice victimized by the politically motivated murders, massacres, and disappearances. First, they suffered inconceivable violence. And they suffered again when those who were responsible for the butchery escaped any legal acknowledgment of their crimes. As one commentator noted, "The underlying message of impunity is clear, both for the victims and the perpetrators: If there is no punishment, then there was, in effect, no crime."[120] Ending impunity and establishing justice, we will show, are the motivations that eventually drove those we interviewed to become active critics of the government and eventually to collectively perceive themselves as Guatemalans.

During the long civil war, the Guatemalan criminal justice system evolved into a bifurcated, parallel system in which the state terror structure operated with relatively little restraint from official legality. Clandestine, state-sanctioned agents applied punitive actions against perceived political criminals in ways not specified in the written law. It was a penal system wherein sanctions ranging from death threats and warnings to sequesters, tortures, and extrajudicial executions were applied with the intent of eradicating anti-state political action. The system of terror "criminalized" social movements (such as the labor movement, struggles to expand education, and land reform endeavors) thought to jeopardize the hegemony of the ruling class, a hegemony that depended upon state terror for its relative strength and durability. The state terror system criminalized political opposition to the point of systematically applying the death penalty to perceived transgressors. In general, such criminalization was a fundamental element of the state terror system, and it was the backbone of the clandestine, parallel judicial-penal system in Guatemala.

The employment of state-sanctioned terrorism in Guatemala affected the criminal justice system and allowed the police, prosecutors, and courts to be accomplices to the persecution. The impunity with which state-sanctioned terrorists operated rendered the justice system meaningless. The structural checks and balances of the "justice" network were impotent in the face of the dominant power of terrorist violence, which reached into all levels of the government and judicial system. In Guatemala, the interests of the state were fortified and defined by the exercise of violence from which no one was guaranteed immunity. Even the presidents of the country had to have feared assassination and overthrow. The procedural strength of the criminal justice system was rendered inept, as terror nullified the impartiality of its members, frightening them into inactivity or usurping them as accomplices in covering up horrific acts.

CONCLUSION

Throughout nearly all of Guatemala's 185-year history it has been dominated by elites who used the law and the criminal justice system to support their own interests. The culture and concerns of an indigenous Mayan population were subjugated. A brief attempt at democracy following World War II was thwarted by the Guatemalan military with the direct aid of the United States. In the years that followed, the military increased its hold over all aspects of life in the country. Attempts at armed overthrow of the existing military state, beginning in the 1960s, were countered with well-funded, U.S.-supported counterinsurgency tactics, which evolved into the state-sanctioned terrorist machine responsible for more than 93 percent of the 150,000 dead and 50,000 disappeared.[121]

Most of those killed and disappeared by the state-sanctioned forces were rural Maya, guilty of nothing more than living in an area that the military categorized as being under guerrilla control. They were slaughtered as part of a "scorched earth" policy that ignored the value of their lives. The perpetrators of the violence committed these horrific acts with impunity, as all levels of the criminal justice system were made impotent out of fear or duplicity.

The government-sponsored terror apparatus was intended to prevent all anti-state actions, whether they were committed by communist guerrillas, common criminals, or peaceful demonstrators. The original progenitors of the extralegal system may not have envisioned such a wide scope for their activities, but once they had started along the muddy path, it would have been hard for them to turn back.

The violence certainly silenced segments of the population. The immunity afforded death squad members by criminal justice system agents was probably in large part an intended outcome of the violence. But the tactics used by the state-sanctioned terrorists had unintended effects. Most notably, they were the impetus for bringing together Guatemalans who demanded an end to impunity and the implementation of justice. This coming together blurred ethnic, geographic, and class lines and facilitated the formation of a popular movement and a collective identity. These communities brought together diverse social sectors of society that previously would have remained disparate, and their union empowered formerly disenfranchised groups. In this process, the communities created the potential for a new Guatemala based on pluralism.

We use the accounts of the survivors of the disappeared to explore their transformations from powerless individuals to political activists. Their stories are filled with great sadness and great courage. The mere telling of their activism to a university researcher put their lives at risk. During the early 1990s, when the interviews were conducted, individuals were still being murdered and kidnapped, taken into the night never to be seen again. The interviewees, however, were not the only ones who had to be courageous. Collecting this information required data collection methods not usually associated with university research. In the next chapter, we describe the process of collecting the data in some detail, a process that closely resembles a tale of adventure and intrigue.

CHAPTER TWO

Access Was Not Easy

The research that forms the core of this book required not only traditional academic strategies and study but also perseverance, investigatory stealth, and ongoing deprivation of Western, middle-class comforts. It often required Frank Afflitto, who did all the interviews, to place himself in physical danger.

Access was not easy. Data were not there for the taking, a source of professional status for the researcher at any cost to the project participants. Ethically, it was important for the safety of the respondents to maintain their anonymity and confidentiality. It was dangerous for them to be seen with a foreigner (*un gringo*) or a stranger (*un desconocido*, literally "an unknown one") noticeably from outside the neighborhood or without the local accent. Persons who agreed to be interviewed and who attributed illegal and extralegal acts to government or government-linked institutions placed themselves at risk of becoming targets of intimidation, disappearance, or assassination.

While the general research process described later in this chapter is extensive, it is hardly exhaustive. Specifics of the research strategy, interview process, and interview schedules might not interest most readers, and thus we include such material in Appendix A rather than here. Before discussing the research process and subjects in this chapter, Frank gives the reader an idea of the circumstances of data collection, illustrating what it was like to research concepts of justice and political activities in the Guatemalan popular movement. Because it is Frank's story, it is told in the first person.

FRANK'S STORY
How I Became Involved

I began working on issues concerning Guatemala in 1980 in Boston and later through coalition work with the American Friends Service Committee in Cambridge, Massachusetts. I became a member of an international support group, the Network in Solidarity with the People of Guatemala, and worked with others concerned about Guatemala and the lack of attention paid to it. In 1989 I began graduate school at the University of California, Irvine, in Orange County, California (an odd place, one might think, for an activist), and became involved with the Guatemala Information Center of Los Angeles. There I met individuals who were connected to the popular movement in Guatemala. With these contacts and some seed money obtained from the university with the help of Professor Roxanne Silver, I traveled to Guatemala to learn firsthand what was going on in the country.

Massacre and Rally—Santiago Atitlán, Sololá

On December 8, 1990, my first full day in Guatemala, I was driven, packed like a sardine in a van with various popular-organization members, to a widely attended demonstration whose main focus was the withdrawal of government security forces from a predominantly Mayan region. I became familiar with various union and university struggles represented by my fellow passengers as we drove together to the rally site and stopped for breakfast along the way.

The demonstration was held in Santiago Atitlán, a majority Tzutuhil Maya community several hours' drive from the capital by the routes we took. At the rally, approximately 45,000 people, mostly Tzutuhil Maya community members from the surrounding villages, arrived to repudiate the killing of fourteen and wounding of twenty-two community members six days earlier by the Guatemalan army. They also came to protest the continuing army and National Police presence in their communities.

The town reminded me of a story I had read as a child about the Norwegians under the Quisling pro-Nazi government who wore paper clips on their clothing as a sign of protest and refused to sit next to occupying German forces on public transportation. In the Guatemalan municipality, the main form of public transportation, the extra-urban buses, were adorned with black flags, symbols of the widespread anti-army sentiment. Buses throughout the country, in fact, were embellished with this silent display of protest.

December 8, the day of the demonstration, entailed a host of activities for me: staying alone overnight in a town with which I was unfamiliar (it was, after all, my first full day in the country); playing with children on the steps of the church from which the speakers and the surviving family members of the deceased victims were gathered; privately interviewing a local elected official who granted me permission to stay and conduct interviews; braving a stereotypical government agent in dark sunglasses who, nose to nose, screamed in my face, "What did you ask of the [official]?" and "Where are you from?"; and giving up my money and warm jacket to some needy informants, leaving me cold and hungry with the equivalent of about seven U.S. dollars in my possession, enough for a one-night stay in the town. The motel I stayed in that night was only $1.20, so I felt that the remaining monies were sufficient for a quick, light meal and transportation to the capital, where I had more funds stowed.

My first day's work produced one interview with a family member of an assassinated man. My second day was not easier. The imminence of the Gulf War had fueled a rise in gasoline prices and, as a result, hiked urban and extra-urban bus fares. The entire country was in the middle of a transportation strike because of the rate changes. Few if any extra-urban buses were running. The dilemma for me was how to get back to the relative safety of the capital with my taped interview, cold, hungry, and with very little money.

I rode a launch in the morning across the lake with a number of uniformed national and military police personnel on board, cassette tape and interview schedule in my shoulder bag, after having successfully bargained for my fee. When I got off the launch on the shores of Panajachel, I quickly made my way toward the road leading out of town and away from the security personnel whom I feared, especially after the previous day's intimidating encounter with a presumed government agent. There was no transportation to be found, so I was forced to walk. I begged one gentleman to give me a ride with his family to the capital, but he adamantly refused. Six days after a major episode of government violence against local civilians, I could not blame him.

I walked from Panajachel north to Sololá, encountering an elderly Kaqchikel Mayan gentleman along the way. We walked together through a hilly area, which I later learned was a post-murder body-dumping ground. My walking companion taught me some words in his language. Later, after buying him and me breakfast with my dwindling funds, I went with him to a Catholic mass in town. After mass he took me to see local religious leaders who offered me transportation to the capital the next day. With no money for a night's lodging and no offers, I told my hosts that I would try to make it myself, and if not, I would be back at 7 a.m. to take them up on the transportation offer. Their proposition was particularly generous because I had told them that I was there interviewing families of the disappeared, and the religious officials were aware that being associated with me placed them in danger.

My elderly guide told me whom to ask for a ride to Los Encuentros (The Crossroads). A K'iché Mayan truck driver obliged me with the hour-or-so ride through the countryside for a relatively nominal fee. At Los Encuentros I negotiated a ride with a local pickup truck owner en route to the capital.

The five-hour ride in the back of the pickup truck was not comfortable. My short-sleeved shirt was no match for the cold and windy 4,000-foot mountains. I spent the time talking with a young Kaqchikel man who worked as a butcher's apprentice and who shared the back of the pickup with me for half the ride. We talked about the enforced disappearances of people, about conducting field research, and about life in the midst of violent social conflict.

Near the outskirts of Guatemala City, I caught a bus into the capital, where I was staying. No one was home and, with no key to get in, I waited outside in the cold for several hours until someone came back and let me in. Nearly forty-eight hours of activities had brought me only one formal interview with a subject and left me with no money in my pocket. I had, however, traveled with informants, attended a rally as an observer, related successfully to community members, and otherwise begun to learn, in flesh and blood, what it was like to be a Guatemalan of humble means.

Children's March

The next day, December 10, 1990, I accompanied a march led by 400 children who had each lost at least one relative to enforced disappearance or extrajudicial execution. Before the march, the children had spent a day or two in the offices of popular organizations making colored cellophane and stick lanterns. White wax candles were lit inside the lanterns to represent the lives and souls of their missing loved ones.

The wind was a challenge for many of the young candle-holders throughout the several-hour march route as the children tended the candles in their makeshift lanterns with a determined gentility. The candles kept burning from the march's origins to the rally site in front of the National Palace in downtown Guatemala City—the seat of the executive branch of the Republic of Guatemala including the office of the president. Along the march route, two young men on a motorcycle sped through the line of marchers, almost running over several children. Hecklers were present along the way, in addition to some vociferous supporters and a mainly silent majority of spectators. As I recorded the sounds of the march and took pictures, barefoot and determined children took up chants. A megaphone-holder called: "Who sequesters, tortures, and kills the people?" and 400 children replied in unison: "The army!"

Several thousand people representing various popular-movement organizations joined the children, held signs, addressed the presidential palace through megaphones, and sang songs about disappeared relatives. Suddenly, the palace's sixty-foot Christmas tree at the back of the crowd caught fire. The popular organizations later claimed that police-inspired *maras*, or street gangs, infiltrated the crowd and started the fire, although some feisty trade unionists and others who attended might have felt a certain sense of righteousness and humor at seeing the outgoing president's expensive Christmas tree go up in smoke in front of hungry, cold, war-orphaned children. The humor, however, soon turned to despair, then panic.

Like a "white Christmas," a moment of peace descended over me as I thought back to my New England childhood and watched the big white flakes of snow-like ash floating around the plaza. But that moment of peace was quickly interrupted as I realized that the ash was burning hot as it flurried and descended on our skin. The children were overwhelmed with smoke and the steady stream of falling ash. Songs and speeches to disappeared loved ones, whom they longed to have home for Christmas, ended abruptly, and a general panic ensued as *mara* gang members ran in and out of the crowd.

As darkness came, widows and children ran to mount public buses. National Police invaded the square, firing shots from all angles. To their credit, they fired over people's heads, shy, perhaps, to kill in front of international newspersons and in the wake of the Santiago Atitlán violence the previous week. In any event, the *mara* youths, before my eyes, pulled Mayan women by their hair off of the buses and stoned the buses with numerous blunt objects, sending glass splinters into the hair and faces of screaming women and children. The sounds of gunfire, smashing glass, and screams were everywhere.

Instead of leaving, I stayed with the last group of demonstrators, composed of several women and eleven children. I believed that I was not in deadly danger and could best serve their safety by staying by their side, as the presence of foreigners has often provided a measure of protection for Guatemalan activists. For whatever reason, our group was not touched by the *maras* as they beat people around us. Gang members ran at our closely huddled group but parted like the Red Sea and did not crash into us. Two government agents, stereotypically attired in tan trench coats and with Uzi weapons bulging from their waists, came up to us and accusingly queried: "This is what you call nonviolent, huh?" The white-haired, balding security agent stared at us for a minute or so before he and his accomplice left.

Several hours later we were rescued by a popular-movement van. I rode half in, half out of the crowded van, clutching a Christmas tree covered with paper-ornament peace doves bearing the names of disappeared persons. I was told that a man who was a delegate of one of the groups sponsoring the demonstration, Mutual Support Group of Family Members of the Detained-Disappeared (GAM), had just been assassinated in a public bus station by unknown gun wielders as he waited for transportation to his home area. Surprisingly, perhaps, that was the evening's only reported fatality.

I got back to the GAM office after a full day of participating in activities and, more importantly, after standing outside for hours and contributing to the safety of the group of children and GAM leaders. I was standing around with hundreds of crowded indigenous delegates and their children when, from behind, a woman grabbed my arm, swung me around, and yelled *¡Compañero!* (companion, comrade) in my face. She was not the only one to have witnessed my high level of participation in the day's activities. From that moment until the wee hours of the morning and all of the following day, dozens of mainly indigenous women gathered around me as my interviews with them as GAM members began.

My actions of the evening had largely been shaped by the moment-to-moment activities. I, too, had felt the need to vent my anger and frustration about circumstances in Guatemala. But there was some calculation to my presence at the demonstration. Access to GAM members and my continuing and improving reputation with them over time had largely depended on my participatory zeal that night and not necessarily on who I said that I was.

PAR METHODOLOGY AS A RESEARCH STRENGTH

My research methodology is known as Participatory Action Research (PAR). It is an interactive methodology that requires the participation of members of the groups being studied. Such participation ideally begins with the inception of the research. Research participants help shape the work by providing information on what is important to them rather than confining their answers to the predetermined belief structures of the researchers. The strategy allows subjects the opportunity to ask questions of the interviewer and to indicate whether they have information on the subject area. PAR's flexible and participatory nature permits the detection and cancellation of erroneous lines of inquiry and of theoretically imposed research designs and a priori explanations of phenomena that constrain observation and thought.[1]

Action research, in general, is designed to assist in the development of a theoretical understanding of strategies of social change. Social systems and social relations are active, evolving, interactive processes that are both cause and effect of transformation. Active participation made me "close" to the data and facilitated my awareness and understanding of social change. Participation was a necessary precursor to data collection.

The flexible and adaptable nature of PAR research methods accounted for the minimizing of the relative importance of some data during the study and the focus on and pursuit of additional lines of data inquiry. I had arrived in Guatemala to focus on the psycho-emotional stressors and cognitive modes of coping that the survivors of the disappeared used. But that soon gave way to a respondent-generated paradigm of civil society's relations with violent law. Specifically, my emphasis on coping and stress was not necessarily the seminal emphasis as perceived by those whose stories are reported here. For them, the main point was a governmental and legal culture and structure that perpetuated illegal acts by never bringing anyone "to justice."

Risks for the Researcher: Reflections and an Example

Interviewing during a civil war while state-sanctioned terror is being used as a counterinsurgency tactic deserves more attention dedicated to covering the safety, ethical, and methodological issues of such research than could reasonably be discussed here.[2] What was of immediate importance to me was that I and the individuals with whom I spoke were also potential targets. In Guatemala, everyone who was not directly involved with the repressive state apparatus was a potential victim of the indiscriminate violence.[3] Moreover, the type of information I gathered (i.e., regarding state abuses and the impotence and complicity of formal law) was likely threatening to the military state, and I feared repercussions. I eventually would have plenty of experiences to fuel my suspicions.

One example of intimidation occurred in December 1990. I was sitting with two women in a sandwich shop in the capital city when I noticed a man who came in and sat in a booth opposite us and diagonal to my position. He was facing me, as the two women with whom I was eating were also doing. My research associates later referred to the tall, lanky, red-haired, bearded man as "a hit-man from Zacapa." Zacapa was the seat of the annihilated guerrilla movement of the 1960s and was known as an area of pro-military, anti-communist zeal. It is now a principally non-Indian province where, due to what many informants attributed to anti-Mayan racism, many "white," "light-skinned" males are recruited for the death squads.

While the man did not say anything, certain features of his clothing, stance, and cold gaze rapidly gave him away to me as someone who wanted to know more about me and/or intimidate me. I kicked the feet of my lunchmates and immediately switched the conversation to a benign topic: a trip to Mayan ruins. We paid and left without finishing our food. We were not the only ones who did that, as the man also left, having drunk only half of his beer and leaving his barely delivered food untouched.

When we walked into the street, an accomplice of the man in the sandwich shop waited outside on his motorcycle so as to block our exit or escape if he so desired. He weighed approximately 250 pounds or more, and struggling to free oneself from his grasp would have posed a difficult challenge. Wearing leather motorcycle gloves that were red, white, and blue with Western-style fringes, he looked like a character out of a surrealistic Davy Crockett movie.

I turned left, with my back to the wall, and said goodbye to the female companions. I had provided myself with some measure of safety and a wide area of visibility. I had also placed myself between the motorcycle thugs and the two associates, who took a route away from the "hit-men," while I stayed there until they were out of sight and then took another route. The two presumed intelligence agents on the motorcycle also went off in another direction.

The red-haired man from the restaurant appeared on several occasions within a short time span when I was a pedestrian on the street, and he also came by the office of a sponsoring organization looking for me. He provided the man at the office, who attended to his request, with a perfect description of me. This information was not told to me until my last day in Guatemala on this trip, January 1, 1991. At a New Year's celebration, while dancing cumbia and downing Scotch whiskey on an empty stomach in an informal atmosphere, the news of how closely I had been watched by one man had a sobering effect. Years later, I was told even more that confirmed my suspicions and rekindled my fears.

Respondent Security: Some Specific Concerns

Certainly, my fear and suspicions were real. But people who talked to me about their experiences were in greater danger than I. In the sandwich-shop episode, the greater threat was to the safety of the two informants with whom I was lunching. Their identification with me, though knowingly accepted by them, probably placed them in a poor light with state-associated agents and made them targets for future questioning.

Many of my informants expressed concerns for their safety. A representative of a human rights organization reported making a number of separate bus trips in different directions before reaching the capital city so that her movements and final destination could not be easily guessed by assassins. I learned similar strategies. I always walked against traffic on the many one-way thoroughfares in Guatemala City. I worried that if I did otherwise, I might fall prey to gun-toting men approaching from behind in an automobile.

In one instance in fieldwork, an informant and I left a small-town house, and the informant wanted to walk together to the marketplace, as a generous host would, not wanting me to lose my way. I elected, for safety reasons, to walk separately, and he agreed to follow that plan. The public route I took to the market brought me into contact with several small army patrols, maybe nine soldiers in all. Had my informant and I been together passing the patrols, we might have been stopped and questioned as to why we were together, as to why I had cassette tapes, batteries, and hand-held tape recorders in my shoulder bag, and as to what was on those tapes.[4] Those would most likely have been unfortunate circumstances for the informant.

In homes, particularly in villages or small towns, my conversations with informants were often conducted in hushed voices, and I invented various pretexts for why a stranger was visiting the home of a local resident. For example, I purchased items from some of those with whom I spoke as an excuse to be in a home, or I attended local soccer games as a justification for being in the area. All these measures were designed to protect my informants' anonymity so as to avoid compromising their security. These precautions were considered minimal ethical measures for the research, given the real dangers present for those with whom I spoke. Lack of such safety measures could certainly have led to the sequester-torture-deaths of numerous persons, including me. The ethical safeguards described here are by far the most important elements of any study conducted with victimized populations under circumstances of continuing victimization and imminent danger.

Participant Observations

The danger my informants and I faced was, in large part, a result of my decision to conduct the research as a participant observer. There were other strategies I might have chosen, but it is unlikely that they would have proved successful. For example, in the industrialized world, researchers commonly solicit subjects by advertising in newspapers and elsewhere and use cash payments as incentives to gain participation. Such a method, however, would have netted me few legitimate takers. The money I might offer could never offset activists' fears that I might be a state agent ready to use the information I obtained against them. Or I could have chosen to simply observe the activities of the groups to which the survivors of the disappeared belonged, the "professional stranger" approach, as it is sometimes called in anthropological circles. This strategy too would have likely limited my access to information. Under such circumstances, it would have been more likely for the activists to identify me as a spy for the military state and do their best to avoid me.

The use of participant observations and semi-structured interviews is an important strength of this study. Key informants helped me to gain an understanding of the phenomena under study. As a participant observer in Guatemala, I had a vantage point that enabled me to comprehend the motives and actions of the survivors of the disappeared as they saw them.

Trust is an important aspect of any social fieldwork, and building trust amidst an ongoing climate of fear was a challenge for me and any field researcher in Guatemala.[5] On a pragmatic level, trust enabled me to talk with the Guatemalans who participated in the study. They had confidence in me and were willing to "open up" so that I might better understand their situations. Several important host organizations eventually trusted me with their private contradictions, such as the presence of drunken or violent members or destructive internecine gossip or frowned-upon extramarital affairs. For some persons to have developed confidence in me on others' recommendations in a relatively short time speaks to the special qualities of the respondents in the sample.

The building of confidence and trust and the ability to offer something back to the interviewed communities were necessary elements of the research process. They were essential for gaining respondent trust and hence access.[6] Moreover, the information that I was given was probably more complete than I could have gathered if I were not trusted and was unable or unwilling to participate. And my understanding of the data was enhanced. It is one thing to be told of intimidation and fear. It is quite another to live it. In a broader sense, I felt that I was contributing in an activist manner to the detailed, scientific exposure of state-sanctioned terrorism.

My closeness to the activities of those I was researching was not without some cost. My approach to the research undoubtedly resulted in a loss of some objectivity. I had taken a decided stance against what I perceived to be Guatemalan state-sanctioned terrorism prior to commencing the field research. As a result, I arrived in Guatemala with a fixed set of beliefs and perceptions that may have clouded my understanding or my interpretation or my ability to disbelieve some of what people told me, especially with respect to the government's "deaf ear" regarding impunity and continuing violence. In addition, my beliefs and the need to build trust directed me to work with certain sectors of the Guatemalan populace and to ignore or avoid others. I only heard one side of the stories, from the view of the popular organizations, and I did not for the most part meet or speak with former or active government or legal officials who might have provided different perspectives. In addition, as a participant observer I ran the risk of changing the world I was studying. This dilemma for researchers was popularized by the TV series *Star Trek*. The space travelers were directed not to interfere in the worlds they studied, but they quickly learned that their mere presence could change things, like it or not. For me, the potential to effect change was an ethical goal of the research, given the plight of those with whom I spoke.

While these comparative weaknesses are evident in the research approach and respondent selection procedures upon which I embarked, they were intended as an ethical stance in the face of what I perceived to be a state-directed campaign of violence. Under situations of extreme human duress, I felt that researching respondents without working with them to change their situation at its source represented indifference to their plight and may have even contributed to their suffering. Whatever vicarious side benefits might have been derived from "getting things off one's chest" during a lengthy interview or through sterile documentation were deemed by me as insufficient in beneficial magnitude when compared with the gravity of inaction in the area of social change.

I, or more appropriately, Paul Jesilow and I took some action to minimize the effects of my closeness to the data. Primarily, this involved adding Paul Jesilow to the research project. He was not involved in the data collection and does not know any of the participants, although he was directly involved in early stages of establishing the research focus. His reading and analyses of the interviews are less affected by the matters to which I was subjected. He is able to bring a measure of objectivity, a necessary component of research, to the work in order to offset my subjective perceptions.

ISSUES IN IMAGE MANAGEMENT

My image was an important commodity in this research.[7] In general, the social position of the researcher affects the type of information learned.[8] Throughout my stays among the Guatemalans, my image was something that was being socially constructed, used at times to favor me or, at others, wielded against me, depending on the situations and contexts. In this respect, my position as a participatory sympathizer allowed me access to areas that would have been totally off limits for other outsiders wishing to examine the intimate thoughts and attitudes of state violence survivors. But, as with most things, the image had a downside. The perception that I was an empathetic activist may have led some people to answer my questions by telling me what they believed I wanted to hear.

La bola, or the roundabout gossip about me, I learned the hard way, was everywhere.[9] There was no confidential relationship, as I was the "other" and would continue to be for some time. As I became more a part of people's lives and became accepted, gossip may have diminished. Perhaps I simply did not hear the gossip, as it was more well guarded so as not to hurt me. Perhaps there really was less speculation about my motives and presence as time went on.

The gossip was important because it played a role in establishing how I was perceived by the different Guatemalan groups. I had to be aware of the images I projected to the varying audiences because those guises affected both access to respondents as well as the kinds of information they would give me. Image management quickly became an important part of the research. On more than one occasion I had to take action to minimize the effect that an image might have on the research as well as on my safety and that of the respondents.

The Guatemalans envisioned an array of social roles for me other than that of a researcher. I doubt that I know them all, but the following depictions of me are imbued with meaning and are the principal selves into which I was categorized.

The Gringo Moneybags

Guatemala is a poor country. Few people have funds for even the most minimal medical care. "Ancient" diseases still flourish there. Scores of persons, for example, were dying of cholera in 1992. The fact that I was from the United States and could afford to fly to Guatemala while most people in the country could not even pay the exit tax of some fifty *quetzales* (approximately nine U.S. dollars at the time) to leave the country was enough evidence to paint me as a "gringo moneybags."

I was not rich by U.S. or European standards. I had come to Guatemala on a scholarship and a shoestring budget that left me borrowing money for my stay and eating tortillas with *chiltepe* chilies and salt for days on end. No matter the stories I could provide of a relatively deprived life nor the struggles I described in putting myself through undergraduate and graduate studies as a "loaned to death" working-class student, the image of one who did not work was salient for some.

The mere fact that I was not bent over in the plantation fields or in the Coca-Cola bottling plant was enough for some people to equate me with Guatemala's economically secure non-Indian (*ladino*) upper class. While this did not bring me major noticeable problems, in retrospect it appears to me that the value of the work I did was diminished in the eyes of those who saw me as an apolitical intellectual who spent his time thinking about things while accomplishing little.

Whatever the case, having pens, paper, a handheld tape recorder, and two pairs of pants instead of one made me *un rico*, a "rich one," in the eyes of many. This was especially true among the poorest agricultural people. This social equation-making amidst the politics of hunger and destitution that comprise the social landscape of Guatemala was a common way of judging who I was. The social comparisons made by persons who came into contact with me were, no doubt, the framework within which my economic status was judged. "If I cannot afford pens and notebooks for my children and he has more than one pen, then he has money" ran the understandable logic.

North Americans and Europeans often did flaunt their money to the dismay of malnourished Guatemalans. One group of Spaniards who reputedly had come to Guatemala to learn of the social situation spent more of their time drinking beer, shooting up cocaine, and wallowing in their sorrow at seeing the effects of economic austerity and death squad–inflicted suffering in Guatemala than they did on any other activities (except perhaps on sleeping off their hangovers). On one occasion, this group of approximately twenty Spaniards went to a women's social project in El Mezquital, one of the poorest slum areas of the capital. There, after being exposed for several hours to dire urban poverty and social organizing among women in the pouring rain, the group, it was reported to me, donated not one Guatemalan cent to the women's project yet promptly went to a downtown bar and drowned their shocked middle-class sensibilities in 500 *quetzales'* ($91) worth of beer and liquor. While one of the group's organizers allegedly paid for his flight by smuggling twelve bags of cocaine back to Spain, what they gave to Guatemala in return is questionable at best.

The images generated by the tourists hurt my ability to do the research. In tourist areas, *gringos* are often seen as hippies, drug addicts, diseased, and of dubious sexuality. *Gringas*, foreign Caucasian women, are stereotyped as whores, and *gringos*, the men, most often are assumed to be *huecos*, literally "holes" or "hollow ones," an unflattering colloquialism for homosexual, an image I had to confront.

The "Faggot" ("Unmanly" Man)

My disposition is usually soft-spoken and somewhat deferential, particularly in new situations with unknown circumstances. My demeanor, combined with my foreign status, resulted in some trade unionists singling me out as being of questionable sexuality. The "ball" (*la bola*) of gossip had gone through its arc and come my way. Seeing this, I realized that an image as "less than a man" could cost me much organizational trust and personal safety.

In Guatemala, there is a continuum of male aggressiveness that runs from being a *hueco* ("faggot," "weakling," "milquetoast," "sissy") on one end to being a *brincón* (literally "jumpy" or "jumper") on the other. A *hueco* might be the guy who gets sand kicked in his face by the big, muscular bully in an ancient Charles Atlas cartoon advertisement. A *brincón* exudes machismo—a certain toughness, an aura of a rebel who is always ready for a fight no matter the odds. In Guatemala, in order to safeguard oneself from aggression, one must achieve a balance between the two ends on the continuum of popular masculinity. Being a *hueco* is to leave oneself open to victimization on the streets and to being used as a dupe for services, such as never-to-be-repaid personal loans by organizational fellows. If one exudes too much machismo, one also is open to victimization, as other men attempt to prove they are tougher. To conduct my research, I learned I must find the balance, shifted and navigated between situations, that would maximize my present and future strengths and minimize my current and future vulnerabilities. The importance of gaining the respect of Guatemalans cannot be overlooked, as a margin of respect meant access to respondents and organizations—and kept me relatively safe on the increasingly violent city streets.

My need for image management became strikingly obvious to me as I passed by groups of male brewery workers, an unavoidable part of my activities in one city. I had to be able to continue such passage uninterrupted.

These unionized workers are better paid than much of the Guatemalan workforce. The exuberantly aggressive masculinity of these laborers was constantly played out in their street antics on breaks and at lunchtime as they whistled at women, guzzled beers, and hung out in boisterous groups.

One day it was necessary for me to pass through eight or so male workers who were gathered on a very narrow side street. Their conversation changed and then silenced as I passed. Behind my back, one of them called out, *Hueco, hueco*. The brewery workers' Westernized (i.e., non-Indian) dress was in contrast to my more nativist wardrobe, reflected in my wearing a colorful woven wool shoulder bag (*morral*), which I wore rather unavoidably in a less than *brincón* manner. I imagined they identified me with other foreigners at the nearby boardinghouse and believed that I was not "man" enough to stand up to their degrading insult and to talk tough.

I was reluctant at the moment of the initial shock of hearing the insult to do anything but ignore it, so I took several more steps away from them. I knew I would never be able to enter into their social circle. An attempt to impart my own personal views of manliness or gender neutrality onto them would be ineffective and foolish. I needed, however, to make an attempt to walk that fine line between *hueco* and *brincón* in order to find my safety zone so that they would think that I was sufficiently strong to come and go through that neighborhood and not be victimized. Taking a gamble, I turned around and marched into their midst. Intruding into the circle, I promptly directed myself to the gentleman speaking at that moment and retorted, "Who are you calling a *hueco*? Who? Who? I'm no *hueco*. Perhaps you are?"

The men were apparently shocked to hear me speak street language, head held high, while risking myself in the middle of the eight burly men. I received numerous apologies and assurances that they were saying that someone in the story they were telling was a *hueco*. "Well, maybe you are," I stressed again and reaffirmed to them all verbally that "nobody calls me a *hueco*."

Rather than playing on homophobia or machismo, I was protecting myself. Public images are part of social relations that relegate "unmanliness" to the characteristics of a person easily targeted.[10] Such images are powerful and dangerous, and to ignore them is interpreted as an unwillingness to confront dangers or challenges and hence is itself a weakness.

My boldness worked. I was never again bothered by any of the brewery workers. Even their stares at my shoulder bag decreased and then stopped. Eventually, I was met, for the most part, by indifferent heads rather than by confronting gazes.

The Therapist

Another image management problem resulted because many Guatemalans did not understand the difference between a research-oriented social psychologist and a therapist-practitioner. Many persons appeared to think that if I did one, then I must do the other. Being from a U.S. university only enhanced the awed effect my educational status had on particularly middle- to upper-class urban people.

"Therapist" turned out to be a role from which I could not escape, as many persons "checked out" their behaviors with me or confided to me their troubles and heartaches, broken love lives, and loneliness. This "please fix me, Frank" attitude was often particularly exhausting for me. I frequently needed support myself. I daily spoke at length with persons who had been raped or tortured or who had witnessed sequesters, massacres, and executions. Hearing so much pain in daily doses, I could not help but take on the pain that informants and respondents were suffering and communicating to me.[11] I also had to worry about the very real possibility of my own demise while collecting sensitive data that alleged government sponsorship and complicity in systematic, long-term violence.

The pressures of being the free community therapist were numerous. Combined with beliefs of my having money, for instance, this image led some persons to want to monopolize my time, to want me to take them to parks and pay their admission fees and on trips to help them alleviate their emotional suffering. While these were noble endeavors, I was constantly working to help various people understand that I had to be mobile and that I was not in Guatemala to "play" and take people on vacations.

The therapist image certainly affected the extent of time I spent interviewing respondents, particularly during the second fieldwork period in 1992. This therapist image, however, due to my perceived empathy and respondents' willingness to disclose personal information, made me privy to significant and intimate details of people's thoughts and life experiences that under different circumstances most likely would have been unobtainable.

The Single Man (with a Plane Ticket to los USA)

My unmarried status created added problems for the research. On certain clumsy occasions, some women employed a façade of being emotionally troubled or having pertinent political information for me so as to get into situations of sexual provocation. At other times I was led into dangerous circumstances that were supposedly political in nature, only to find out that my fervor had been manipulated in order to get me close enough for flirtation. Sexual tension is a powerful manipulative tool in the field,[12] and it is a potentially dangerous side effect of continuous human contact under certain circumstances.

Part of my attraction was undoubtedly intertwined with images of me as a person with money as well as that of a sensitive provider of therapeutic conversational understanding. Because I was going back to Los Angeles and I was single, I was fair game for young women wishing to go to "los USA," which, from their perspective, promised freedom from want. The opportunity to play Casanova, however, was not tempting. It was often an awkward, unwanted mess.

The Religious Fanatic

Religion is a major issue in Latin America, and Guatemala is no exception. My religious activities may have affected subjects' images of me and influenced their answers. I could be seen to pray with some persons and wear a cross and other religious symbols. Religiosity, for some staunchly ideological atheists, along with my soft-spoken modal disposition and my unwillingness to be a chronic flirt with the opposite sex, caused some persons, I am sure, to look upon me as an ascetic.

I worked in some largely atheistic organizations. Some trade unionists, for example, might not have agreed with anything but staunch atheism. My religious image most likely kept me out of their inner sphere of close contacts and left me marginalized. Moreover, my work was likely devalued by them. For others, as I knelt next to them in a church or cathedral, lighting a candle and praying for the safe return of their disappeared loved ones, the value of my work may have been enhanced. Overall, I believe that my own visible religiosity was positive for most informants and organizational contacts. This is because I could be seen as someone who followed his own convictions and who was not easily swayed by others' opinions or wants.

Overall, I believe that my own religiosity did not serve as an inhibiting factor in data collection. For the most part, for people with whom I prayed or went to a Catholic mass, the image of me as a religious humanitarian who practiced social transformation was likely a welcome and comforting image. My normal practice of wearing a religious symbol was most often viewed favorably by subjects and associates and placed me within an understandable world in which I appeared less foreign.

The Guerrilla

To numerous security officials and citizens I was probably seen as a communist guerrilla, or at least a sympathizer. Many Guatemalans were indoctrinated to believe that gringos were the guerrillas' "fifth column," agents acting for the rebels from within the country. The image was likely widespread among the military. Civil Patrol leaders and army personnel, according to one of my respondents, warned people to be on the lookout for the guerrillas, blond men with long hair tied back in ponytails. My own physical appearance of short, dark hair and moustache served to aid me in eclipsing such an image. However, for certain government agents, the very fact that I walked with barefooted Indian widows who accused the army of sequestering their husbands was certainly enough for me to be branded as a Guatemalan guerrilla. The guerrilla image was understandably dangerous for my respondents and me.

I made conscious efforts to limit the growth of the guerrilla image. I was an unarmed researcher and attempted not to break Guatemalan law nor to discuss the armed rebel organizations. If someone brought up the guerrillas or offered opinions on the decades-old civil war, I listened to them and took mental notes. I refrained from adding my opinion, in order to construct a fragile margin of safety around my work.

The CIA Spy

In war-torn Guatemala, where government agents and guerrilla sympathizers mingled on the same streets, it is not surprising that some people might have seen me as a CIA spy. For them, the fact that I was from the United States, asked questions, and blended in well with popular organizations made me a likely candidate for being a CIA agent.[13] The CIA had more than a minor interest in Guatemalan affairs and was actively involved in teaching government agents the counterinsurgent methods used by the death squads.[14]

The image of a CIA spy most likely caused potential informants to be slow in trusting me or to never trust me. Intimacy with certain organizations increased through time, especially during the 1992 fieldwork. Such intimacy grew to the point where, with some organizations, I would be a familiar part of informal steering committee meetings and at times would even be sought for advice on organizational matters. Because my ties and access grew with the organizations with whom I spent the most time, this CIA image was probably more limiting at the outset than at later points of the fieldwork. Its likely effect on the data collection was to cause some people to avoid me completely or to tell me only so much of their stories.

THE POPULAR MOVEMENT—WHO WERE THEY?

My participation in activist organizations gave me access to virtually all of the persons I interviewed. Those with whom I spoke may have been atypical of survivors of the disappeared and more representative of persons who somehow became constituents of popular-movement organizations. Activities of these groups were directed toward ending the chronic state-directed injustice in Guatemala and promoting the ascension of civil society over military supremacy.

The focus in this book is on the actions the individuals took and not on the organizations to which they belonged. Much of what is reported here addresses the quiet revolutionaries' activities prior to their association with any group. The groups, however, did provide me with access to individuals and in that regard shaped the type of individuals with whom I spoke by influencing the selection and self-selection of interviewees.

The most active, broad-based, and significant organizations of the early 1990s were members of the UASP, Unidad y Acción Sindical y Popular (Popular and Trade Union Unity and Action). The UASP was formed in 1988, and many of its member organizations were major trade unions, organizations of survivors of violence, and gender-based and rural constituencies that did not necessarily belong to outside coalitions.

Some of the organizations with which my respondents were associated arose in direct response to the actions of state-sanctioned terrorism and included the Mutual Support Group of Family Members of the Detained-Disappeared (GAM), Family Members of the Detained-Disappeared of Guatemala (FAMDEGUA), National Coordinating Body of Guatemalan Widows (CONAVIGUA), and the National Council of the Displaced of Guatemala (CONDEG), among others. But the research also extended to individuals associated with organizations pushing for cultural and economic equality. These groups tended to view cultural role definitions as state-dominated and, at times, Eurocentric. They focused their attention on people who were politically peripheral, such as the Maya, women, and slum dwellers. Examples of organizations of this type were the Mayan group Majawil Q'ij and the Mayan women's sectors represented by Mamá Maquín. This latter organization organized Guatemalan Mayan women who were in refugee camps across the Mexican border.

Economic deprivation was the third broad area of popular-movement activity from which the respondents were drawn. This deprivation was characterized by lack of access to sufficient legitimate sources of income, which in turn limited access to health services, transportation, education, nutrition, and Guatemala's legal system. The principal organizations that focused on this area were the trade unions that made up the UASP. These unions drew their members from the semiprofessional and labor sectors of society. They were often allied with university student and reform-minded Christian movements that were also members of the UASP, such as the Association of University Students (Asociación de Estudiantes Universitarios) and the Symposia for Peace and Life (Jornadas por la Vida y la Paz). These university and religious sectors were multi-issue organizations that in their activities addressed all three issue areas covered by the UASP and other popular-movement groups.

The people I interviewed may have been inclined toward group participation, as mentioned above, and their employment situations may have allowed them to participate in activist organizations. I did not collect information that might have shed light on these matters. Qualitative researchers in general encounter similar constraints.[15]

Usually I attended steering committee meetings or met with specific organizational representatives before talking with members about interviews. In such meetings, I described my research and asked for concrete suggestions on how we could work together and as to what role I could play in activities that focused on their organizational objectives. My participation in their activities before I conducted interviews was a way for people to get to know me and gain confidence and trust in me before sending their vulnerable members to be interviewed. I also got to know the organizations' members and learn which of them were knowledgeable about the topics I wanted to discuss and to build rapport with them.

The connections to organizations among most of the people I interviewed was convenient in that it allowed access to several persons at the same time. They did not have to be group members. At times, they were individuals who were receiving services from the organizations, or they were from the same communities as the organizations' members, because people I interviewed took me to speak with others they knew. Some people approached me to be interviewed. All persons contacted in these ways were attentive to my inquiries, and only one person refused to be interviewed in the nearly five months of direct fieldwork. Such a response rate may suggest the fundamental desire of Guatemala's survivors of state-sanctioned abuses to express themselves.[16] The Guatemalans' willingness to talk also may have reflected a favorable reaction to my stringent efforts to preserve respondent confidentiality, anonymity, and safety as well as the eventual trust built into the relationships among the popular-movement organizations, the potential respondents, and me.

The fact that the people I interviewed often lived near each other considerably reduced my travel time and expenses. But, as with many factors in research, proximity had its disadvantages. The respondents' geographic and cultural homogeneity somewhat limits the generalizability of the findings of this study. That is, the people with whom I spoke may not be representative of like-situated individuals who live elsewhere in the country.

I conducted interviews exclusively in the capital city and in the central and western highland departments (similar to states or provinces) of Sololá, Chimaltenango, Quetzaltenango, and El Quiché. I interviewed many people in the capital who were from other departments, such as San Marcos, Suchitepéquez, Huehuetenango, Retalhuleu, and Escuintla. But the individuals with whom I spoke represented neither the total cultural universe of Guatemalans nor the total universe of survivors of the state-sanctioned terror that began in the 1960s. The people with whom I talked were more representative of persons who had experienced abuses by state authorities since 1980. This is because the more recent disappearances, massacres, and army and police counterinsurgency campaigns were centered in Guatemala City and the Maya-populated departments of the central and western highlands from which my respondents were drawn.

The interview subjects likewise did not necessarily represent the cultural backgrounds of all Guatemalans who had been the victims of state-sanctioned violence. I did not speak the indigenous languages and could only conduct interviews in Spanish. I was usually unwilling to use interpreters because they would have threatened the confidentiality that I promised those I interviewed. I simply could not control interpreters' future behavior. In approximately 15 percent of the interviews, however, I did use the help of native Indian speakers who could translate into Spanish at least some of my questions and the respondents' answers. Such help was usually provided by a trusted group or a family or community member who was in the vicinity at the time of the interview. Overall, I did not interview non-Spanish speakers or persons with very limited Spanish ability. I visited and consulted informants from other ethnolinguistic Mayan groups throughout the course of my fieldwork but did not include them in the current analyses, as they did not formally become respondents through interviews and audio recordings. Sufficient evidence is available to believe that this approach excluded a large number of Guatemalan family members of the disappeared who speak only indigenous languages.[17]

All eighty persons I interviewed in 1990 and 1992 had suffered illegal or extralegal rights violations at the hands of state-sanctioned security forces or institutions; these violations included assassinations and disappearances of family members and/or friends, witnessing of loved ones and other persons being raped, tortured, and mutilated by security forces, and death threats and the accompanying fear of death. Almost all of them reported disappeared or executed family members. Many of these respondents had multiple family losses. Several rural Mayan women had lost up to fourteen family members, including their husbands, to extrajudicial execution or enforced disappearance. A majority of the respondents also gave specific information on non-kin losses. The few who did not have a disappeared or executed family member included a Kaqchikel Mayan woman who was raped as a virgin by an intelligence agent, a trade unionist who was sequestered and tortured, and a K'iché Mayan man who with his family was kept in a filth-filled latrine for more than two weeks at an army base for refusing to participate in the "voluntary" Civil Patrols.

About 80 percent of the interviewees were women. It was generally the men in their families who had been targeted for violence. More than 80 percent spoke as their primary language K'iché, Kaqchikel, Kanjobal, Mam, or Tzutuhil. Spanish was their second or even third language. There was a vast difference in the ages of the people with whom I conversed. The youngest were teenagers, but I also talked with people as old as ninety. They were, for the most part, unschooled. Almost one-third of their number had spent a year or less in a classroom. While the remainder had gone to school longer, their attendance had been short-lived—on average, only four years. But eleven of the eighty had made it to college, three of them graduated, and one of them had become an attorney. In general, the subjects of this study did not substantially differ with respect to these demographic characteristics from other survivors in Guatemala.[18]

INTERVIEWING

Most of my conversations with Guatemalans that form the core of this book took place during the final days of the civilian government of Vinicio Cerezo Arévalo in December 1990, as well as during the civilian government of Jorge Serrano Elías in the summer of 1992. The 1990 interviews took place during the election fervor for the presidential runoff between the two top candidates, Jorge Carpio Nicolle, who was later assassinated by paramilitary agents, and Serrano, who won. I was in Guatemala for one month in 1990 and for two and a half months in 1992. But I collected general data for one week in 1993, for eleven months in 1995 and 1996 while I worked on an unrelated project for the World Health Organization, and for one week in 1999.

The actual interviewing was a painful process for me but even more so for the interviewees. Their stories were real and tangible, and the events they described had lasting and defining effects on their lives. The survivors continued to look for their missing family members in crowded rural and urban marketplaces, city streets, and public buses a decade past the abductions. And there were those whose family members were murdered. One woman told of a brother who was sequestered and later found slain. Holes had been bored into his back as if from a carpenter's drill or meat hook. His abdomen had been flayed with razor blades, among other mutilations. Many moments of the interviews were filled with sobs and uncontrolled crying.

The interviews had much to do with victimization and suffering as well as with political and cultural transformation and resistance. As we spoke, I made sure that the Guatemalans knew that they could stop the interviews at any time. I wanted them to take their time, particularly when issues were painful to discuss. It was important to me that they feel comfortable with the interviews. They were able to delve as deeply or as superficially into a story of abuse or loss as they chose; this floated between discouraging some from providing place or person names or specific dates (measures to protect them from ever being identified) to prompting and probing others to clarify certain details.

I was concerned that the interviews might be trauma-producing, and the last thing I wanted to do was to victimize these people again. They had enough painful experiences in their lives. Because of this, it was ethically essential to conclude the interview process with a focus on their gains and capabilities instead of solely on their losses. I wanted them to realize that they had valuable insights to share and to recommend to others. This strategy was especially important in Guatemala, where no large-scale programs existed to attend to the psychosocial needs of persons victimized by state-sanctioned traumatic processes. While researchers under other circumstances might be able to provide respondents with referral information, a confluence of conditions made that nearly impossible in Guatemala.

CHAPTER THREE

Chronic Ambiguity

The military state's strategy of intimidation through terror arguably worked with the vast majority of the Guatemalan population. No statistics exist on such matters. But it did not work with everyone. For some individuals, it had the opposite effect. Rather than cowering in fear, they became political activists, quiet revolutionaries working to end impunity of the perpetrators and ultimately to transform their country's legacy of violent discrimination into a future of pluralism and justice.

It is, in many ways, the ambiguous nature of disappearances that started the quiet revolutionaries on their journeys to activism. At first they were unsure whether their loved ones were seized by government agents or were the victims of other foul play. "Ordinary," apolitical kidnappings and murders occurred with regularity in Guatemala, and armed guerrillas were also directly responsible for a small portion of the civilian disappearances.[1] The family members turned to governmental authorities, namely the police and army, for help in finding their newly missing loved ones but received none. Emotionally distraught and with seemingly no place to turn, they prayed to God to help them. They were poor and powerless, and they felt they had little to lose by continuing their endeavors to discover the truth. They asked God to protect them. As they continued their efforts to find their missing family members, they met other people in similar circumstances. Some of these individuals were also seeking more general human rights reforms. They became a support system for each other and discussed, among other things, the growing popular movement. We begin their chronicle in this chapter.

The quiet revolutionaries were transformed from victims who turned to God for justice to populist workers seeking justice in the name of the disappeared. It is clear that few of these individuals were activists before their family members were seized. At the time, many were poor Maya, working with other family members on their own and neighbors' small farms. Some lived in the cities, but few, if any, were in powerful positions. Their daily activities were simple by Western standards. Life for most of them, regardless of whether they lived in rural or urban areas, was a determined struggle for survival, sunrise to sunset, day in and day out. For our subjects, it was the best of times.

LIFE BEFORE THE TRAGEDY

A seven-day work week regulated the lives of most Guatemalans, including those in this book, in the years prior to the slaughter. The daily toil for basic existence in the rural areas started in the fog of the early morning. Men arose to the clap-clap-clap of the women of the family making tortillas. A cacophony of roosters, which sound almost ghoulish in their intensity and reach, echoed across the mountain valleys of the highlands and helped the family women awake before the men. To begin the day, the women served a coffee substitute, *pinol,* made from burnt grains of dried corn, or a hot corn porridge drink called *atole* (they could not afford to buy coffee; even those who grew it on their land could not afford to drink the cash crop). They bathed in small groups at a stone sink called a *pila,* with a built-in scrub board on one side and a deep reservoir for water storage on the other, or they opted to bathe in the rivers and streams, and some made a weekly trip to the *temescal,* a shed-like sauna structure for two or three persons, particularly popular in the northwest highlands near Mexico. Standard breakfast fare and smells were produced by warm tortillas that failed to burn the Mayan women's calloused hands, chili peppers (especially a tiny, pea-shaped favorite called *chiltepes*), some mashed tomatoes with spices (called *chirmol*), and perhaps an egg or two. This basic fare, if available, was accompanied by the ever-present black beans, which were boiled with a pungent herb called *epazote* or stinkweed. The poorest peasant often just had tortillas with nothing to put on them—no meat, no beans. The communal feast almost ritualistically was consumed with hands aided by folded tortilla wedges with which they scooped up everything. Chickens pecked at any crumbs they found and defecated around the feet of those gathered at the table, generally outside, under an awning of some sort.

Following the morning meal, the rural men took to the fields, or in fishing villages, the men took to the sea, lake, or river. The women and children might also go if there was a harvest or other pressing short-term agricultural need at the time. During the coffee harvest, for example, many males and some females left their towns and went to the coffee *fincas* on the coast to pick the beans. Other family members may have headed off to hunt with slingshots draped over their shoulders. Some others may have gathered wood or drawn water—often chores for the children, since they were seldom in school. Youngsters also helped with the morning dishes or played with a soccer ball or tied up bundles of rags in the mud or dust, respectively, of the rainy or dry season, sucking on lollipops or sugarcane stalks whenever luck was with them.

Those members of the family who worked in far-off fields or had no time to walk home for lunch took their food for the day with them. Large, corn-dough, meatless, and unseasoned tamales called *tayuyos*, maybe a couple of boiled eggs, a plastic container of *chirmol*, and tortillas were standard fare for work-time belly filling away from home. Days were often split between work on subsistence fields that supplied their daily meals and cash crops to pay for the increasing number of goods such as clothes and drinks that they could not produce.

The cool of the early evening usually saw families gathered for the collective consumption ritual. They felt fortunate if the meal consisted of fresh hen soup, a few turnips, and other vegetables. But in Guatemala, as elsewhere, the men often stopped on their way home to passively defy the family nutritional rites as they gathered for smoking and joking and the downing of bootleg rum called *kusha* or the mostly warm beers of the countryside or Coca-Colas, orange Mirindas, or "Sevens" (7-Up).

Religious gatherings or neighborly visits also characterized the early evenings. Once the sun set—between 7 and 8 p.m. year-round this close to the equator—it was bedtime. Women, however, remained up and often washed and mended clothes by candlelight or kerosene lanterns, chatted, hung the clothes to dry, and fed the family poultry and dog the leftover tortilla bits or the dried, stale ones in their entirety. Late to bed, early to rise was—and continues to be—the lot of the rural women of Guatemala. But in general, both sexes shared heavy loads of responsibility for family maintenance and survival.

The residents of these rural villages were unlikely to see themselves as Guatemalans. Anthropologists as late as the 1970s noted that Maya identified with their village communities, and most gave little import to the idea that they were members of a larger nation. They were firmly Catholic and had a belief in saints as local protectors, which they summoned through ritual. They were suspicious of outsiders and maintained a strong Indian identity.[2]

URBAN LIFE BEFORE THE TRAGEDY

Urban life in the misty wee-morning hours of Guatemala City, El Quiché, Chimaltenango, and Xela was punctuated with a cornucopia of urban wake-up sounds: the vroom, vroom, vroom of ancient, former U.S. Bluebird school buses as their drivers raced from one bus stop to the next combined with the clack, clack, clack of unbalanced aluminum wheels attached to wooden carts of *chicleros*, cigarette and gum sellers—displaced Indians, for the most part—as they traveled over uneven cobblestones and eternally unrepaired broken pavement.

Simple breakfasts, often a bit heartier than those consumed in rural areas, were eaten in haste and with less ritual than those among the fieldworkers. Once finished, the urban Guatemalans entered the black-smoke-filled streets and poured into the buses, which competed for fares at the frequent stops. As in many urban centers during rush hour, people filled every possible space on the public vehicles, forming essentially two lanes of bodies facing outward in the aisles. Bodies rubbed against each other, elbows poked, and the most polite of the urban Guatemalans said *con permiso* as they passed and tried to get a seat or at least a more comfortable space in which to stand before the bus jerked along to the next stop. The riders might also have barnyard animals on board—sometimes hens in their arms but more often pigs, goats, and roosters in the luggage compartment below the bus floor or on the roof of the extra-urban buses. The *ayudantes*, or fare-collecting bus workers, whistled at women on the sidewalk and called to each other, vying for fares, yelling out the routes like evangelical Baptist preachers, *Colonia Venezuela, Nimajuyú, Maya, Maya, Maayaaaaaaaa!* Buses abounded with thieves and ass-pinching or crotch-rubbing rude men, and competition for seats or space often led to tension, if not arguments.

The offices, factories, stores, and large vegetable and meat markets filled with workers beginning their days often by six or seven in the morning. Many workers who lived in the shantytown neighborhoods that ringed the city had been awake for some time. They often had to take two or three buses to arrive at their jobs, and they spent substantial portions of their day's meager salaries in the process.

Managing basic services was characterized by long queues at the banks, the phone company, the electric company, government ministries, and the grocery store, in addition to the need to compete for public transportation on an often exhausting daily basis. Bus madness, black-smoke clouds, and the off-key roar of old engines continued into late evening, as second-shift and nightlife workers made their way home after the day's wage earning, often in an atmosphere of tremendous insecurity. Urban crime levels were—and continue to be—astounding, especially rape, armed robbery, and assaults, and many urban Guatemalans lived, worked, and came home in fear. The urban Guatemalans then and now traded the relative availability of subsistence foods in the countryside for urban luxuries such as electricity, semi-running water, movie theaters, bars, pharmaceuticals, and store-bought foods such as ice cream, sodas, chips, and baked goods.

No matter the hardships they faced, compared to their future, it was still the best of times. In the coming years, many of the rural communities, maybe 700 of them and their inhabitants, were obliterated. Maybe a million individuals fled the country. Some 150,000 civilians, mostly rural Maya, were savagely murdered, and an additional 50,000 individuals, from throughout Guatemala, were disappeared.

WHY WERE THEY MURDERED?
COUNTERINSURGENCY TARGETS

The savagery in Guatemala grew from the long civil war in the country. Disappearances and assassinations were part of the military government's counterinsurgency scheme. Those Guatemalans who lived in areas where guerrillas were active witnessed untold brutality. The violence was a tornado, indiscriminately grabbing and killing uninvolved rural residents and guerrillas alike.

It is not our intent to retell the violence that was practiced on thousands of innocents in Guatemala. There are other books devoted to such matters.[3] But we depart from this practice to tell a survivor's tale of his family's demise at the hands of the army. We do this so that the reader has a sense of the Guatemalans' despair at the situations around them and of the brutality that had entered the lives of villagers in many of the western and central rural areas in the early 1980s. The horror he describes was the usual lot for many in villages that the army believed were infested with guerrillas.

> At six in the evening, the military commissioners and the army, who were more than 9,000 men, encircled the village . . . Without saying even one word, they arrived at the houses to machine-gun my family. They killed my father, who was 74 years old. Then they killed my brothers, who were 26 years old and the littlest one, who was 12.
>
> Then, they began with the women. For example, my mother wasn't killed with firearms or knives. They made a sharp, pointed stake from wood. So then, they began to torture her in the stomach. Also, they

stuck it into her here in the neck, in the eyes, and they stuck it into her mouth as well.

So then, what they said to her, or, that's to say, what they asked of my mother was me. My mother knew that I was inside [the house]. But she denied knowing my whereabouts. "I don't know," she said. So then, they killed her by pure torture. By kicking her. And they also drew a knife. So then, they cut off her ears, a piece of her nose, while she was alive.

So then, my mother herself . . . I could hear her really well [asked], "What do you men want from us? We are poor people. What is it that you want from us?" And so they said to her, "You people are pure guerrillas. You are pure communists. But what we want from you, we want your son." That's how they spoke to her.

So then, they went to grab her once again, my mother, and . . . she was 64 years old. And then, they went to grab my wife. And they did the same thing to her, with the stakes. And she was carrying [in a woven cloth called a *rebozo*] a little girl who was eight months old. So then, they began to torture her. "Tell us where your husband is. Hand him over and you'll go free." But, with many kicks, and from the stake, lots and lots of blood was flowing from her stomach and in her face as well. When they were giving her those tremendous kicks, they did it with our daughter attached to her as well. And they were pulling on her hair, and they would stand them up. So then, they killed her, and when they killed her, because the girl was belly down on top of my wife, when they stuck the stake into her, they killed the two of them, because they drove the stake into the stomach of the both of them.

And after this assassination, this massacre, they pulled her and they dragged her inside the house and they lit the house on fire. So then, what they wanted to do was . . . in addition to the bullets, in addition to the tortures, was to burn them. I was present. I was inside the house. But they [the army] didn't see me.

But when they killed my parents and everything, what I did was to go outside. And they began to shoot all over the place. That's when I was able to escape from their hands. Though, in any event, they hit me with gunfire. They hit me here, and here, and they hit me here, and here. I fell right down.

Such executions in rebel-controlled areas were common at the height of the terror and conducted by the army to deter others from joining the rebels and to kill at least some guerrillas who might be unlucky enough to be at the wrong place at the wrong time.

Mass executions were less likely to be used in areas that were not dominated by the rebels. In such communities, the state-sanctioned forces employed selective violence, such as disappearances, against those they perceived to be armed rebels or their sympathizers. Residents of "pink" villages were particularly well aware that the violence in their communities "started because . . . there were guerrillas and the guerrillas are against the army. So then, that's when the sequesters and everything began."

SURVIVING A DISAPPEARANCE

The survivors of the disappeared and murdered who were interviewed for this book utilized various coping measures to deal with the losses of their loved ones. We argue throughout this book that their search for their disappeared loved ones and their pursuit of justice for the murdered and disappeared, including their participation in the popular movement, were facets of these coping measures and that these steps were consistent with their culture.

The quiet revolutionaries employed a wide range of ameliorative and self-empowering responses to the daily challenges set before them as family members of the disappeared and murdered in Guatemala. Many of these, from a traditional Freudian psychotherapeutic or Bowlbian attachment-and-loss perspective, would be viewed as pathological responses.[4] Daily crying bouts, lighting of candles and incense, the fabrication of home memorials or shrines, and doting on the lost family members ten years after the disappearances would all seem problematic to many traditionally trained Western psychotherapists. But it is important to view the measures the Guatemalans took from their cultural framework and not from ours. Joy Ufema, a pioneering death-and-dying specialist, recently noted in this regard that she likes "to remind people who have rules about grieving that we will grieve until we are done. For some, that may be weeks; for others, years."[5] In the broadest sense, adaptive coping with the loss of a family member might be anything one deems relevant, as long as it does not further debilitate the surviving family member. The construct of debilitation itself can only be understood in its cultural context.

The consideration of how to define or distinguish culturally appropriate long-term coping strategies is important because of the need to avoid the imposition of Western ideals and definitions on other cultures where they may be inappropriate, if not harmful. Remarriage, for example, is often praised as a sign of recovery in Western academic literature on widowhood and coping,[6] but it may not have been an appropriate adaptation to the loss of a spouse for rural and especially Mayan women in the western highlands of Guatemala. Such women conformed their sexual behavior to an ideal that held that a woman would be a virgin at marriage and should share sexual experiences with only one man through the course of her life. It is not surprising, then, that many of the rural women consistently expressed the desire to not remarry even though they had not seen their husbands in years or knew them to be dead. "I'll never put another man at the head of my children" was a common comment from women separated from their husbands.

Beyond the cultural constraint, there were numerous other reasons women in Guatemala did not remarry, many of which have been cited or proposed in other studies of Guatemalan widows.[7] The slaughter certainly decreased the number of eligible men in many Mayan communities. Men did not want to marry widows who already had children and other family obligations. Male subjects in this study noted that Guatemalan norms demand that the woman be a virgin when arriving at marriage. The relatively few surviving males, as a result, tended to pursue young virgins for marriage rather than previously married women with children and economic problems and limitations.

The men also distanced themselves from such women because of the social belief that the women must also have done something wrong to have gotten themselves into their current situations. If your family member was a *mala gente* (bad person or one of the bad people), the pseudologic goes, then you must be too. Some women may have preferred the autonomy of being newly single to marrying men who may have wanted to thwart their newfound independence and demand the attention some women would rather have reserved for their children. Fear may have played a role in women not remarrying. Many of the respondents, both men and women, expressed deep concern in the interviews about losing more family members to murder and disappearance. Remarrying, if at all possible, would have once again left them vulnerable to losing new mates in similar fashion. Such fearful vulnerability was pervasive, and the interviews are rife with such notions.

Remarriage apparently makes little sense in terms of adapting to the traumatic loss of a spouse for a large segment of rural Guatemalan women, given the culturally derived standard of a woman having one man in her life and a myriad of related traditional values and daily circumstances. To some extent, to remarry would have been to deny one's culture, to deny one's own identity and existence but most importantly to deny the existence of the disappeared. Illustrative of our point is the daily ritualization practiced by many of the quiet revolutionaries of identifying with lost family members.

In not atypical stories, one preliterate urban mother of a disappeared son carried a little notebook and counted each day, hour, and minute of her son's absence after more than a decade. She reported still looking for him at bus stops and in the people who got on the bus as she rode it, as well as in crowded marketplaces and other public locales. Another woman left her house each evening for more than half a decade to see if her sons were coming up the hill. Such behavior must be considered in the context of traditional Guatemalan views of marriage, family, and community relationships that typify areas of central-western Guatemala where fieldwork was performed. For these women to remember their husbands, their sons, their daughters every day is a reaffirmation of their identity represented in their blood ties and communal institutions. While the physical presence of the loved one has been separated from the communal and familial setting, the blood ties that person represents have not. The disappeared men are still the fathers of their children. The brothers of the disappeared fathers are still the children's uncles. The kinship networks or blood ties do not vanish.

The value of family is forever. Just as one does not replace his or her children if they are missing, one does not replace a husband who is missing but still "with" the family. A family is created on a permanent basis, and the cosmological cultural world of the traditional Maya does not necessarily preclude contact with the missing or dead, as we will explain in more detail later. Through cosmological worldviews, dreams, acts of remembrance, the worked land, and the children (the seeds of the union of the man and surviving woman), the man is still a part of the family, even during what may become a permanent physical absence.

Daily remembrances, while obviously a source of sorrow, appear to represent an adaptive response in the particular social milieu. The strategies appear successful at helping family members serve the memories of their missing loved ones in a dignified manner and in maintaining and reinforcing shattered blood and community ties that are essential to their identities. It is an understandable strategy in the face of the prolonged slaughter and daily crises that questioned and threatened their identities, both individually and collectively.

"IS HE ALIVE OR DEAD?"

The perplexity surrounding disappearances led many not only to activism but also to a new, collective identity. "Is he alive or dead?" they wonder. "Will she return? When?" "Where is he?" "Is she being tortured?" For them, the resolution of the chronic ambiguity associated with the enforced disappearance of loved ones was often the greatest motivating factor for eventually joining one of the human rights groups. Even those quiet revolutionaries who knew of or witnessed their family members' deaths did not completely escape some of this ambiguity. They wondered where the bodies of their murdered relatives were buried, and some worried if they had suffered much before their deaths. The quiet revolutionaries movingly and almost universally illustrated these themes.

Consumers of modern media regularly see on newscasts individuals who have missing family members, and the viewers are told about the efforts such individuals are making to alleviate their anxiety about their missing loved ones. In May 2001, the parents of a federal intern in Washington, D.C., appealed to television news audiences for help in finding their daughter. The young woman's disappearance and her romantic involvement with a congressman continued to occupy headlines until the events of September 11, 2001, replaced them. After that, one of the leading stories was the anguish experienced by family members of those missing in the collapse of the World Trade Center buildings. More than a year later, some families still denied that their loved ones had died in the tragedy. For these families, as for the quiet revolutionaries, the chronic ambiguity of the disappearances impeded family members from the enactment of culturally relevant rites and practices that may be necessary for grieving.[8] The parents of the murdered intern buried their daughter and entered that process. The quiet revolutionaries similarly sought to learn the fates of their loved ones. If they were dead and properly buried, then the surviving family members could begin the grieving process. If they were alive (the desired outcome, of course), they could reunify their families.

The examples we have presented here from the United States differ in one major aspect from the tales of the survivors of the disappeared and murdered in Guatemala. For the most part, the United States activities were the actions of individuals or family members. They may have used efforts to find their loved ones as coping mechanisms to live with the ambiguity of their losses. But those efforts never developed into what academics call a social movement. Such movements involve, according to one commentator, "collective challenges by people with common purposes and solidarity in sustained interaction with elites, opponents, and authorities."[9] Pictures of missing children on milk cartons are not evidence of a social movement because such efforts to find kidnapped children are not opposed by people in powerful positions. In fact, they may be supported.

There are examples in the United States in which social movements were the outgrowth of people facing losses. The efforts of the father of Polly

Klaas, a child who was murdered by a released inmate, led to the enactment of California's Three Strikes Law. Likewise, individuals who founded Mothers Against Drunk Driving used their efforts to cope with the deaths of their own children.[10]

Most applicable to our story were the efforts of U.S. family members of the missing in action and prisoners of war from the Vietnam War who demanded an accounting as part of any peace process. These family members and especially the wives drew on supportive elements in the surrounding social milieu, among other significant factors, in developing coping strategies for indefinite, unresolved, war-induced separation.[11] Ambiguities led them to oppose the United States' solution to the Vietnam War and to foster a social movement to demand information about their missing loved ones. In turn, their involvement in the social movement caused a collective identity shift, from wives and relatives of soldiers who supported their government to members of groups that opposed it. A similar ambiguity drove the Guatemalans to take action.

ALLEVIATING ANXIETY

In many cases, only the initial, acute sense of loss produces more stress than the prolonged ambiguity regarding the whereabouts and fates of the missing. About one-third of the quiet revolutionaries interviewed in this study believed their disappeared relatives were still alive, even after a decade. The focus of their activities, as expressed by many throughout the interviews, was the hope of finding a living relative among the tens of thousands of the nation's disappeared. Among these individuals were ones who were told that their loved ones were dead but who tenaciously believed otherwise. "They tell me he's dead, but I'm not convinced" was a common sentiment. Somewhat more than 40 percent of the quiet revolutionaries knew, or firmly imagined, their family members to be dead at the time of interviews. The remainder were unable to state that they imagined their relatives as dead, but neither could they decisively state that they thought that they were alive. They often left that decision in the hands of a divine power. "Only God knows," they would say, or they simply acknowledged their confusion and inability to decide upon one fate or the other.

Persistent ambiguous thoughts typified all family members of the disappeared, irrespective of the imagined fates of their loved ones. They relied on a number of mechanisms to try to decide whether the missing could be alive or dead, including information from dreams and socially derived cues such as family advice and local gossip.[12] But as we shall show, these fell short of relieving their anxiety.

DREAMS

Indians trust to a great degree in their dreams, and conclusions about disappeared family members were frequently based on dream experiences. Traditional Indian beliefs assign profound levels of cosmological and existential significance to dreams; they serve as mechanisms to facilitate the visitation of beings from the spirit world or as a means of telepathic communication via spirit means.

The quiet revolutionaries, including *ladinos,* often reported dreams and in many cases used them as the bases for their decisions on whether their disappeared loved ones were alive or dead. Illustrative were the dreams of a Mayan woman who had lost her husband, son, and three brothers-in-law to forced disappearance. Her husband came to her as she slept and told her that he was dead. In the dream he asked her to pay for his Catholic mass in honor of his spirit and his memory, as is the tradition. Contented that her husband was dead, she asked God her son's fate. Her son then came to her in a dream. He spoke with her and reassured her that he was alive and that he would return to her in five years but said he did not know where his father was. She then dreamed that her three brothers-in-law were still alive, apparently in some type of forced labor camp.

This woman's story is important because it embodies the stories of all respondents who discussed their dreams from a traditional perspective. As well, her example is important because she dreamed missing loved ones both alive and dead and, as did many traditional Guatemalans, felt that she communicated directly with her missing relatives. Her traditional belief held that dreams are divine knowledge and that she could communicate with her disappeared relatives in dreams via divine intervention. She looked to such communications, particularly from her son, to ameliorate the chronic ambiguity that gnawed at her daily psychological reality.

While Western ideology might argue that it is unhealthy for this woman to maintain the hope that her son and three brothers-in-law may still be alive and might advise her to "let go," it appears that such styles of continual contact with the missing relatives are in no way pathological and are, in fact, adaptive in the cultural milieu. Expectations of human behavior vis-à-vis bereavement and the assumptions related to "recovery" are culture-specific; refusing to let go may be normative mourning behavior in cultures that do not subscribe to postmodern perspectives of bereavement.[13] Perceived dream communications and relative frequency of ruminations about the missing family members may represent constructive and adaptive coping mechanisms at work, especially for traditional Guatemalans, as opposed to being signs of compromised mental health or symptoms of distress.

The relative importance of previous cultural traditions in determining adaptive styles of coping can be seen in the cosmological significance of dreams for rural and traditional respondents and the roles such dreams may play in alleviating or structuring family members' chronic ambiguity in a meaningful way. A traditional Freudian perspective would typically view such dreaming about disappeared family members as frustrated wish fulfillment, akin to children's dreams of eating strawberries after having the delicacy earlier taken away from them, or a youthful male's nocturnal passions.[14] Or a typical Bowlbian view based on stage theories of recovery from loss might conceptualize these dreams as possible unhealthy ruminations in which the persons suffering the losses are stuck in a phase of yearning for lost attachments.[15] There is no convincing evidence, however, that traditional Western psychological or philosophical models of dream interpretation or of the letting go of losses implied by such models are valid when considering the population under study and their relationships to their dreams, their family members, and their perceived cosmological reality. A traditional Western model of dream interpretation cannot account for how these persons viewed their dreams and the importance that these played in their lives, especially as individuals with disappeared family members.

Dreams, in the vast majority of cases, served as the only post-disappearance communication between surviving family members and disappeared loved ones. They were a means for the family members to accept the death of a disappeared one as divine knowledge. This may have erased some of the family member's psychological responsibility in accepting as dead a disappeared loved one, without proof, amid conflicting cues.[16] But the dreams did not fully alleviate their anxieties or allow the expected grieving process to begin. Many individuals dreamed that their missing loved ones were alive, which only created additional questions as to where they were and how they were being treated. Unanswered questions remained for those who had dreamed that family members were dead: Where is the loved one buried? Have animals eaten him? How did she die?

CUES

Dreams were not the only mechanism that the quiet revolutionaries used to try to determine whether loved ones were alive or dead. The chronic ambiguity that forced them to forestall the grieving process and closure (in the nomenclature that has become popular in the Western world) also drove them to make guesses about missing relatives based on socially derived cues. One factor, for example, was their own set of experiences, or those they had been told about, with the forces who they believed had taken away their loved ones. "Look," one reported, "we know the hands into which he's fallen [and he] didn't fall into angels' hands, right? We know that they're criminals. They don't feel their souls!" Based on his knowledge, he concluded that "no, he's not alive."

Several persons received some news of their disappeared relatives, and this information became part of the accounting they used in trying to decide the fates of the missing. In general, such information had come from friendly or compassionate military sources. As many local youths were forcibly conscripted into the Guatemalan army and Civil Patrols, military barracks and bases where sequestered persons were often brought were not always places where anonymity of prisoners was feasible. News that a disappeared relative was alive days or even months after the sequester could always be considered evidence that the person was still alive. But it did not relieve the anxiety, as the possibility remained that the family member had died in captivity or was being horribly mistreated. One woman described detailed news that was passed to her, including a note from one of her sequestered relatives, sent through the father of some friends of the military personnel who were allegedly holding five family members captive for two months by that time:

> Those who know my relatives say that there they are, and they make hand-signs to the other soldiers who know [the relatives] as if to say "They're in there, all locked up! They're blindfolded." . . . and [the girl], they shut her up inside an old ambulance, in the sun. Sun, darkness, and rainwater passed over her there, all shut up inside an ambulance . . . Because the soldier told me where they had [the girl] . . . There she was sitting for three days. They give her a little cup of water. And three days later they give her one tortilla.

The results of such cues, however, were never able to relieve the anxiety. The family members had certain experiences with the authorities, had heard stories, and had perhaps spoken with others in the social environment, all of which often created a body of conflicting cues that maintained the family member in a state of ambiguity. Moreover, the accounting of such cues had a psychological toll on those who utilized them. The value of each cue had to be measured and evaluated amid intense emotional anguish against conflicting cues, all of which were considered significant because they concerned the variety of possible fates of disappeared loved ones. In the end, the quiet revolutionaries could only wonder. "I don't know if she died or not," the woman concluded about the incarcerated girl. "Only God knows."

CONTINUING AMBIGUITY

References to God, the authority of dreams, or an accounting of often disparate cues failed to quell the quiet revolutionaries' anguish regarding their disappeared family members. If the sequestered loved ones were "imagined" alive, there remained the possibility of being reunited with them, and that hope might have helped the quiet revolutionaries' psychological health.[17] But with it came guilt and anxious torment regarding the treatment the disappeared were receiving at the hands of their captors.[18]

The tortures meted out to real or potential opponents of Guatemalan military governments are well documented and horrific.[19] Rarely a day passed during the fieldwork without the announcement in the national media of violent murders or disappearances. People in the streets frequently talked of army abuses such as rape, especially in rural areas. In common parlance the soldiers were labeled *cuques,* a shortened version of the Spanish word *cucaracha* (cockroach). And many of the quiet revolutionaries had felt for themselves or seen the brutality. Numerous survivors reported witnessing public punishments of army prisoners before they were disappeared to fates unknown. By far one of the least severe examples taken from the testimonies gathered for this study was offered by a woman who, along with a town full of people on an election day, saw her husband with his hands tied behind him, kneeling in the back of a jeep, being beaten in the chest with rifle butts by soldiers. The testimonial and academic literatures are replete with examples of such public punishment of prisoners in Guatemala.[20]

The constant, systematic abuse of the population by state forces created turmoil in the minds of the quiet revolutionaries. Individuals who imagined themselves one day reuniting with living family members also simultaneously imagined missing members in involuntary captivity being tortured. The survivors felt guilty when eating or when warming themselves because the individuals in captivity must certainly have been deprived of those basic comforts. Cues were, once again, used to make guesses, this time about the nature of the treatment the missing received. In a country and time when many went hungry due to significant inflation and regressive tax levels on basic consumer items, it is not surprising that one of the survivors of the disappeared imagined the missing to be "suffering a lot, because in this

Guatemala, they treat you like an animal. He's suffering the consequences. I don't even think he eats. If they have him alive, they don't even feed him. And if they do, it's a few crumbs of bread."

Individuals may have tried to soothe anxieties over the treatment of the disappeared by concluding that they were dead. They may have found relief in no longer imagining the daily suffering of family members and were consoled to know that their disappeared family members were, at last, dead.[21] Such consoling cues, fed at the time by the frequent discovery of cadavers nationwide (and the more recent opening of some of the nation's more than 170 registered "clandestine" cemeteries) or by rumors of "bone lagoons" and other areas of cadaver dumping, appear to also have brought with them psychological costs. The loss of family unity and the permanent loss of the disappeared individual from the family system existed irrevocably. But such thoughts also were accompanied by chronic ambiguity for the quiet revolutionaries. They wondered how family members died, how much and long they had suffered before death, where the bodies were, and who was responsible. They longed for traditional burial and mourning rites and fought thoughts of mutilation or of dogs eating the bodies of family members they now could imagine as dead. These are not small matters for traditional Maya, who believe that without proper burial, souls are caught in the empty space "between earth and the afterlife, condemned in time between death and the final obsequies."[22] The anxiety they felt about these matters comes across clearly in the words of one of the quiet revolutionaries:

> I say, I wonder where they tossed him? And perhaps some animal ate
> him and I didn't know about it. I, who loved him so much, to just have
> him tossed away like that, and to not even know where the remains
> are. Perhaps some animal ate him. In the end, I never rest from these
> feelings. Sometimes I sit and wonder if he's dead, how is it that I don't
> know where he's buried? Because of all the work that's going on now
> to exhume the remains [in the clandestine cemeteries] . . . I think a lot
> about him, how I could find him and take him out [of a clandestine
> cemetery]. Put him in a cemetery as is our custom. But this is
> hard on me.

The quiet revolutionaries almost all faced chronic ambiguity and anxiety over the physical whereabouts of their missing loved ones. This is true even if they knew their family members to be dead. Some of their anxieties may have been personal. A father, for example, responded to his wife, who had complained that he ignored his living offspring, with the retort that his missing son "is not a dog." Perhaps the father feared that he too would be ignored if disappeared. But much of the anxiety the quiet revolutionaries felt was rooted in culture. Their feelings and desires seem to differ little from those of modern Western family members who have had a child kidnapped and long to have the child returned. They too have a psychological need to begin the grieving process. The quiet revolutionaries also wanted to enact traditional rites such as placing flowers at gravesides. One expressed the deep sorrow of uncertainty:

> The advice I have [for others] is that when you've lost a loved one [to death], resign yourself. At least you've got them there. Once in a while, you go to leave them a bunch of flowers. On the other hand, I don't know . . . if he's alive or . . . I live with that, right? This is what I've spoken out about, because others have told me their children were killed, and they go and bury them and all, but they've got them. On the other hand, me . . .

The pain caused by uncertainty led survivors at times to prefer knowing that their loved ones were dead, to wish, as one said, to "find my daughter, even if she's dead, just to find her."

WOMEN ARE OVERREPRESENTED

Women were overrepresented among the quiet revolutionaries. Since men were the primary victims of the disappearances and slaughter, it seems reasonable that women would be overrepresented among survivors. But there are less obvious reasons that led to their active participation. One is associated with gendered identities, in particular women's commitment to the mother identity.[23]

In general, identity plays a role in behavior.[24] Some experts on the subject argue that individuals' various identities (for example, mother, wife, schoolteacher, daughter) are arranged in a hierarchy and that behavioral choices are associated with the location of the identity in the array.[25] Thus a woman for whom the mother identity takes precedence would usually choose to spend time with her children as opposed to spending time with other individuals.

Throughout most of Guatemala, women had access to few personal identities other than wife and mother. Men had identities as father and husband, but they also were wage earners and leaders of communities and families. For women to let go of the missing meant relinquishing their identity. If their family no longer existed, then who were they? If they were no longer wives and no longer mothers, they had no identity. Moreover, within the cultural framework, "good" mothers and wives do not simply give up on children and husbands. Accepting loved ones as dead and "moving on," when seen through the cultural lens of these women, would be to identify one's self as a bad individual. Men had roles that were meaningful to them other than as fathers or husbands from which they could gain self-worth. For example, fathers of the disappeared could give up on finding children alive while maintaining positive self-images as wage earners.[26]

The gendered identities of the men and women did not always result in greater anxiety among the women. We noted the instance of the father who answered his wife's pleas to quit the search for a son with the comment that the boy was not a dog. It was the father, for whatever reason, who was driven to not surrender. But this example also illustrates the salience of the mother role for the woman. She urged the father to let go of the one child in order to save the others. Women's anxieties about missing husbands can be seen similarly. Given the uncertainty as to how they will feed and clothe their children without the family wage earner, the women were often unwilling to accept missing husbands as dead. It seems reasonable to assume that the anxiety felt by survivors of the disappeared and murdered was more intense and prevalent among women.[27]

It is also likely that the chronic ambiguity triggered an eventual identity shift in the women from wife or mother to identities that also included wage earner and political activist. The interviewed women's hold on their culturally accepted identities was tenuous at best. They clung to their beliefs that they were still wives and mothers. But the conflicting cues filled them with anxiety and left them in a state of normlessness. Before the disappearances, they knew their roles and how they were to behave. But the disappearances removed such certainties in their lives. Under the circumstances, the women were more likely to be predisposed to accepting a new identity. Although not a perfect analogy, we offer the tale of a Zen master who is approached by a potential student. The master offers the student tea before the first lesson and proceeds to overfill the disciple's cup. "Stop, my cup is full and can hold no more," cries the student, as the tea flows onto the floor. The teacher replies that the student is as the cup: so full that he will not be able to learn anything new. The disciple, the master implies, must first be emptied of previous beliefs before he can learn the new ideology. Similarly, the women first had their former identities damaged before they could take on new ones. If the disappeared were known to be dead, the women might have assumed the identity of widow and during normal times followed a well-trodden, culturally acceptable path. But the chronic ambiguity and the times prevented them from adopting a widow's identity and kept the women open to other possibilities. A comment made by a quiet revolutionary who had several disappeared family members nicely illustrates the process: "When I got married, I knew nothing about business," she began. "So when I was left alone, I worked hard in the fields. [When] one has no money, one works like this and earns a few cents. My children were small. And after my sons went away, I worked even more because their children were small. And here I am right now [at a movement office], struggling for my family, those who are disappeared." She moved from an identity that focused on wife and mother to one that included worker and activist. The inclusion of the new identity was an outgrowth of her struggle to resurrect her family.

ALLEVIATING ANXIETY THROUGH ACTION

It was chronic ambiguity that drove the quiet revolutionaries to action. It was not necessarily or exclusively the loss of a spouse, a child, but the need to do something toward ending the relentless ambiguity. The anxiety they felt was perhaps not so different from that felt by the Calvinists whom Max Weber described in his classic work *The Protestant Ethic and the Spirit of Capitalism*. Calvinists believed they were predestined for heaven or hell but had no idea which destination awaited them upon death. Weber argued that Calvinists threw themselves into work to relieve their anxiety about this matter. Eventually, independent business came to be seen as a calling particularly acceptable to God. This change, Weber argued, led to the creation of the modern Protestant businessman.[28]

We argue that the quiet revolutionaries were galvanized to try and find the missing, to join family members' support groups, and to eventually seek justice for their loved ones as members of political action organizations as coping mechanisms to relieve the anxiety caused by the ambiguous nature of their losses. The work allowed them, at least for a while, to forget the situation that was their daily existence. In addition, the ambiguity and anxiety the quiet revolutionaries felt was not limited to thoughts about missing family members but "spilled over" into other behaviors and their daily interpersonal social relations.[29] In war-torn Guatemala, the quiet revolutionaries realized that what had happened to their family members could happen to them and others, their children, their grandchildren. The quiet revolutionaries' participation in political activities also helped alleviate this anxiety and fear while it simultaneously placed them in greater danger for repression. Together, these circumstances served as precursors to the establishment among the quiet revolutionaries of a collective identity as Guatemalans.

CONCLUSION

The quiet revolutionaries whose stories are told in this book do not represent everyone who had a disappeared family member or who did not know where their family members were buried. Linda Green interviewed Mayan widows who were not active members of social movements. The Kaqchikel women responded to the violence against their loved ones by becoming ill. Their illnesses, Green forcefully argues, were representations of "the horrors that they had experienced" and "a refusal to break ties with the person who was killed or disappeared."[30] To not feel pain, Green's respondents reported, would be to forget their family members' deaths. Their illnesses, Green posits, "will not go away until there is justice."[31] There were, among the interviewed, a considerable majority of persons with such symptoms. Their illnesses, however, were not the focus for these quiet revolutionaries. They responded to queries about their health, but allowed to speak on their own, they discussed their commitment and work to end impunity.

The people whose accounts we report here were more representative of individuals who, for whatever reasons, were active members of, were receiving services from, or were otherwise connected to popular organizations in the early 1990s. Most interviews, as discussed in Chapter Two, were obtained through organizational contacts. The people in this study were not randomly selected for inclusion. Rather, they chose to be interviewed. They may not even have been representative of others in the organizations. There is the possibility that people sought to be interviewed who were significantly more distressed or had more of a psychological need to disclose their thoughts regarding their traumatic experiences.

The stories told here may have been atypical, even when compared to those of other members of their own families who had also experienced the loss of relatives. In addition to the possibility that the individuals may have been more inclined to group participation, they may have had more opportunities to participate than did other members of the family or other survivors of the disappeared. Many of the interviewees were unemployed, with time on their hands. Moreover, they may have been those persons of the family system who were more distressed by the disappearances. Their relationships to the missing and how they viewed them certainly played some role. Or the quiet revolutionaries may have been more daring or determined in terms of risking political participation during dangerous times or simply more inclined than other family members to think that the disappeared relatives were still alive. No information was collected from nonparticipating family members on such matters. This does not seem unreasonable given the dangerous times in which the interviews were conducted. Such efforts would have likely, at some point, placed the quiet revolutionaries in critical danger.

It is plausible that the interviews themselves produced the results. The questions were designed to assess components of theoretically derived social-psychological constructs as well as to gather data related to respondents' memories and perceptions of traumatic incidents and situational elements of the trauma. The interviews were designed to elicit qualitative and quantitative data regarding activities and ways of thinking that would typify respondents' coping responses to their losses and solutions to the problems they encountered as family members of the disappeared. The interviews focused on their ideas and activities for changing their individual and group social situations. Details of the interview instruments and their backgrounds are described in Appendix A. Other ideas about group participation might never have arisen during the interviews because the questions did not pertain to the individuals.

Having said all that, then, what is there to say about the quiet revolutionaries? Were they a small group of people Frank happened to interview and who were unrepresentative of the social and psychological processes going on among other Guatemalan social movement members? Perhaps, but the opposite seems more likely to be true. We are not the first to suggest that the ambiguous nature of disappearances gave rise to a social movement. Alison Brysk notes a similar process at work during the struggle for human rights in Argentina at about the same time. Disappearances "temporarily paralyzed resistance," she writes, but "eventually stimulated protest precisely because [they] blocked the resolution of intolerable family uncertainty and loss."[32] She notes that groups with family ties to the disappeared became some of the most influential figures in the Argentine human rights movement and that the movement began with the mothers of the disappeared who gathered each day in silent vigil in the plaza across from the presidential palace.[33] Much that occurred in Guatemala and Argentina was similar. But the scale of killings and disappearances in Guatemala, estimated at 150,000 civilian murders and 50,000 disappearances, dwarfed the

9,000 disappearances that occurred in Argentina. From Brysk's example we can assume that the quiet revolutionaries were representative of a sizable group of Guatemalans who became members of popular groups.

In the process, we will argue in later chapters, they came to see the atrocities, both those that were personal and those against all Guatemalans, as acts of injustice.

CHAPTER FOUR

Seeking Justice

As with family members in the industrialized world who have missing relatives, the quiet revolutionaries made exhausting efforts to learn the whereabouts of their loved ones and, in particular, whether they were alive or dead. Those quiet revolutionaries whose family members were known to have been murdered certainly wanted to recover the remains of their relatives, but this was less of an initial driving force toward political action than were disappearances. For the survivors of the disappeared, their actions during the first hours and days after the events catapulted them to eventual involvement in the popular movement.

The family members turned to governmental authorities, the police, and the army, for help in finding their newly missing loved ones. At first they were unsure whether their relatives were seized by government agents or were the victims of common crimes. Family and friends began their inquiries at local and far-flung state institutions where they hoped to find the disappeared. But they were met with threats meant to frighten them into inaction. These initial events helped shape their perceptions that injustices were being committed against them.

Fear was a common element in stories from survivors who sought information about the missing. It often shaped the interactions they had with officials who supposedly held the key to open the door of information. "In those days," a survivor recalled, "you didn't inquire about the whereabouts of the disappeared."

A Mayan woman described in broken Spanish how she went to a military detachment to look for her husband with the wives of other men. They demanded that the soldiers read the list of those captured. The military men rebuked the women and declared, "Your husbands are pure illegitimate subversives." The soldiers told the gathered women that if they read the list, the wives would have to stay there, prisoners as well. The women had little choice. Further action would have only hurt the welfare of their children at home and done little if anything to stop the presumed torture and end the unlawful detention of their husbands.

Economic fear acted as a de facto deterrent to family members' efforts to learn about missing loved ones. Some survivors of the disappeared, to make a living, served the economic wishes of military personnel. As with military bases throughout the world, poor people gathered outside the encampments and sold whatever items soldiers might buy. The poor merchants were dependent on the goodwill of their customers. Without it, they could not have fed their families. Survivors told of instances in which individuals encountered soldiers whom they presumed guilty of sequestering or killing their loved ones. They related feelings of impotence and fear. One young indigenous woman, for example, described the sequester and disappearance of her father perpetrated by masked men in army uniforms. Soon after the sequester, as she sold cigarettes, gum, and candies as a *chiclera* near the local army detachment, she was surprised in the midst of her grief when a soldier approached to buy a cigarette. She recognized him by his height and coloring as one who had participated in her father's sequester, though his mouth at the time had been covered by a handkerchief. During our interview she expressed the agony she felt at having to sell him merchandise. She imagined her father inside the garrison being tortured to death while she was outside selling a cigarette to a man who had removed him from the family. The poverty of this survivor and others in her circumstances helped shape their perceptions of injustice, as articulated by a Mayan woman: "It's not just, because one ends up being a widow and then has to look at how to resolve that situation . . . how to gather a few cents here and there."

For respondents who dared investigate, their searches were fraught with the potential for imminent violence. Family members received anonymous letters warning them to "stop looking for our disappeared family members because we were going to end up in the same conditions as them." The situation left some complaining:

It's not just. It's not just, any way you look at it . . . They only threaten you and everything. Well, they wouldn't be the ones threatening, if they weren't the ones responsible for these things! They don't have to be threatening anybody. Any one of us is free to look for his or her family members in hospitals,[1] in detention centers, wherever you have an idea that they may be keeping them.

WHERE ARE THEY?: MISDIRECTION

The quiet revolutionaries who continued the search for their disappeared loved ones met with multiple disappointments. The best they learned was admission as to the whereabouts of the missing, but even this did them little good. An indigenous woman who attributed the disappearance of her two sons to the military described how, when her first son was taken away, a soldier admitted that the army was keeping him in a local makeshift headquarters. "They are detained inside," the soldier told her, "but we can't talk about this, because this thing is very serious." She concluded that it was impossible to glean any other relevant information through military channels.

Establishing blame provided surviving family members with a starting point for their searches for the disappeared. Authorities, however, rarely admitted to the disappearances, despite overwhelming evidence to the contrary. A man who worked on a plantation lost his son to a disappearance that hundreds of plantation workers witnessed, as it took place on payday. Witnesses said that "they took him inside the office, they tied him up . . . and they shoved him into a car," the father reported. "Two military persons were in the back of the car from [a nearby] detachment. They took him away. After about two hours, they returned once again in the car, but this time without my son." The father continued:

> That day I immediately went to the military detachment, to ask the sergeant. I said "Good afternoon" to him, entered, and I said to him, "I've come because of this problem. Yes, that's how it is. Right here and now they've just gotten done telling me that you [the army] took my son prisoner." "Us?! It wasn't us!" They denied it. "Fine," I told him. "Because the people who gave it to [attacked] my son were seen, and it was you [the army]!" "No," he told me. "Go to the police and ask them!"

The father recognized that the sergeant was lying.

The survivors of the disappeared uniformly characterized what they regarded as noticeable attempts at misdirection. Their hunts for missing family members were often temporarily exhausted by participation in wild goose chases. These calculated deceptions, according to the survivors, were attempts to derail their activities and to wear them out in their pursuit of accountability and evidence. Typical of comments were those made by a woman who had traveled numerous and circuitous miles in search of information:

We went to the military detachment [far away] on the coast, because they told me that there he was sequestered. And I arrived there at the base, and the colonel there told me that they had no one, not one of the sequestered. And that it was better that we didn't stick our noses into these things, because then it was the family members that suffered the consequences.

In another typical instance, a father was told that his son was already dead, so he and his wife mentally prepared for finding their son's cadaver. The situation turned out otherwise. Upon buying a casket and arriving at the morgue, the body laid out on the slab was not that of their son. He and his wife returned home, financially and emotionally drained. One woman described receiving deceitful telegrams from military authorities raising her soon-to-be-dashed hopes of ever finding her disappeared family member. When she got to where he was supposedly detained, the soldiers told her that he was not there. Rather, the soldiers taunted her that she could find him in the local morgue.

Taunting was common and increased the survivors' misgivings when addressing legal authorities. Probably the most common retort from police officers toward many urban women was that of "Aahh, your husband, he went off with some other woman." Some family members were similarly told that their loved ones had run off with the guerrillas. One woman, after having the family's chief breadwinner disappeared, sent a telegram to the police, who responded to her that she should apply for employment with them. When she went to the police station, what she found waiting for her was not what she desired. The officer who was her employment contact "tried to get in and make moves" on her. "I was looking for an honorable job," she continued. "I wasn't looking for someone to go to bed with." She felt humiliated to have looked for work from the very persons whom she suspected of sequestering her husband.

In a rare case, police officers were suspected and eventually incarcerated and tried for the sequester-torture-murders of two university students. A relative of one of the two murdered students described the actions of the police investigators early in the process. They wanted to know "if we were willing to give them money for the sequestered" or for their travels while supposedly investigating the whereabouts of the two students. The relative continued:

On the third day after he was sequestered . . . two family members went directly to the police to ask them what it was that they had investigated related to the sequester. And the only thing that the family members got out of them was being made fun of, being mocked. The police began to mock the family members, chanting slogans that the university students used in their demonstrations. They laughed at them. And, kind of as the last straw, the chief of the police began making statements like how was it that our family members would leave the house without letting us know beforehand where they had gone; that [the student] should have told us where he was going. And then he stated that they had no information on the sequester.

In this case, the president of Guatemala interceded on behalf of the police and requested that the family members of the missing not claim that the police were involved. He was "certain that it hadn't been them." The president promised that the authorities "were going to 'make justice.' They were going to mobilize people to see who it had really been."

Official high-level denials and cover-ups were, from the quiet revolutionaries' perspective, part of the misdirection used to mock the survivors and exhaust their energies. One woman described her group's efforts to locate the disappeared after President Vinicio Cerezo Arévalo—the first civilian president since 1970—came to power in 1986. The quiet revolutionaries were hopeful that his election signaled a change in Guatemala, that there was now an opportunity to learn about their disappeared family members.

> We asked for an audience with him [Cerezo]. So then, he said "Yes, I'm going to look to see if they're there [confined]," he answered us. He told us, "Yes, I'm going to give you the names of those who are still alive. And those who are dead, I can't do anything about that." So we were left, all of us, with some shred of hope. And then it came to be two weeks later, which was the day he was to give us the names, and he denied everything. He told us "I never said those words to you." Even the reporters that were there said they'd written down that he had said he was going to give us the names. And at the very hour of truth, he denied everything. And later on, he simply didn't talk to us.

Perhaps the quiet revolutionaries are correct in their assumption that this was simply another effort at misdirection. But there are other explanations. Foremost among these is that the quiet revolutionaries misread the situation. There had been no opportunity for change. The newly elected president had been honest with them when he stated his intention to reveal the whereabouts of the disappeared. But he might have learned that he could fulfill his promise only by sacrificing his own life. Many powerful individuals in the country, particularly in the military, opposed the release of such information and could have made it clear to the president that he would be providing it at his own peril.

ECONOMIC BARRIERS

Having exhausted themselves with personal efforts to find disappeared relatives, many quiet revolutionaries attempted to recruit the assistance of those in the judicial system. These efforts "came to be a gesture of protest and a challenge to the residual fiction of a legal system."[2] In general, however, poverty made it difficult for most of the quiet revolutionaries and other Guatemalans to use the justice system. The mere cost of traveling to the capital city to file a report was problematic for most Guatemalans. A round-trip bus fare from an interior city to the capital could cost upwards of a fortnight's wages for an agriculturalist or several day's wages for an industrial worker.[3] "We couldn't make any kind of official complaint," a torture survivor from a western city noted, "because we are far removed from the capital city." The cost of traveling back and forth was, in his words, "very difficult."

Money is also necessary to hire attorneys in Guatemala, just as in the United States and elsewhere. The procurement of court forms and official seals needed for filing court documents likewise depends on financial ability. A Mayan woman, when queried about how one with no money goes about attempting to punish those who had killed her husband, retorted, "That's how they get away with killing, because there's no money." The survivors felt that their pleas for justice were ignored because they were poor.

Individuals characterized justice as a market-rate piece of merchandise, something brokered only within the bounds of a financial transaction. The relative of an assassinated university student was quite poignant in his assessment of justice as a commodity: "Justice isn't seen as the product of some act, but rather as something that's worth something to someone. Justice gets paid for." He concluded that justice is "applied for the benefit of those who have the money."

Tales of corruption filled the survivors' accounts, and the quiet revolutionaries held extremely negative perceptions of legal officials and the legal system in general. The use of positions of legal authority for self-enrichment was a common theme in their stories. The occupational corruption was seen as determining and undermining the legal process and reducing the possibilities for achieving justice through legal procedures.

Bribes given to judicial authorities were the principal element of circumventing procedural justice. The survivors saw the illegal payments to court functionaries and judges as a class issue, since they were unable to afford them, but rich and economically powerful individuals could purchase favorable outcomes for themselves. One Mayan woman described the search for her disappeared son: "I went to the Supreme Court, and I want[ed] them to fix this thing with my son. And what they responded to me there was 'If you have the three hundred [quetzales],[4] we'll fix it right here and now.'" This request for a hefty sum of money from a poor woman effectively served to constrain her access to legal recourse. On hearing this story, another Mayan woman commented, "Three hundred quetzales . . . that's what they do to someone so that someone doesn't say anything. They know that you don't have money." A plantation worker had a similar story. He described going to the courthouse after visiting many military and social institutions in search of his disappeared son:

> They think they're the lords and ladies of life itself, and bribing them is what it's all about. If you've got money and you arrive at his door with some problem, it'll take you a few thousand to "fix" it. There it is. That's it in a nutshell. But a poor person, right! With what [do we pay them] if we have nothing?

In general, poor, indigenous quiet revolutionaries described numerous incidents that made it clear to them that law was a commodity beyond their meager means. A Mayan man reported extortion attempts by military operatives in a rural, mainly Indian area. He said the soldiers wanted the local people to give them money so they could eat at the local diners. "They leave the law behind and try to take the money from us," he said. "They say that the money that they receive as their salary isn't enough for them." If the local Indians did not buy the soldiers' meals, the soldiers would "go tell on us"—accuse them of subversion—at the military base. Once the suspicion of the army was aroused, the community members knew that they would be open to broader forms of victimization, including assassination. Not surprisingly, this man saw the requests as unjust, particularly given the poverty of his community: "We don't have anything to give them!"

Many of the Maya attributed to racism as well as their poverty the procedural ineffectiveness they experienced. Justice, for these persons, was based on genetic lineage and social class. Their perceptions that courts permitted neither the use of their languages nor translators in proceedings contributed to their inability to access the justice system. Racism, they rightly concluded, worked against them in all matters. Forced military recruitment was portrayed as anti-Indian racism. "Oh, how I wish that all who are *ladinos* and everyone would be grabbed [into the army]!" exclaimed one Mayan man. His wish, however, was unfulfilled. He added, "What happens is that only the indigenous are the ones who get grabbed."

OTHER PROBLEMS

It is doubtful that money would have bought justice for the survivors of the disappeared, even if they could have afforded the officials' prices. Accessing legal resources in Guatemalan society by initiating a court case or seeking out an attorney has often been dangerous, and entering the legal system in human rights cases has put complainants' lives in jeopardy. For our informants, the pursuit of justice in official legal forums was something to be weighed among additional, perhaps contradictory options. One of these alternatives was the incitement of further injustices. A trade unionist from a western region, after being sequestered, tortured, and released, described the dilemma:

> Although one presents the denunciation and wants to see what can be done about it, never, never is justice done for one. And not only that, it could be that, when one goes to make the denunciations to the press, to the government, what the government brings about is your disappearance.

He placed his decision to "let it be" in the context of the ongoing union organizing and the fear of adversely affecting it. For this man, a greater justice was served by furthering the development of the trade union movement. Happily, it also spared his family additional suffering; before his release, the torturers threatened his children as well. He reasoned:

> If we go around making these kinds of denunciations and everything, we wouldn't be able to do anything else. The only thing we would have ended up achieving would have been that our base, our mass members, would have been intimidated. And what interests us is that the trade union movement keeps on going forward and that it not be intimidated by these types of things happening.[5]

But such cases also presented risks to authorities who might try to fulfill their legal duties. Fear was a strong determinant in the decisions of state employees to not pursue wrongdoers. One woman described how she approached the local military commissioner, a civilian-military liaison, who stated that he would not investigate the disappearance of her son by the army. Though his proper role would have been to approach local military personnel, investigate the allegations through their channels, and get back to the woman alleging the sequester, the commissioner refused. The official told the quiet revolutionary, "No, he wouldn't do any investigating because they could also take him away."

The lack of investigation by the authorities left the survivors of the disappeared suspicious that the police were involved in the sequesters. From their perspective, justice was unlikely if the police were the perpetrators. Justice would be achieved if the police helped them locate the missing and even more so if police caught the abductors, no matter who they were. But when a police force that was supposed to investigate disappearances only made threats against family members for demanding investigations, justice was unlikely. That the same force failed to investigate the disappearances was further evidence for the interviewed that the system was unjust.

Even when investigations were conducted and suspects detained, the family members were sure that justice was not done. Most of the murders and disappearances in Guatemala were the work of the military. Guatemala's long history of military personnel being tried exclusively in military courts for alleged crimes against civilians—and being consistently absolved—was more than sufficient evidence for the survivors that justice was not being done. There seemed to them little chance that the villains were to be punished:

> Here in Guatemala, there are various cases. There's the assassination of three people in Guatemala City, where two soldiers were found responsible and then "escaped." Now they run free. And they say, "Oh, look, we're going to catch them here. We're going to catch them there," and everything, and, you know, but . . . we don't really hear of it. Nothing happened. Nothing concrete. Why? Because they are military personnel.

Impunity reigned.

NAMING AND BLAMING

It was important to the quiet revolutionaries to establish, at least in their own minds, why their family members had been murdered and disappeared and who was responsible for the acts. Without such knowledge, the assumed deaths and disappearances of their missing relatives were without meaning, random acts that might be best attributed to "God's will."

In general, people desire to understand the world around them. They infuse meaning into circumstances as a means of maintaining sanity. The death of a family member is commonly a time of great sadness, but it is made more bearable if we understand the circumstances. "She lived a long life" is a common comment made at the passing of a grandparent. The length of the life of the recently departed loved one helps the survivors to understand the death. In contrast, the death of a young child is difficult for any parent to comprehend. The parents might, through their tears, ask, "Why did this happen to my child?" Establishing causality and responsibility allows the parents to focus their attention on such matters and may make it easier to accept the death and complete the grieving process. The naming of a cause or an offender and the establishment of blame, in this regard, gives meaning to the death. "Naming and blaming," as some academics have called it,[6] were important components of the process leading to the quiet revolutionaries' conceptions of justice and their eventual involvement in the popular movement.

WHO WAS RESPONSIBLE?

Determining why a family member had been murdered or disappeared, as with many questions in Guatemala, was fraught with ambiguity. The quiet revolutionaries, at the time of the interviews, were in general agreement that the violence was the outgrowth of the country's lengthy internal conflict. But naming such a general cause as the driving force behind their missing relatives' fates probably provided them with little satisfaction, and they were left wondering "Why?" They turned once again to cues in their social environment in their efforts to name a more specific cause.

In the most general sense, the survivors blamed the military government for the violence. A common exclamation from the interviewed was "Oh, how I wish that the government wouldn't do any more killings!" The government was seen as ultimately culpable for their plight, according to a Mayan woman—who reported having been raped by a military intelligence agent—"because they prepare these types of people, inhuman savages." More specifically, the violations were attributed almost entirely by the survivors to the state's security forces, in particular to the army. A typical statement was "It's the army, the ones who do all that killing . . . They killed my sons, they killed my husband, they killed my neighbors, they killed my son-in-law, everybody."

In rural areas, the paramilitary Civil Patrols, which were seen as the local power base of the Guatemalan army, were often assigned blame. Members of these units were the only citizens organized on a local level who could legally carry guns, and those guns were available to them for a variety of purposes, according to the surviving family members, including extermination of co-villagers. The fact that some persons had the ability to kill fellow community members, the argument went, led to killings. One widow provided evidence that for her was conclusive that the Civil Defense Patrol was involved in her husband's disappearance. She fingered the local unit leader as the main culprit:

It was the commander of the Civil Self-Defense Patrol. He is now dead, but there are other paramilitary men as well who are working on following the same footsteps as that murderer. By the light of day he carried his arms and he obligated the civil patrollers to follow him, to go to sequester, to go to assassinate, to rape the women, the girls in the villages. He, during his life, had eighteen women. And that is corroborated by the people themselves. And we know it, because he, with his weapons, he felt more manly. And so then, in front of us, he did these things. For that reason we know it.

In the rural areas, the survivors of the disappeared and murdered were likely to believe that their family members had been wrongly targeted as rebels or rebel supporters. During enactment of the scorched-earth policy of the 1980s, the military used a wide brush in painting individuals as active revolutionaries. Some of the selections were predicated on old animosities. Members of groups pushing for land reform, for example, were targeted for disappearance and execution because influential plantation owners considered any agriculturalist rights group as a front for the rebel movement. The elimination of the organizations' members and leaders served the long-term interests of the landowners by removing any opposition to their practices.

In general, any anti-government sentiment in the rural or urban areas was enough to get one labeled a guerrilla during the scorched-earth period. Time and time again, interviewees reported that loved ones had been seized because they refused to be silent in the face of whatever injustices they may have perceived. At the time of the interviews, family members of the disappeared recognized the connection between being outspoken and being labeled a rebel. "When people go about finding out what their rights are and demanding them," stated one man, "then they are accused of being guerrillas." Another man, referring to the worst epoch of violence, reported that "ten years ago, to speak about human rights was to label yourself a communist, a guerrilla."

The family members of some of the disappeared understood the use of military force against the rebels and, to a limited extent, comprehended the use of counterinsurgency tactics. They did not condone the use of violence against activists, but they were more likely to see the cause-and-effect relationship between political activity and disappearance. But there were also survivors of the disappeared who believed that their relatives were labeled as rebels and seized despite their lack of political involvement. In a broad sense, the difference between the groups was, for some individuals, the difference between family members of the urban disappeared and rural survivors.

RURAL VERSUS URBAN

Rural Mayan widows acknowledged that the violence took place in a context of counterinsurgency warfare, but they maintained that they knew nothing of the supposed political involvement of local friends and family members. One of these women lamented, "We didn't even know what color [were the uniforms of] the one side, nor what color was the other side."

The labeling of family members as guerrillas prior to their disappearances created some ambiguity for their rural survivors. They provided evidence in support of their beliefs that their loved ones were not rebels. But the language the survivors used indicated that they had at least some doubts as to their family members' innocence. One widow commented on the general category of those who were labeled guerrillas and then disappeared: "But it's not certain that they are guerrillas." She continued, "At least, I never saw my husband with a gun. I couldn't even kill a chicken in front of him because he didn't like it. He pitied them." Another woman, whose brother was disappeared after the army accused him of being a guerrilla, argued that her sibling's alleged rebel status "was not certain because he never liked to stick his nose into politics nor into any problems. He only liked his job." These two disappeared family members probably were not active rebel fighters or sympathizers, but their survivors' evidence in support of this position was weak. Not carrying a gun, pitying chickens, not expressing an opinion, or liking one's job were probably characteristics found among guerrilla supporters as well as innocents.

In the city, university students and trade unionists who were victimized were involved in political action and social-change activities, and this was often known to the quiet revolutionaries. These persons had to explain their activities and beliefs to their family members, and so their family members knew about the causes for which the disappeared were acting. A surviving family member of a labor leader seemed well acquainted with the motivations for unionization: "Unionism is all about watching out for the rights of the worker, the rights which are often forgotten by the business owners. They are trampled upon . . . and the union has to see, at times, that their rights are respected."

Mass media, population density, and word of mouth all made for more urban exposure to the violence phenomena and to the stories of persons working against the government. The urban survivors of the disappeared on the whole were more politicized, more politically savvy, and perhaps more activist-oriented than rural people. The words of the wife of a disappeared trade unionist illustrate this sophistication. She explicitly located her husband's disappearance within a class battle between labor and "the capitalists [who] always want to have you under their heel." Her use of the term "capitalists" and reference to class struggle indicates a level of political knowledge that goes beyond a rudimentary understanding of events.

The disappearances and murders were relatively unbearable for the rural widows. They were unable to find meaningful reasons for their family members' demise and were less likely to display the psychological resilience that some of their more politically savvy urban counterparts exhibited. In this regard, the establishment of causality and responsibility, at least in their own minds, likely helped the urban quiet revolutionaries better cope with the loss of family members.

TWENTY-SEVEN ARE DISAPPEARED

It was most often during the telling of disappearances that family survivors went to great lengths to establish blame, as if they were presenting evidence in a courtroom against those who had sequestered their loved ones. We once again deviate from our practice to not focus on the murders and disappearances in order to underscore this point.

On June 21, 1980, twenty-seven trade unionists, delegates of the National Workers Central (CNT), were sequestered and disappeared in broad daylight in downtown Guatemala City. Among them, an interviewee reported, "were five women, two of whom were pregnant." The union leaders had gathered to conduct a memorial ceremony for one of their number who had been murdered that morning. The sequestering force, according to several people, numbered about sixty plain-clothed, armed individuals who blocked and rerouted traffic in the heart of the city as they surrounded the building in which the union leaders were meeting.

The unionists were on the top floor of the two-story building. The armed force entered the building through the first-floor door by using a Ford Bronco to ram open the entrance. The type of vehicle was important to the quiet revolutionaries, as it was evidence to them as to whom the perpetrators were. As one of their number noted, the Bronco was the vehicle of the National Police, the type of vehicle "in which they took them away." The respondents bolstered their arguments by reference to two young persons who were able to flee through a window onto the roofs of the neighboring buildings and escape. These were the only persons on the inside of the offices who were witness to the invasion and who survived to tell.

Individuals described in detail the scene they encountered the day after the abductions. "All of the window panes were in pieces," a woman recalled, "chairs thrown to one side. The purses of the women [were strewn around the office as well] . . . giving us the impression that everything had all been thrown together." The disarray and chaos of the union office were not the only reminders of violence. "There were some pools of blood that were very big. And furthermore, we found a . . . spent shell cartridge." Another family member of a disappeared trade unionist remembered that "there were pistols. I believe we found two, and blood that we found there, spread out on the floor and on some chairs."

The armed men who had entered the union offices, according to our informants, were members of the former detective division of the National Police (*judiciales*, Judicial Police). The informants had not actually seen the abductions. Rather, their identifications were generally based on anonymous witnesses' testimonies, deductions from information reported or gathered at the scene, or the patterns of violence previously observed in Guatemala. They pointed to their evidence: the types of vehicles used in the sequester, the modus operandi of the sequesterers, the scope of their actions, the close proximity of the Judicial Police headquarters to the union offices, and the targets of the disappearances—union leaders. A woman's account typified the surviving family members' deductive reasoning: "There were witnesses who said that they stuck them into some Broncos that they used to use before and that the Judicial Police had taken them away." She continued, "Their [Judicial Police] offices were only two blocks away from where they [the unionists] were . . . We were told that the one who commanded the group [of sequesterers] was [name], who was, at that time, [title] of the Judicial Police."

Unnamed witnesses who were on the streets or who observed the events from their windows were identified by the survivors as corroborating their viewpoint. One survivor related that "many people saw all that . . . that there were cars of the Judicial Police that were there."

For some of the people, there was no need for concrete evidence in order to identify the perpetrators. For them, almost all injustices were attributable to the Judicial Police because, they argued, "in those days, it was the Judicial Police that was most likely to do those damaging deeds."

Many quiet revolutionaries were not content with naming the conglomerate of the Judicial Police; they needed to blame an individual. One said, "We always knew that it was the [police] chief under the [President] Lucas García government who was most repressive toward the trade union movement . . . the very head of the Judicial Police." Still another family member of the disappeared unionists attributed the sequesters to the military president of the time, General Romeo Lucas García.

Other family members of the disappeared unionists saw the abductions as part of a class battle. For them, the actual perpetrators were agents of an upper class. While the blame might be shared by certain individuals, it was more directly affixed to an entire social class. The words of a relative of one of the disappeared trade unionists reflect this view:

> What I believe, more than anything else, is that it was the business-owning class [who oversaw the disappearances] . . . my disappeared [relative] was in the directive of a particular union. At various times, the factory manager there had threatened him. He had even called my [relative] one last time and told him that . . . if they didn't give up on this thing, [he showed my relative] a pistol that the manager had in his bag. For that reason, to whom I assign the blame is the business-owning class. They try to find some way to skim some lives from off the top in order to see if the union movement comes tumbling down.

The establishment of blame for the disappearances of the twenty-seven contributed to the quiet revolutionaries' deductive reasoning in that it allowed them to also guess a cause for the loss of family members: they were disappeared at a union meeting by agents of the business class; therefore, the logic went, they were disappeared because of their union activities.

THEY OWED NOTHING

An oft-repeated Guatemalan saying is "He who owes nothing fears nothing." The Guatemalans are referring to freedom from societal debts or social responsibilities. In contrast, those who have committed some sort of transgression are deserving of punishment.

Important for the quiet revolutionaries' reasoning was establishing that their loved ones were innocent of any wrongdoing. Otherwise, the abductions and murders might be rightly deserved. For the quiet revolutionaries, their missing family members had owed nothing. Yet they were punished by sequester, disappearance, torture, and murder, and these penalties were administered by an extralegal system comprised of the legally authorized security forces and their paralegal and extralegal allies. As a result, respondents systematically denied that their loved ones deserved the fates that they encountered at the hands of the authorities. The comments of a Mayan widow about her husband's murder and the murder of numerous other villagers by the army were typical:

> If you're guilty, then you deserve what you get. But he wasn't guilty of anything. He wasn't mixed up in anything. And he didn't deserve it. That's what hurts me, because if my husband had been up to something and had been mixed up in something, then he would deserve what he got. But since there wasn't anything going on, everyone who they did that to, didn't deserve it.

The rural widows often contrasted the innocence of murdered and disappeared husbands with the guilt of their executioners. In the words of one woman, "The ones who didn't owe anything were taken away, and the ones who owed weren't touched." For her, not only was the apprehension of those she perceived as innocent unjust, but the fact that physical punishments were meted out against those not formally accused assisted in fashioning her perception that a grave injustice had taken place. She grieved that "they gave them a bad killing."[7] The widow continued, "They tied them up with barbed wire, their hands behind their backs. They tied their shins up with wire. And by this barbed wire, they say, they lifted them up and threw them into the trucks." For this woman and others, the horror that their loved ones endured prior to their deaths was undeserved and the punishment unjust.

Surviving family members bolstered their arguments that many of the murdered owed nothing by referring to groups of victims who they believed were particularly innocent, such as the pregnant women in the case of the disappeared twenty-seven. One woman reported that the army and military commissioners burned homes in her village to kill the residents. Along with the horror of watching neighbors and family members burn to death, she was appalled at the killing of children and the elderly. "The thing is that the people who died hadn't done anything wrong," she protested. "There were children, elderly, old people who haven't done anything wrong!"

Refusing to participate in the nominally voluntary anti-guerrilla Civil Patrol units was a common reason for the victimization of men in the rural areas. A woman reported that her husband had moved from their village to the capital city after receiving death threats for not having been willing to perform Civil Patrol duties. He was killed anyway. "They took him as if he were any John Doe from a subversive organization."

As poor people, agriculturalists wishing to shirk patrol obligations juxtaposed the needs of their families with those of the military leaders. Family came first. For this, from their view, they were unjustly punished. One explained:

> When "the man" says there's an order and that everyone has to patrol because the guerrillas are coming, if the men say "We don't have time because we have to provide for our households, for our children; we have to work for them in order to have sufficient corn and beans," they accuse them of being subversives. And for that, they persecute them, and for that, they kill them.

The disfavor felt by the Guatemalans toward the Civil Patrols made the local military units prime targets to be made scapegoats for violence in rural areas and contributed to survivors' perceptions that the punishments were unjust. A widow claimed that her dead husband and other members of his Civil Patrol were murdered by the army. She explained that he and other local village males were conducting their Civil Patrol duties in the evening, and they came upon a number of massacred civilians. They were blamed by the authorities for the slaughter, which she and other village women claimed they did not do. In essence, according to her, they were framed, and other local persons working with the military perpetrated the mass murder. The Civil Patrol members had owed nothing.

Quiet revolutionaries who had an urban upbringing perceived the killings and disappearances as particularly unjust because they involved the destruction of the best of society; the best sons and daughters of the nation were the ones being systematically eliminated. Their view stood in sharp contrast to the labeling of the same persons as *mala gente* by state forces to mean revolutionaries or politically oriented social undesirables. Surviving family members admitted that their relatives and community members were "fighters" in society and were most certainly raising a ruckus in certain circles, but they saw this combative spirit as altruistic. A mother said her son told her that "he was a member of the student association here, from the university . . . [and] he supported the poor persons and everything. These were his ideals. For that," she concluded, "they sequestered him."

The deaths among society's cream was viewed by surviving urban family members as particularly unjust when juxtaposed with their good deeds. They were most often described as exceptional persons who were justly fighting the good fight. The family members focused on the almost angelic goodness of the victims; the only crime they committed was their good-heartedness. A quiet revolutionary bemoaned that "they've killed many young people, many useful students, many useful men, useful for Guatemala." They were tortured and killed "for watching over the people, for looking out for the poor." Their deaths and disappearances, according to their surviving family members, were unjust because they were selflessly contributing to the wider community, an extremely admirable trait in Guatemala.

The urban survivors often contrasted the horrific treatment of their loved ones with their perceived goodness. A mother who had lost a student son to illegal detention and subsequent disappearance described the details of her son's torture as related to her by others who were also detained. "Their bodies had been repeatedly cut with razor blades. Lit cigarettes had been used to burn their feet, and electric-shock prods had been inserted into their rectums." To her sorrow, her son was not released along with the others and remained disappeared. She eloquently contrasted the tortures with the altruistic goodness of her son, who she believed had died because he demanded better desks and more quality teachers at his school:

> In my way of thinking, [it was] because he was a very intellectual student. He didn't let them get away with lies. He was very astute. He liked to do favors for those who needed them. And he liked to unite with his *compañeros;* and in whatever student strike that they had, he was right there demanding better conditions. For that, it was probably that . . . for those ideas, not bad but good, that, when he received his teaching title, he wanted to serve his country, serve as a citizen, not as a delinquent nor as a thief.

A fellow respondent similarly contrasted the goodness of those eliminated with the brutishness of the perpetrators of systematic violence.

> There are human beings who are quite merciless. They don't think about the damage that they're going to cause, carrying away useful people without thinking about the fact that they are even fighting for them . . .

for a better future and everything. They are human beings who are not interested in any of this, [only] that they pay them so that they carry away the intelligent people, the intellectuals. And they [the detainees] are human beings, as well, who are men who look out for [their fellow] human beings so that there [will] be equality, so that there [will] be peace, and more than anything else, for respect for human rights.

Whatever weaknesses the disappeared and executed may have had in life vanished with their deaths and left their survivors looking for justice. "I witnessed how they were tortured, how they were burned," a quiet revolutionary anguished. "These are roots, banners, and flags of struggle for me."

SEEKING JUSTICE

The family members of the disappeared established for themselves a moral accounting in which their missing loved ones had been punished for assumed crimes by the extrajudicial forces. The government was found wanting in the moral equation. The alleged crimes, the quiet revolutionaries preached, were not investigated prior to punishments being meted out. The act of taking someone away before investigating guilt was foremost in many respondents' minds and, at times, overshadowed concerns about the fate of their missing relatives. "They killed them or they didn't kill them," no matter the final outcome of the sequester and subsequent disappearance, "but, by what right did they take them away in the first place?"

To this moral accounting the survivors of the disappeared added the weight of law. One of the survivors explained:

A transgression is dealt with by judging the person. For that reason the authorities exist. There's law here in Guatemala so that persons are judged. That's the way it should be! Not just carting someone ignorantly away as if he or she were a dog. Like a dog! So then, the law has to judge first in order for there to be a punishment assigned. Not to disappear them, as they do with them. And that's what pains me. That there's no law here in Guatemala. Let them judge us as to whether or not we owe anything!

Similarly, another woman whose husband was disappeared commented:

It's not just! Because they didn't investigate whether he was guilty or innocent or something. They just killed them. That's what I say.

Because if they said to him, well, you know, "Why did you do that?" or "We have a witness who saw you do such and such," it's his problem for what he's done. Then they can kill him or punish him. But just killing like that . . . you don't know if the person caused some kind of problem or not.

At times during the long civil war, the Guatemalan government established institutional mechanisms to lend a measure of legal authority to its actions. There were survivors of the disappeared who were aware of the efforts but found them wanting. One recalled that "in the year 1982, Ríos Montt was in power. The special military tribunals were created, and lots of people were executed by firing squad without having had a logical trial, a correct trial." He was critical that defendants were brought to trial in less than twenty-four hours before anonymous, hooded judges who summarily found them guilty. Execution by firing squad quickly followed and then burial in unmarked, mass graves. "That was a clear violation of human rights," he concluded.

It is unclear as to when the survivors of the disappeared began to incorporate perceptions of the legal system into their moral accounting. Perhaps the survivors of the disappeared who lived in the capital city at the time of their family members' abductions were politically more astute and recognized the absence of formal legal authority prior to the tragedies in their own lives. Poverty-stricken rural Mayan widows were probably less likely to immediately see the lack of law in their husbands' disappearances. The rural widows may have acquired their perceptions of a lawless Guatemala while trying to locate their missing loved ones or after speaking with popular-movement members. For us, it matters little.

The point we wish to make is that the executions and disappearances kindled a desire for legal justice in some survivors. This small flame was fanned into a blaze by the further injuries they faced as they sought information about missing loved ones. In the long run, their searches led them, through diverse routes, to participate in the social movement to end impunity, as this quiet revolutionary explains:

I united with the Mutual Support Group with the proposition of finding them, because their whereabouts were, in reality, unknown. I had already done so much. I even went to speak with the President. I went to speak with the Chief of State. I went to the Secretary of State. I spoke with the Police. They sent me to G-2 [military intelligence]. I even went to the International Red Cross, bringing to them documents that showed that my son had been taken into custody by the National Police, because it even came out in the national newspapers. In all of the newspapers it came out, with photos. I put in paid ads, and I've never gotten an answer on his whereabouts. Even the Archbishop went and said he'd handed in paperwork to the proper authorities and he could do nothing more for me. Only that there was a little group starting, a group of mutual support, and that I should direct myself to that group. And for that reason, I'm still here now.

JUSTICE AND IMPUNITY

Through the years, the goals of the quiet revolutionaries changed. At first, their individual efforts had been aimed at resurrecting their families through the return of the disappeared or, in the case of those who knew their family members to be dead, to learn the whereabouts of their loved ones' bodies. Their sense of justice led the former to argue that "alive they took them away, alive we want them back." As time passed and the likelihood of finding loved ones alive diminished, the quiet revolutionaries loosely banded together to form a movement to end impunity. The desire to find their disappeared loved ones still troubled their thoughts, but they gained some relief from joining with others in an attempt to gain justice for the disappeared.

Justice was often conceptualized by the quiet revolutionaries as a "right to know." They argued that murders and disappearances had been endemic in Guatemalan society, and the impunity granted the perpetrators of these crimes was one of the principal injustices Guatemalans consistently faced. Denying them the right to know the whereabouts of their loved ones collectively punished family members and entire communities.

For the quiet revolutionaries, the right to know the identities of the perpetrators of state-sanctioned human rights crimes was a call for implementing the law as written, something that they perceived as never occurring. They consistently declared that respect for life was a necessary element for the existence of any type of justice in Guatemala but that such respect could only be fostered if there was legal accountability for acts of violence. Demands by the quiet revolutionaries for the right to know was their most consistent strategy for bringing to fruition their vision of justice. Once this knowledge was obtained, their logic held, all else would follow: prosecution, forgiveness, healing.

The quiet revolutionaries resisted efforts that they believed might undermine their struggle to achieve the right to know, that is, justice or legal accountability for their loved ones' fates. In the early 1990s, for example, the Guatemalan government raised the possibility of reparations for the family members of the murdered and disappeared. The quiet revolutionaries generally rejected such ideas. They argued that "life has no reparation; not in any corner of the world does life have reparation." Justice could not be achieved through money, their logic told them. "All the world's money wouldn't be enough, because life has no price." For this individual and others, the proposed governmental payments to the victims' families as a remedy for the killings were as unjust as the killings themselves.

Some individuals talked about forgiving and forgetting, alluding to a sense of inevitability in achieving the right to know the whereabouts of missing loved ones. But most quiet revolutionaries pursued a goal to obtain accountability for the loss of their relatives.

The cornerstone of Guatemalan impunity was the lack of legal punishments for wrongdoers. It was the survivors' harshest reality, seemingly more important in their anguished evaluations of the justice system than the original murders and sequesters of their loved ones. For them, the failure to apply legal sanctions only resulted in more violence. "They never punish them, so they keep on doing it" was a common sentiment. "They're not afraid, because they won't be punished." An interviewee supplied an example:

> There are two police officers who killed some students. After having jailed them, after having had them in jail for quite some time, they were submitted to a process of law. So then, what resulted from that process of law is that they found that there was no problem against them, and they absolved them. Now, those guys go out into the street, and with more strength, and with more power, they're going out to do their villainous misdeeds.

The quiet revolutionaries' desire for punishments was synonymous with wanting the law to be applied as written and intended. Otherwise, the rule of law, considered important in democratic countries, was undermined. "Laws need to be applied," and failure to do so bred disregard for the legal order. "They just continue doing what they're doing," one reported, "and they don't respect the law." The theme of respect for the law as written was addressed by many family members. For them, the problem was not with the law itself, but in the systematic lack of implementation of that law.

Impunity consistently superseded the written law, according to the quiet revolutionaries. The ability of state-sanctioned forces to use unchecked methods to achieve their ends meant that written law had little, if any, power. Threats to use violence became the law. An elderly rural woman explained. The army came to her village and told the community "that we shouldn't get mixed up in a certain thing. 'Because if you're going to get mixed up in that one thing, then the violence comes back again.'" After describing these threats, she admitted that she was "pretty scared" because besides the army, "there's nobody there" to implement legal order. She characterized the army's violence and threats of violence as the only law available. "There's the law!" she exclaimed, referring to the military's threats. The injustice of army-propagated violence to this woman was the direct antithesis of the law as she desired it, while it was the law as she lived it. The impunity from punishment enjoyed by the military meant that their actions became law.

CONCLUSION

Despite the many obstacles placed in the path of the survivors of the disappeared, many of their number continued with efforts to achieve an acceptable justice. The survivors' experiences with state authorities, however, only increased their sense of injustice. Their pursuits became aborted attempts so prolonged that they eventually saw the legal system as anything but a tool for achieving their goals. Their pursuits were met by a string of injustices that impeded their searches but eventually led to their involvement with the popular movement. They argued that procedural justice did not exist in Guatemala and that the justice system was ineffective. It was collectively viewed as rife with corruption, wholly ineffectual in relation to its purported role, and generally inaccessible to the majority of Guatemalans.

It is clear from the testimonies of the quiet revolutionaries that they perceived the disappearances and murders of their family members as extralegal punishments administered by agents of the established governmental, political, and law enforcement systems. Agents of the state and allegedly in some cases the private sector deemed the activities of their relatives politically criminal and subversive of state order or a threat to individual profit. Activists and union organizers were unconstitutionally detained and disappeared or tortured and murdered to punish them for their opposition to the status quo. At the same time, the government-sanctioned violence was aimed at deterring agriculturalists, would-be unionists, and social do-gooders from taking up the banner of social transformation. Since those who were designated as enforcers of the legal code were those deemed guilty of

meting out extralegal punishments and committing crimes against humanity, true justice was not to be achieved in the short term.

Justice, for the surviving family members of the disappeared and murdered, was to be found in finding their relatives (or their relatives' bodies)
and the future empowerment of civilian legal institutions over armed security forces. They felt they had a right to know the whereabouts of missing loved ones and to know the identities of those who had exercised the
violence. Furthermore, they wanted "trials and castigation for the assassins
of the people." They felt that they were right in pursuing legal accountability for the sequesters. Their missing loved ones had been denied, from
their perspective, the protection of the law, as extralegal assassinations and
disappearances bypassed legal procedures. Justice could be resurrected if
those same legal procedures were used to uncover and punish the guilty.
It was important to them to use the legal system as opposed to vigilante
activities or armed rebellion: "We don't want vengeance; what we want
is justice." They aptly recognized that social order required that justice be
reinstituted.

Impunity created among the quiet revolutionaries an atmosphere of fear,
personal and communal insecurity, and a sense of impotence. Impunity fostered a lack of respect for established legal and security institutions. For
the quiet revolutionaries, the successful use of legal procedures would have
allowed the written law to operate in its intended fashion and defeat impunity. Stability and social order were expected outcomes. Implementation of
such goals, however, was beyond the efforts of individuals and required a
social movement, which we describe in the next chapter.

CHAPTER FIVE

The Social Movement to End Impunity

Our principal interest throughout this study has been the mechanisms that led people to participate in a social movement to end impunity in Guatemala. Our focus in previous chapters has been on individual actions of the quiet revolutionaries—how they experienced, managed, and responded to the disappearances and murders of those closest to them. In this chapter we move from individual accounts to the macro-level social movement and examine three essential components of that shift: the psychological mechanisms the quiet revolutionaries implemented to live with ongoing ambiguous situations; the formation, evolution, and manifestation of a broadly defined social movement; and the development of a collective identity that we (and others) see as the link between individual motivation and eventual social action.[1] All of these elements emerge in this chapter, but we note them here to make clear our intention to tie together these matters. To discuss these concerns we will often use data that we have already noted. But we also will look beyond the borders of Guatemala to experiences elsewhere. Indeed, these are macro issues.

SOCIAL MOVEMENTS

Social movements involve "collective challenges by people with common purposes and solidarity in sustained interaction with elites, opponents, and authorities."[2] It is generally accepted that social movements begin in response to some sort of grievance in the society against the government or elites. Such discontent is universal; all societies have members who are not fully satisfied. Utopia may never exist, and the Judeo-Christian and Muslim telling of creation suggests it never has. Eve's convincing words to Adam on the matter of the apple showed her dissatisfaction with the Garden of Eden and its architect. Muslims believe Adam and Eve were equally guilty; Eve's and Adam's temptation to eat the fruit from the one forbidden tree represents their discontent with not having access to all that was available in that paradise. The suggestion is that from the beginning, people have wanted what they knew or imagined that they did not have.

The related challenge we face in this study, then, is to determine the circumstances under which grievances will galvanize social movements. Attention has centered on learning the factors that give rise to individual participation in social movements. To put the matter succinctly with respect to the quiet revolutionaries: Why did they become involved while other survivors of the disappeared and murdered in Guatemala remained inactive?

Writers have generally explained individual participation in social movements as the result of rational choice and opportunity.[3] Proponents of the rational choice model argue that individuals will participate if there are incentives for them to do so. The model is not so clear-cut as a utilitarian model that might argue that individuals weigh the costs and benefits of participation and decide to take action when the incentives outweigh the deterrents. There are benefits that seem difficult to measure, such as the satisfaction one might obtain from participation in a cause that he or she believes to be just.[4] Writers have posited that some individuals might consider a goal so valuable that they choose to participate if they have any chance of success.[5] There is also consideration of individuals who turn the rational choice model somewhat on its head. They participate, according to at least one scholar, because they realize that under some circumstances the collective good would never be achieved if everyone reasoned as the rational individual.[6] They choose to participate precisely because there are few incentives to do so, sure in their knowledge that if they did not do it, *no one* would.[7] They protest because the action represents the kind of person that the participant wants to be.[8]

It has become commonplace to discount the role that psychological states such as alienation and frustration may play in movement participation.[9] It would be a mistake, of course, to totally discount psychological considerations, and other authors do note such.[10] This is particularly important for us because we have argued that psychological elements must have played some role in the quiet revolutionaries' continued efforts to uncover the whereabouts of their disappeared or murdered loved ones.

Collective identity is an alternative explanation to the rational choice model.[11] It is the link, many suggest, between individual motive (the potential to act) and actual participation in a social movement.[12] Authors of an article in the *Annual Review of Sociology* in 2001 define "collective identity" as

> an individual's cognitive, moral, and emotional connection with a broader community, category, practice, or institution. It is a perception of a shared status or relation, which may be imagined rather than experienced directly, and it is distinct from personal identities, although it may form part of a personal identity. A collective identity may have been first constructed by outsiders (for example, as in the case of "Hispanics" in this country), who may still enforce it, but it depends on some acceptance by those to whom it is applied. Collective identities are expressed in cultural materials—names, narratives, symbols, verbal styles, rituals, clothing, and so on—but not all cultural materials express collective identities. Collective identity does not imply the rational calculus for evaluating choices that "interest" does. And unlike ideology, collective identity carries with it positive feelings for other members of the group.[13]

Holders of the identity see their actions as positive and righteous.[14] Collective identities, proponents contend, push people to participate in social movements.[15] We will return to these matters in the coming pages.

POLITICAL OPPORTUNITIES

The quiet revolutionaries definitely had a grievance against the government. They wanted to know the fates and whereabouts of their missing loved ones. They wanted to know why their relatives had been taken away or murdered, and they wanted to know who was responsible for the violence and to see the culprits punished. They knew their cause was just and their goal valuable. Many disregarded the low odds of finding their loved ones alive, and they did not care to listen to those who tried to dissuade them from their activities. Efforts to find the missing—or even their mortal remains—and obtain justice for them had become obsessions that were rooted in the survivors' own need to subdue their mental anguish.

Yes, the quiet revolutionaries had a grievance. But a grievance is not enough to establish a social movement.[16] Not everyone who has a grievance and wants to participate in a larger related cause joins a social movement. In general, there must be perceived opportunities and resources for a social movement to begin as well as for individuals to participate.[17] One of the older enunciations of this idea comes from Tocqueville in his comments on the French Revolution: "When a people which has put up with an oppressive rule over a long period without protest suddenly finds the government relaxing its pressure, it takes up arms against it."[18] Simply put, people must have some hope of success for a social movement to begin. The actual likelihood that the participants' goal will be achieved may be unimportant. Nancy Naples, who has extensively studied social activism in the United States, noted that community workers she interviewed were able to instill in others "a belief in the ability to overcome" obstacles that in fact they were having little practical and measurable "success" at overcoming.[19]

Potential activists must believe that an opportunity for success exists. People who eventually become members of social movements are hopeful individuals who believe that their participation will make a difference.[20] Such was the case when the quiet revolutionaries were interviewed in 1990 and 1992.

PERCEIVED OPPORTUNITY

The election in 1986 of President Vinicio Cerezo to head the first civilian government in more than fifteen years seemed to signal a change in Guatemala to those who would join social movements. In part the perceived alteration resulted from a lessening of hostilities between the revolutionaries and the government. The URNG, prior to the 1986 elections, rightly recognized that a military victory was not possible and initiated efforts at political negotiation with the new government.[21] The new political climate gave people hope for finding some of the disappeared alive and for ending impunity. The optimism is evident in the previously described visit of survivors of the disappeared to President Vinicio Cerezo. The failure of their visit to uncover any useful information indicates that the perception that opportunities exist need not be uniformly valid. That is, social movements may begin because people believe they can succeed when in reality no such opportunity exists.[22]

The election of a civilian government in Guatemala in 1986 was in part a reaction to world pressure. In particular, in the late 1970s, U.S. president Jimmy Carter withheld aid from Guatemala based on the country's poor human rights record. The episode demonstrated that the world was watching events in Guatemala and would react to violations of human rights. This provided another opportunity for the growth of the social movement. Leaders of various Guatemalan groups turned to the international community for funding, protection, and the listening ears of an influential audience.

The Guatemalans' plight made waves on international circuits, which in turn was used for leverage against the military and others in power. The quiet revolutionaries were well aware of this and during our interviews often spoke of international support. An indigenous farmer credited the pressure from "many international letters" for causing "these threats against us to have calmed down a little." The Guatemalans saw that they were being watched, as another interviewee noted, by "many North American friends now, taking pictures . . . Thanks be to the North Americans, to the Germans and everyone, to the Europeans, because they came here to see how things really are, to see what has really happened here."

There was recognition at the time that a certain amount of safety was to be gained by demonstrating before an international audience. A *ladina* explained:

> We seek solidarity of those who come from many countries over here, because the army's afraid of them, and they come to help us here in Guatemala. Because of [international solidarity], I see that they help us plenty here in Guatemala . . . I have learned through the violence, and through not having our rights respected here in Guatemala. And through people like yourselves [in international solidarity], life is respected a little more in Guatemala. If it wasn't for people such as yourselves, we'd all be dead here in Guatemala.

The presence and assistance of people from outside Guatemala provided a reason for the quiet revolutionaries to believe that their efforts might be successful, and this gave them hope for change.

> I say that perhaps we'll come out with some kind of solution which will be the best for all of us. If things continue the way they are now, with international support to Guatemala, I believe that the situation will get better. Because before there was none of this. There was no type of help in Guatemala. On the other hand, now there's lots of help. And I ask of God that we advance. And that they'll be declaring against these assassinations and against those ingrates that sequester and everything.

International attention and Guatemalans' hopes for change continued into the next presidential election cycle, in 1990. Presidential candidates made promises that seemed to indicate a coming transition to less draconian government strategies. Cerezo's successor, civilian President Jorge Serrano, began negotiations with the URNG in early 1991,[23] as both sides realized that a military solution was improbable—a conclusion that was not missed by the quiet revolutionaries. One commented, "Perhaps the current negotiations exist because power is not so well defined, not from one side or the other." The change in state-sanctioned violence was accompanied by a partial loosening of the army's institutional worldview and strict us-versus-them counterinsurgency model.

THE PAN-MAYAN MOVEMENT

In some ways a popular social movement against Guatemala's government was already showing signs of life long before the election of a civilian government. A pan-Mayan movement had begun more than a decade earlier in Guatemala with the goal of improving conditions for the indigenous peoples of Latin America.[24]

A "pan" identity is not a linguistic or cultural identity; rather, it has been described as "the development of bridging organizations and solidarities among subgroups of ethnic collectivities that are often seen as homogeneous by outsiders."[25] Asian is a pan identity that encompasses numerous disparate languages and religions. Latino is a pan identity composed of people who in some large part share the same religion and language. Mayan is a pan identity covering more than twenty languages. Native American is a pan identify for hundreds of nations with different languages and different religions.

A pan identity can serve political purposes. For example, Native Americans in the United States have held strong tribal identifications that have hindered the development of a pan-Indian identity and thus kept them fragmented. Tribes often must compete with each other for federal funds, a process that keeps their interests divided. Sometimes, however, Native Americans work to blur tribal differences, as they did in the 2000 California initiative to allow gaming on reservations. Opponents of the law wanted to convince voters that it would benefit only a handful of people. Advocates for the initiative described it as serving all Indians; television ads stressed that gambling profits would benefit all California tribes, even those that did not have gaming facilities. In this fashion, the proponents created a pan-Indian identity that voters supported. If the opponents of the initiative had been able to convince the public that the law primarily would benefit only a few tribes, the voters might have rejected the initiative.

The pan-Mayan movement from its infancy was more than simply an effort at cultural resurgence. The vast array of prolonged victimizations had generated a litany of grievances against the regions' governments. The problem for the leaders of the young movement was how to get their voices to have an impact in the halls of their governments.

Indigenous Americans are historically the poorest and least influential members of their nations. In Latin America, racism against Indians defined their appearance as threatening or subhuman, or at best, invisible.[26] Under such circumstances, there was little optimism regarding the success of a social movement to improve the plight of the Maya. Out of necessity, the pioneers of the movement turned to an international audience. There, as an expert on the subject notes, they were able to turn weakness into strength.[27] Their cultural and racial differences had made them politically marginal at home, but these characteristics had a much different impact in Europe, the United States, and Canada: "it marked them as fascinating, exotic, and romantic."[28]

During the early years the Indian rights movement met with only limited success in most areas, and not every grievance against the Latin American governments on the pan-Mayan movement's extensive list played well to the international audience of the 1970s. Human rights advocacy, as evidenced by U.S. President Jimmy Carter's withholding of aid, had some momentary impact. And activities that centered around environmental issues gained some appeal.[29] For one reason, the industrialized world easily associated ecological preservation with elements of indigenous cultures' ties to the land.[30] In a memorable U.S. television public service announcement portraying the evil of littering, Iron Eyes Cody, a Native American actor, witnesses a trashed landscape; the television viewer then saw a close-up of the actor, in full native regalia, as a single tear descended his face.

The environmental card proved a successful avenue for the Indian rights movement to reach an international audience. The strategy of linking environmental issues to Indian rights allowed the social movement's concerns to be placed under the heading of environmental issues on the agendas of major international players such as the World Bank and the Congressional Human Rights Caucus. It also granted tribal peoples access to organizations such as the Inter-American Development Bank that had been criticized for ignoring the social consequences of their actions.[31] The environmental card gave Mayan activists entry to the world stage at a time when their other goals, such as political rights and social equality, were unable to attract attention. A quiet revolutionary commented in 1990, "Five years ago, that did not exist here. Nor did the word 'the environment' exist, nor 'ecology,' nor 'human rights,' nor 'promotion of human rights.' This body politic is something new. It has been recent."

By the mid-1980s, a pan-Mayan movement had spread throughout the region and beyond. The movement's foremost goal in Guatemala by then was to end the slaughter of the Maya. Mayanists years later still could not, as Kay Warren has noted, "given the widespread killings and repression . . . safely deal with political violence in their own public writings in the early 1990s."[32] In Guatemala, the environmental linkage was used by quiet revolutionaries to add a measure of safety to their condemnations of the killings conducted with impunity.

The connection between ecological issues and survival of the Maya was evident to at least some of the quiet revolutionaries. "Our dignity, as human beings, should be respected," one said. "We have the right to life," he continued. "We have the right to live in peace." He associated his feelings about humans with the ecological argument made in favor of biodiversity. He concluded with a question: "If animals have the right to life, why not human beings?"

For this man and other observers, the level of killing rose to the level of genocide.[33] Whole villages were wiped out. Whether the soldiers were intentionally practicing genocide or survivors saw it as genocide at the moment is unclear. Can there be a scale of genocide? At one end we find state-directed, systematic efforts to exterminate specific groups, such as was the case in Hitler's Germany. At the other end, we find indiscriminate killing by state-sanctioned forces, facilitated by racism, as was the case with the Serbian massacres of Bosnian Muslims in the 1990s. It is at this latter end of the scale, if such a scale exists, that the survivors of the disappeared and murdered placed the actions of the Guatemalan military. As one stated, "If they are in the army, it's to care for and watch over the nation . . . and not to be massacring so many indigenous persons."

Recognition that racism against the native people contributed to the killing was evident to many of the quiet revolutionaries. They believed that the government saw little value in their lives, a belief they supported with evidence. A Mayan woman described how the Kekchí-speaking president of the early 1980s, General Romeo Lucas García, offered to settle a land dispute between a plantation owner and some Indian squatters who had entered a small piece of his "wide expanses of land to sow their corn." Rather than "bothering" with the court system to have the trespassers removed, President Lucas responded to the landowner's telegram for help by sending

> him a telegram back telling him that he would send out to kill two or
> three Indians, and with that the problem would be resolved . . . that he

would have sent such a telegram, saying that he [the landowner] should kill two or three Indians to resolve the problem, that's not just. And that's the president!

There was, among the quiet revolutionaries, an understanding of how the racism directed against Guatemala's Indians led to their slaughter. One Mayan respondent explained that "they don't take us into account [as we would like] . . . But we see that they take us into account as savages. Right? So, with that, they no longer fear killing a person." Another individual added that indigenous victims were defined as subhuman: "They would only kill them, the same as with an animal. Like a dog that passes by, and you shoot it to make sure your gun is working properly. Just to satisfy your curiosity." Sentiments that reduce opponents to less than human are common in wartime and allow an enemy to be targeted for annihilation.

The quiet revolutionaries, particularly Maya, asserted that their lives had worth. They opposed the definition of themselves as "animals" and propagated the message that "I am man; I am human." Other members of past movements for civil rights have acted similarly. It was an often witnessed theme in the United States during the civil rights movement of the 1960s. It is a call for equality based on membership in the greater human community and for dissolving the prejudices that divide us.

The quiet revolutionaries, by 1990, categorized the largest portion of victims of the killing as Indians or Maya. We cannot be sure that during the killing of the early 1980s the interviewees would have recognized that the army was killing mostly Indians. For one reason, they may not have had any idea about what went on outside their own villages. But more importantly for our story, our subjects may have come to identify themselves as Maya years later, during their time as members of the popular groups. At first they may have seen themselves as members of one of Guatemala's many specific indigenous groups or as residents of particular villages. Earlier anthropological research suggests that such self-views predominated. One of our main arguments is that the slaughter during the scorched-earth period eventually led indigenous individuals to join the popular movement and to assume a pan-Mayan or pan-Indian identity.

The point is that a pan-Mayan or Indian rights movement had developed prior to the activism of the quiet revolutionaries. The achievements of the Mayan movement had an impact on individuals who later were attracted to the movement to end impunity. They saw an opportunity for success and believed that their participation might make a difference.

LESSONS FROM ELSEWHERE IN LATIN AMERICA:
WOMEN LEAD THE MOVEMENT

Guatemala was not the only country with an authoritarian government where fledgling popular movements gained support because the world was watching.[34] Argentina experienced similar events. A military regime held power in Argentina from 1976 to 1983. During these years, the government fought an anti-guerrilla "war" that resulted in the disappearances of about 9,000 civilians and the torture and release of several thousand more. The acts, as in Guatemala, were committed by the military and paramilitary death squads.[35]

The movement in Argentina began with mothers of the disappeared who gathered in silent vigil in the plaza across from the presidential palace and who became known as the Madres de la Plaza de Mayo. As occurred later in Guatemala, the women originally met while looking for their disappeared children. These women were later joined by other groups. But family-based human rights groups occupied the most influential positions in the Argentine movement.[36] Family, particularly grieving mothers trying to locate their missing children, became important in the protest movement precisely because they were fulfilling socially legitimate or expected roles.[37]

The role of motherhood and other female roles were also important in other social movements against authoritarian governments in Latin America during the period, including mothers in Nicaragua during the Somoza regime and later the Contra War, as well as mothers, sisters, and daughters of the disappeared in Chile and elsewhere.[38] Jo Fisher, who studied women's participation in the Latin American movements, concludes:

> Before the coups most of these women had been housewives, tied
> to the home by children, with no political experience and little
> interest in the world outside their home and families. Military rule
> shattered this world, forcing them to take on a more active role in
> public affairs.[39]

The same phenomenon was evident in Guatemala and was part of the opportunity structure that gave rise to the social movement.

The existing ideology about women in Guatemala and elsewhere in Latin America held that women's proper role was with the family and that the public sphere was the domain of men. "The housewife," a Mayan woman explained. "She doesn't have to be in the court looking for a disappeared relative. She is supposed to be in the kitchen." Women in Guatemala were granted power as long as the issue centered on the family.[40] This ideology, of course, was not limited to Latin America, nor was it new.

Women have long used their power within the home to protest events in the world of men. War shatters women's ability to be housewives and can force them to take an aggressive role in politics. In ancient times, Athenian playwright Aristophanes tells us that the women of his city withheld intimate favors from the men until they agreed to end war making.

Women also have used their accepted roles to enter the world of men. For example, middle- and upper-class women successfully gained entrance into the police occupation in the United States during the early 1900s by arguing that the special qualities of womanhood should be celebrated as a valuable difference between men and women in police roles. One of the female pioneers in the occupation argued that "no woman can really be a good policewoman, unless she works as a woman and carries with her into a police department a woman's ideals."[41] The college-educated women were able to gain a foothold in the occupation prior to 1920 by concentrating on maternal issues such as the care of juveniles.[42]

Numerous scholars have studied the transformation of individuals into social and political activists.[43] Here we build upon their work and heavily borrow from it. In analyzing the motives of the quiet revolutionaries, in particular the female Maya, we find resemblances to the transformation of poor women of color in other countries as well as that of Euro-American women in the United States whose political actions were sparked by their attachment to gendered identities.[44]

In Guatemala the women among the quiet revolutionaries perceived their protest actions through the cultural lens that gave them power over home and family. Their activism might have been influenced by the resurgence of Mayan cultural values as part of the pan-Mayan movement. Archeological evidence suggests that prior to the Spanish conquest, Mayan women actively participated in politics and society, but their involvement was limited by gender roles.[45] Their participation in economic matters was affected by their maternal duties; they needed to work near home so they could care for small children. This association with the domestic world molded the shape of their accepted roles in the public sphere. Matthew Restall finds a similar pattern in the Spanish colonial era in Guatemala. Both women and men inherited land, but women were more likely to receive the land upon which a home sat, while men inherited cultivated and wooded land. Women acquired livestock that were kept near the house, while men inherited cattle and other animals that were maintained at a distance from the domicile.[46] Women held power within a circumscribed area, as did men. On occasion, the women used their position to protest actions of colonial authorities. In 1795, "during a typhus plague . . . a group of Ixil Maya women seized the town church and held hostage the parish priest, a Spanish doctor sent to treat the sick, and his assistants." The women's actions were based on their role "as guardians of custom, especially social rituals regarding death."[47] The resurgence of Mayan culture may have influenced some of the quiet revolutionaries to reassert their right to protest matters associated with their gender role.

Protest by women in Guatemala that was connected to gender-specific concerns strengthened their ability to mobilize for action. It allowed them to identify their goal as right and those who opposed them as wrong. Because their position had cultural resonance with the general population and most likely with many in the army and the ruling elite, they were more successful than political opponents who based their opposition to the government on less widely held beliefs, such as economic equality. The women framed their arguments in such a way that it was acceptable to "constituents, antagonists, and bystanders or observers."[48]

The women, and those who joined them, protested against activities and situations related to their maternal or family roles—most notably the disappearance and murder of husbands and children, but also such realms as children's feeding, housing, clothing, and health. They did not challenge the dominant ideology that women's primary interest should be the welfare of their families and that men should handle public matters. This strategy allowed the women space to protest, while predominantly "male" issues in Guatemala—union activity or university protest, for example— were crushed.

As time went by, the women added other issues and framed them within acceptable gender roles. They added protest against violence by focusing on how it destroyed the family, or they attacked sexual violence against women by ridiculing or questioning the machismo of men who would take advantage of vulnerable women. By this method, the women were able to legitimate their protest by couching it in the acceptable gender ideology of Guatemala.[49] This is not to say that the strategy was calculated. The views they held were honest. As with all of us, they were, to one degree or another, part of their cultural milieu. The women were raised in the society and perhaps had not questioned its tenets. One woman drew this distinction:

We don't have the courage that men have. This is my idea, that they have more courage, more experience. One, as a woman, no, [but] my form of thinking says that, like this group here, working together, everything together, then we could do something in Guatemala. But, separately, we could never get anywhere. My hope is founded in the group. To help them as they help us, so that there's a change. Because if we don't get together, there'll never be change.

She used the culturally accepted notion of women as weak to inform her decision to join the social movement. The contrasting image of the strong, aggressive, macho male might have worked against males' individual entrance into movement groups.

The quiet revolutionaries' objection to the leftist armed revolution may have reflected the women's gendered role. The leftist guerrilla leaders could have been committed to gender equality and yet seen the solution within the framework of male ideology.[50] That is, "women would be liberated through their incorporation into the labor market."[51] Equality, from this perspective, means equality of interests. Matters of gender or ethnicity are subsumed into class issues.[52] Equality for women, under such circumstances, means a loss of status as a group needing protection.[53] Most of the female quiet revolutionaries, poor women with children to care for, had no desire for such equality.

It was from their offspring that the activist identity of many quiet revolutionaries sprang. Being a good mother, as discussed earlier, was of primary importance to them.[54] They generally were much more concerned with how to raise their children after the family's primary source of income had been disappeared or murdered. Their criticisms of the government were not based on economic ideology but couched in their daily needs, values, and identities as mothers. Their accounts highlighted such matters. "Ah, the children want their food, want their things; they want all their clothes washed, and I can't even afford soap" was a common sentiment.

In general, social movements' goals and methods reflect the character of the place in which they occur,[55] and the movements often are galvanized by events that are less visible than the ones that become the focus of protest.[56] In Guatemala and elsewhere in Latin America, issues of family provided women with an unexpected opportunity to protest.[57] "The unity of women is very interesting," commented an indigenous widow as she reflected on her own and others' involvement in a widow's organization. She explained:

We are working so that we help each other as women. To give ourselves ideas and also to have some mutual coexistence in order to calm, a bit, our pain. And it is something that, well, that women [in the group] perceive; that it exists. But despite the fear, we feel valor and high spirits to continue working, although we're widows. But we have the conviction to continue collaborating with other widows. Our fear exists. But we watch over each other quite a bit. And we also believe that if we don't do it today, then, who [will do it] for our children tomorrow? I've learned to shake off the fear. I have learned to become a bit more self-assured, and I have learned to improve in my work. I have known other people who have helped me psychologically, not economically, to avoid, to confront more problems. I have learned very good things. To live with others, to share, to dialogue, to understand the plights of others as well. And my very difficult situation helped me as well. Or, let's say, for that very same reason I learned that I should demand my rights. Also, I learned that the dignity of other persons has to be respected. Because before I didn't know it and I didn't understand it. But now I know that it's very important in living as humans. And that the dignity of women also [has to] be respected. And that helped me discover [enlightenment]. When I lived in my house, well, I didn't have worries. I didn't think that certain things were going to happen. I didn't think. Only about my children, care for them, feed them, keep them clean. I only thought about these things. But now on my path, it is different. Now I think about the future of my children and about the present as well. I think about the situation that they are going to live [in]. I think about how I can work so that they can continue studying. So that they don't have to suffer that which I have had to suffer. And so that they don't have to walk the same path down which my husband had to suffer. About myself, perhaps something very important. You could say the shaking off of oneself. You could say that, for the moment, I've forgotten about myself. And I want to do something for others. That is what I've learned now.

During times of widespread, socially grounded threats to health and home, "women's performance of apparently traditional female roles can lead them to take revolutionary actions on behalf of their families and communities."[58] Nancy Naples coined the term "activist mothering" to describe and document such a process.[59] To extend this image somewhat, it is evident that the quiet revolutionaries, both men and women, were engaging in some form of "activist parenting" or "activist family maintenance." Individualized preoccupations for one's own before the quiet revolutionaries' involvement with the movement were supplanted by a form of "care for one, care for all" social mothering or parenting in which they respected and felt everyone else's losses and successes. Caring and mothering had left the "confines of a bounded family unit,"[60] and it was projected onto a national plane. Their interests were not just for their own families but all Guatemalan families. Their inclusion of others in their preoccupations for health and welfare facilitated their eventual assumption of a national identity.

Social-movement and historical circumstances eventually changed and led some quiet revolutionaries to refocus on home life. By 1992 women's participation in Guatemala's social movement to seek justice or accountability for the disappeared had somewhat waned from the 1990 level. Some of the women had given up hope that they would ever find their missing loved ones and had abandoned the organized search. In 1990 there had seemed to be an opportunity; the political climate gave people hope for finding some of the disappeared alive, but two years later, for at least some of the female quiet revolutionaries, that hope had mostly evaporated. Some of the women had remarried, while others had been coerced through violence into silence, and still others were just too busy trying to feed their children and could not participate because of economic reasons. One woman who left the movement noted in December 1990:

> I've learned plenty, because perhaps one who has her husband takes care of the husband. But when they are no longer there, one has to see about the children and to move forward. To work as a man and a woman at the same time. I was left alone, my girl was only three years, and my son was not yet born. I was left pregnant. And when my son was born, I was all alone, because I had to work. I was working in a cafeteria, where they paid me three *quetzales* per day. But the advantage there was that they gave me food for myself and the children. Thus, I raised them, carrying him on my back. And my mother's been helping me these days. But now, in January, she told me that I had to take charge of the children. And my situation will become more difficult because now I won't have anyone's help, just me, working for the children.

Their personal identities as mothers were of primary importance for many of the women who abandoned the popular movement. The movement for them had been a means to resurrect their families. They had not accepted a new social identity. Their desires were for traditional families in which husbands provided the daily tortillas. A researcher has found this longing among Brazilian women as well: "Given the intense struggles that single mothers constantly waged to ensure household survival, it is not surprising that women would look back with nostalgia to a family system that provided them with greater support."[61]

A Guatemalan interviewee's comments in 1990 reveal her motives for joining and perhaps a growing skepticism:

> I only come to this group because they say there's a solution to all this, that they can reappear alive, and that we have to struggle for this. It's a toss-up as to whether they're alive or whether they're dead. Only God can know for sure whether they're alive or whether they're dead, only God; that's right! Everybody says that we have to struggle so that, just like that, one day, they reappear alive.

In Guatemala, women did want to return to home and hearth, and many did. But the extent of killings in Guatemala altered the roles of at least some women in the country. The killings of males and displacement of hundreds of thousands of Guatemalan families as a result of the violence resulted in women going to work outside the home.

There were few opportunities before 1990 for women to make a living. They were involved in the informal sector as vendors in the marketplace. But in Guatemala, women traditionally worked in their homes or as domestic servants. Motherhood was their primary identity, and there were few alternative identities to which they had access. The need for women to earn a living, however, plunged them into new areas of employment and social protest. Women became active participants in labor-union organizing in Guatemala in response to the exploitation of workers in export assembly plants called *maquilas*. Women composed the majority of the *maquila* workforce, in large part because they had to support their families, starting with their parents and younger siblings. The minimum daily maquila wage was almost twice that of domestic workers. Women took the jobs and then formed unions to fight for better working conditions.[62]

During the time Frank was in Guatemala, he witnessed women's struggle in the trade union movement against machismo and the sexual subordination and objectification of their gender. These women had other social identities besides motherhood. They were also breadwinners and social activists. A woman associated with the union movement remembered that

> when I was left alone, I began to work [outside the home]. So then, when I began to work, I began to learn, let's say, in some parts, just what was exploitation and discrimination in the very same jobs. And often, as they say here in Guatemala, one has to leave things be, to

keep quiet about the things that one sees and all that. Acting like that, they let you keep your job. I have had experiences like that, in different jobs, let's say, of discrimination, exploitation, and, let's say, insults and abuses—plenty of such experiences.

Gender transformation also occurred in rural areas of Guatemala as a result of the widespread killings, combined with the pan-Mayan movement. For nearly one hundred years, Kaqchikel Mayan women have been tourist attractions. Visitors have wandered through their communities in hopes of seeing how the indigenous people live. The women realized that the tourists could be a source of income. They allowed the visitors to watch them weave and then sold the tourists the finished products.[63] The pan-Mayan movement increased the number of tourists visiting Guatemala,[64] and many found the Maya to be intriguing.[65] Tourists, however, do not necessarily see the real world of the Maya. Rather, they are presented with an idealized depiction, which is controlled by the women. The performances presented to tourists show an idealized Mayan world in which gender roles are clearly delineated. Women take care of the home, do the weaving, and care for the offspring, while men do the farming, pay the bills, and deal with people outside the home. Increasingly, it is the presentation of home life, including the sale of woven goods—items that are generally controlled by the women—that is producing economic wealth for some Mayan families. This has somewhat altered gender roles in communities, primarily because many women now are the chief providers for their families. As the value of the women's labor has increased, men have begun to support them by helping with the domestic duties. The consciousness of the Mayan women has also been raised as an outgrowth of their labor. In the course of their presentations to tourists, the women engage in conversations with their worldwide visitors. The subject often turns to gender differences in the Mayan community and the subjugation of women—a topic to which the Mayan women return after the tourists have left.[66]

The removal of men from the households meant thousands of women were forced to assume the mantel of breadwinner. After a death squad killed her husband in 1979, a widow and her daughters gave up on the subsistence family farm their loved one had slaved over to feed them, and they turned to weaving and selling their woven goods to support themselves. The women proved successful at their new endeavor and soon were among the leaders in their community.[67] The story of these women is atypical in that most widows did not prosper, but it does exemplify the need to which women had to respond to support their families.

Economic opportunities for women expanded in Guatemala as a result of the extensive killings and slowly opened the way for the acquisition of identities apart from that of mother. A poor economic situation in the country during the years preceding and following the peace accords increased male unemployment and further expanded opportunities for female employment in the maquila industry and other low-wage export sectors. These occurrences, combined with women's active role in the various social movements, had the unintended consequence of partially redefining gender identities. Women were no longer confined only to motherhood but had the potential to be breadwinners as well. "I learned how to do these jobs because I don't have money," one of the interviewed Mayan women began. "But they all laughed because what courage I had to work like a man. And I am a woman. [But] it's a happiness to work, because knowing how to work can get one by in life. Not that well, mind you, but one can get by."

Because there had been some change in gender identity in Guatemala does not necessarily mean that the trend will continue unabated. In the United States during World War II, women went to work and were viewed as capable of handling many occupational duties that previously had been denied them. But following the war, returning soldiers took back their jobs, and women returned to motherhood and domestic duties. Such a transition for women back to the mother identity in Guatemala has certainly been slowed by the greatly reduced number of men in the population. But what will occur when gender ratios become more equal remains to be seen.

The new identities women could assume affected participation in the social movement that was designed to achieve justice for the disappeared. Resurrection of their families or discovering what had happened to missing loved ones were factors that had driven many women to join the movement. These motivations were intricately linked to the women's identity as mothers. During the early 1990s, women left the movement when the likelihood of finding loved ones alive and resurrecting their families seemingly decreased. In the later 1990s, many women demobilized because they had other identities besides mother available to them. Frank observed this change in the identities of those who were active in the grassroots movements in the differences among the female activists he met in 1990 and those he met two years later. The women in the popular movement when Frank returned in 1992 were less likely than those he met in 1990 to see the motivation for their activities as the resurrection of their families. Rather, in 1992 the women's demands were dominated by calls for the reintroduction of democratic institutions. Women remained a vital element in the social movement to end impunity, albeit not always in the same numbers or for the same reasons as in 1990.

COMING TOGETHER

The mass killings and disappearances in Guatemala by state-sanctioned forces were intended to eradicate any anti-state political action. The very nature and function of state-sanctioned terrorism is to inhibit the growth and development of political movements opposed to the state and its national project.[68] State terror in Guatemala, through the use of death squads as extralegal security and penal forces, was intentionally clandestine. Essentially, the state utilized the death squad forces to hide its responsibility for the political repression. The Guatemalan authorities' use of clandestine forces was designed to provide them deniability. The government, when faced with protest, could always deny involvement and blame the atrocities on other forces such as the guerrillas or common criminals. The objective was to suppress protest while not providing political ammunition to opponents of the ruling class. Revelations of government sponsorship or complicity in repression could always be used by movement leaders to attract new members to the cause or to increase the solidarity of the group.

In general, the actions of government officials to restrict political protest have been identified by academics as important factors in the development of social movements as well as influencing individual participation.[69] "Conflict sets boundaries between groups," sociologist Lewis Coser has noted, "by strengthening group consciousness and awareness of separateness, thus establishing the identity of groups within the system."[70] In Guatemala the system of terror criminalized any social movement thought to threaten the ruling-class hegemony—a dominance that depended upon state terror for its relative strength and durability. The state terror system criminalized political opposition to the point of systematically applying the death penalty to perceived transgressors. The killings and threats of violence against would-be protestors were meant to silence opposition. But it had the unintended effect of creating a substantial number of potential activists.

Death squad activities galvanized the popular movement. The diffusion of the violence throughout Guatemalan society created cross-cutting ties—networks of survivors—and a homogenization of values among large segments of the population. Thus, a social movement came into existence that had a unifying goal probably best described by the interviewees as justice for the disappeared.[71] But the movement pursued other, somewhat secondary, issues that were direct results of the ubiquitous use of disappearances, murder and torture: the rights of union members, indigenous people, agriculturalists, and students, to name a few.

The pursuit of secondary issues had been, at best, minimally successful as separate social movements. The Mayan movement had fared a little better than the others because it had linked its agenda to that of environmental groups and had gained some institutional support among world organizations. The insurgent groups, however, had been largely unable to mobilize support among diverse sectors of the population; nor were they effective at developing means to broadcast their ideals into the wider Guatemalan society.

Insurgent groups usually find allies among members of other social movements who help spread the message.[72] In Guatemala, however, barriers of social class and race hindered such alliances. University students were mainly drawn from the middle and upper classes. Unionists were working-class, while agriculturalists were largely Mayan and the object of national discrimination. In the fragmented society of Guatemala, members of one group were unlikely to have much contact with individuals from another, given their socioeconomic, cultural, and linguistic differences. They simply did not socialize in the same circles, and thus there was little opportunity for information or influence to cross from one organization to another.[73] If anything, their differences meant the groups were often at odds. The ubiquitous violence changed all that by creating links or bridges between the various insurgent groups, uniting people from all walks of Guatemalan life in their demands for an end to impunity and in their unceasing clamor for justice.

The state-sanctioned violence created what academics call "weak ties" between individuals. "Tie" refers to contact between individuals. The strength of a tie is related to a number of factors, such as the amount of time people spend together, the emotional intensity of their relationships, the extent of intimacy they share, and the things they do for each other. People with strong ties are usually good friends who see each other often, share values, and favor similar activities. In contrast, individuals who have weak ties are usually acquaintances. Strong ties do not facilitate the diffusion of ideas. Certainly good friends share ideas and, if one learns something new, we can expect that in short order all members of a friendship network will soon have learned the information. But since such networks are limited in size, the diffusion of the new information will be limited. That is, we can only have so many good friends. Weak ties are not so constrained. Each of us is likely to have scores of acquaintances. Information shared with them is likely to be broadcast in ever-widening circles as they tell their friends and acquaintances.[74]

Each of the various "secondary" social movements in Guatemala (union, student, agriculturalist) had consisted of members with strong ties to each other. Each movement was made up almost entirely of members drawn from one social class. The state had long utilized murders and disappearances against all these groups as a means to repress them. In addition, there is evidence that nongovernmental forces utilized similar tactics to eliminate old enemies and cloaked their actions in the ubiquitous violence that was occurring. For example, plantation owners had murdered promoters of land reform, plant owners did the same with union organizers, and business owners took the opportunity to eliminate competitors.

The ambiguous nature of disappearances, and murders to a lesser extent, drove the interviewees and other individuals to try to learn what had happened to their missing loved ones. While looking in hospitals, morgues, and government offices, they met other survivors. The extent of the violence meant there were many thousands of individuals seeking information. Given the number of people, it is not surprising that they met others in similar circumstances.

Their personal identity and status as survivors brought them together and overrode distinctions that had kept them apart, bringing together a *ladino* plantation worker from Escuintla, a *ladina* lower-middle-class housewife from the capital city, a preliterate and predominantly monolingual rural Kaqchikel woman, an urban *ladino* trade unionist, and a K'iché Mayan university instructor. As they talked and shared information, they became aware of organizations heavily comprised of communities of survivors. The survivors attended meetings, and soon these organizations drew increasing numbers of individuals who had weak ties to each other. These individuals became bridges among the secondary social movements, which facilitated the diffusion of movement goals among a large portion of the Guatemalan population.

The effects of weak ties were evident in the words of a twenty-five-year-old woman who was a college-educated trade-union worker. She had been a schoolgirl at a specialized, career-oriented secondary institute during the height of the slaughter in the early 1980s without direct awareness of the violence: "The truth is that I don't really remember, myself, because I wasn't mixed up or involved with [these things]. I didn't really know, in reality, the problems of people who lived in Guatemala as I do now." Her relatively high socioeconomic status had kept her isolated from the general Guatemalan population and in the dark about what was occurring outside her small circle of friends. She surmised that "the reality of Guatemala is they tried to cover up from us" these matters. She learned from other quiet revolutionaries that "various people have been objects of various violations to their human rights. Mainly, it's been the people in the rural areas, the people who haven't had studies. With them, these cases are even more prevalent."

An expert on social movements has surmised that because "resistance to a risky or deviant activity is greater than to a safe or normal one, a larger number of people will have to be exposed to it and adopt it, in the early stages, before it will spread in a chain reaction."[75] This is exactly what occurred in Guatemala. The earlier movement groups had consisted of communities made up of cliques whose members had ties to every other member of the clique but not to activists of other communities. This severely inhibited organizational efforts, and spreading the message through means such as leafleting had little effect. People simply did not take such advertising seriously, and there were inherent dangers in being caught with such materials. The message must ultimately be communicated from person to person.[76] The quiet revolutionaries became those personal ties. The fact that they were weak ties was crucial to the diffusion of the message.

In the dangerous world of Guatemala, social-movement participants needed to trust each other and their leaders. The quiet revolutionaries were able to assure each other that leaders were trustworthy and if necessary to talk to the leaders and other members of the group about potential participants. This is how Frank obtained access to interview many of the quiet revolutionaries. Individuals vouched for him to leaders who in turn commended him to others for interviews. Weak ties were also indispensable to the diffusion of the social movement in racially segregated Guatemala; weak interracial ties are an effective means to bridge the social distance between racial groups—Maya and *ladino* in the case of Guatemala.[77]

As long as the individual social movements consisted only of members with strong ties to each other, the insurgent social groups remained fragmented and were easily repressed by state forces. The weak ties among the quiet revolutionaries that resulted from the ubiquitous violence were indispensable to the integration of the social movements. Eventually, the weak ties among members of the different groups masked or blurred the boundaries of the various secondary movements.[78] Moreover, the memberships became interdependent, and by this process they overcame "basic cleavages," as Coser describes the term,[79] and improved the various individual movements' chances for survival. Preliterate Mayans needed the assistance of educated city dwellers for court cases and for reaching out to the international community or, on occasion, to flee to the relative safety of the cities. The city dwellers needed the Maya, who comprised the largest number of victims, because the urban movements lacked members and strength because they focused on middle-class or union issues and organizational goals. The repression cut across community lines, and ultimately, so did the response. The rise of interdependence, in terms of members all helping each other search for the disappeared and accountability, contributed to the strength, growth, and survival of the movement.

GAINING MOMENTUM

By the time Frank arrived in Guatemala in 1990, the social movement for justice for the disappeared and murdered had begun. State forces were attempting to repress the civil society–based insurgent movement but were hampered by the groups' methods. In the 1980s, individual or small numbers of survivors confronted officials and demanded accountability. Taunts, misdirection, and threats to use violence against the few, isolated protestors ended the confrontations in favor of the state authorities. But the united movement groups were able to mount much larger protests and borrowed the strategies of social protest used elsewhere in the world. The pre-Christmas march to the presidential palace by schoolchildren carrying lighted candles illustrates the successful use of a strategy of nonviolent protest. The well-organized protest was designed to attract a significant audience from within Guatemala as well as internationally. The organizers recognized that the state forces would be unlikely to use lethal force or to seize demonstrators, particularly young children, in full view of international camera crews and visitors. The international presence, which included Frank, prevented the use of some violence against the demonstrators. The only fatality occurred that evening away from the scene of the march.

Use of an international audience to protect protest activities gained further impetus in 1992. At the time of the five-hundredth anniversary of Columbus' arrival in the Americas, much attention in Guatemala and worldwide focused on the adverse effects of his "discovery."[80] This helped call attention to the plight of the Maya and furthered solidarity among the quiet revolutionaries. The *ladinos* among them were awakened to the history of abuse against the indigenous population, and they supported the Mayan agriculturalists. One *ladino*, for example, complained that it was not right for the Maya to be

> attacked as criminals when they really have a right to ask for the things they were asking for, because the land was taken away from them five

hundred years ago. And they need that land to be returned to them, because they are the only owners.

The quincentennial also was used to consolidate the pan-Mayan identity by defining a historical conflict between the indigenous population and groups of European descent, which strengthened "group consciousness and awareness" among Mayan quiet revolutionaries and steeled their resolve to overcome the long-standing oppression.[81] A Mayan explained the strategy:

This is a chain of events five hundred years long. But it's not over yet. So much is spoken about what happened five hundred years ago, but I say it just goes right on happening, especially the discrimination against us, the indigenous people. For the government, we are the backwardness of Guatemala because we possess a culture, because we defend what is ours. Yes, clearly, if we demand our rights, we are a danger for Guatemala. And it's better off for them if we just keep being a cheap source of labor in order to make them rich . . . We are the largest population, and each time they continue trying to exterminate us. But, as the saying goes, they kill one and a hundred more arise, such that they cannot finish us off. And they use so many kinds of politicking to destroy us. But I feel that the more that they continue destroying us, more and more consciousness is being created.

In December 1992, as an exclamation point to the year's events, Rigoberta Menchú received the Nobel Peace Prize for her book and work documenting the slaughter of indigenous people in Guatemala, and she returned to the country after a decade in exile. Suddenly, a member of the social movement, a survivor of those murdered, was one of the most celebrated individuals in the world. Guatemala was center stage.

The new strategy of mass demonstration reduced the danger to movement participants. Fear still existed among the quiet revolutionaries, and they took numerous precautions when they were alone or in small groups. They took circuitous routes to movement activities so as to mask final destinations or always walked against traffic to prevent assassination or sequester from behind. But overall, participants in mass demonstrations were relatively safe compared to protestors in earlier years. The change meant an increase in the number of willing protestors, which further swelled the size of demonstrations, and gave greater incentives for participation.

BECOMING GUATEMALAN

A camaraderie developed among the movement members, and there was a certain sense of celebration among participants following a demonstration. Prestige, attention, and approval were the rewards granted by the quiet revolutionaries to new participants who braved the repressive acts of the state. It was so for Frank following the December demonstration, when a woman grabbed his arm, swung him around and yelled, ¡*Compañero!* It was his participation that gained him access to GAM members that night, and his continuing and improving reputation with them largely depended on his participatory zeal. In Guatemala (as elsewhere), taking part in social movement activities despite repression resulted in rewards for participants and led to increased protest.[82] Efforts to harass demonstrators did not cause them to give up their fight. Rather, it often strengthened their resolve and gave them confidence. They had survived the state's efforts to deter them and knew they could do it again. "Some people consider [our efforts] bad, and they look down upon us," commented one. "But that's not the majority of people. Rather, there are others who also understand that this is a struggle. They call it a sterile struggle, but we know that it's constructive."

The quiet revolutionaries rightfully believed their actions would lead to improving the general welfare of Guatemalans. Under such circumstances, experts on social movements have noted, they felt they should be treated with respect, not derision. One result was that activities designed to stop them were seen as immoral and increased support for the movement, even from individuals who had not suffered at the hands of the state security forces.[83] The impact of the acts of repression on members of the various secondary social movements was to create empathy among them and further drive them toward integration. A student whose uncle had been assassinated makes this point:

> It's a pity that blood had to raise the consciousness of the people. Because this blow [assassinated uncle] that was dealt us made more vivid and real all the violations of human rights that were going on in the country. Because we'd always heard about those kinds of things. We'd always see them on television and everything, but we had never lived it. And we had never seen it up so close. I have encountered *compañeras* who have traumas just like this. The army has killed their fathers or killed their mothers. They have raped their sisters. *Compañeros* who have lived in the flesh what it's like to be detained. We have seen other young people who have these kinds of problems,

here in the university. It's principally the people from the countryside. Because . . . I have study mates of mine who come from faraway places. And there, for being places that are more enclosed or isolated, this type of violence occurs more. Because out there, it's the army who rules. And they do and undo just as they please, and the police as well.

The murder of the student's uncle had made real the violence that she had only previously witnessed on television. Violations of human rights committed by the army and police against rural villagers were now understood as acts committed against people who were her *compañeros*. Another woman expressed this widespread view as well:

I'm not afraid because I do it to find out not only about my son, but about the children and family members of all the *compañeros*. I've learned that not only we are the abused, as there are more violations of human rights in the highlands. And my anguish extends there, to the highlands, to all the *compañeros* there. Not only do bullets kill them, but malnutrition, and they sleep on the floor. They don't have food to eat. There's no work. And all this causes me anguish because I'm a human being equal to them.

At least in word, there was a blurring of the distinction between social classes and ethnicities. Indigenous and *ladino*, "I take those two words as one and the same," replied an urban working-class *ladina* when asked to which ethnicity she belonged.

The success of the demonstrations increased members' commitment to the cause and garnered public support, further strengthening the movement.[84] The increased size of movement activities fed members' confidence that their protest was meaningful, effective, and viable. The same message was broadcast to bystanders, which attracted more of them to the movement. The growing numbers of protestors meant that individuals were increasingly safer, which in turn led to more members. In general, of course, there must be some point when all potential protestors have joined a movement. But in Guatemala, the numbers of potential participants had been swelled by the scale of violence.

The murders and disappearances in the fragmented Guatemalan society had the result of turning the old adage about "divide and conquer" on its head. The survivors of the omnipresent violence united in an effort to end the killing and to achieve justice for its victims. They came to see the problems of others as their problems and began to speak in terms of "we" and "us." The problems of indigenous people became the problems of university students and unionists. State security forces' efforts to suppress the movement for justice for the disappeared and murdered only increased the bonds among the members.

Continued acts of repression against members of the social movement further fueled societal discontent with the existing political order, particularly among the quiet revolutionaries, who saw their political aims as just and their tactics as legal. They were unwilling to accept the status quo as legitimate. Rather, they urged implementation, as they saw it, of the legitimate legal order and its institutions. Their participation in the social movement had melded them into a group, which they incorporated into their self-view or identity. No longer were they only Maya, unionists, students, or even survivors of the disappeared and murdered. They still held these identities. But their calls for changes in civil society they made as Guatemalans, and those who opposed them they viewed as enemies of the people. "The congressional deputies say that they are the fathers of the fatherland, but they are not Guatemalans," one said. "They don't have a nationalist consciousness. They don't love their country." Another said, "For me, it's so easy," continuing:

I've thought many, many times that, for me, it's for all the people of Guatemala, all of the children who suffer; all of the women who are widows, all of that. If all of these were in liberty in Guatemala, then my life would also be in liberty. Because if other people suffer and if I am in a life of luxury and all, then my life has no worth.

CONCLUSION

Political activity in Guatemala was directly tied to identity. The women, in particular, did not have to give up their identities—stop being mothers or wives—in order to become activists. Their activism was a natural extension of their status as wives or mothers. The threats posed by the disappearances "to family health and community survival disrupted the taken-for-granted fabric of their daily lives, politicizing women who had never viewed themselves as activists."[85]

It is apparent from Guatemala and elsewhere in the world that traditional female roles can lead women into nontraditional actions on behalf of others and themselves. Moreover, the actions of women are not limited by ethnicity or social class. Euro-American working-class women at the Love Canal toxic waste site began their journeys to activism when they "began to suspect a connection between the invisible hazard posed by toxic wastes and their children's ill health."[86] And middle- and upper-class Protestant women became involved in the early twentieth century in efforts to prohibit alcohol and child labor, as well as join the police, as efforts to protect the family and children.[87]

The quiet revolutionaries, often the women, were engaging in some form of "activist parenting" or "activist family maintenance."[88] Nancy Naples, in her research with low-income and working-class, largely urban women of color in the United States, has described how activism itself, for the women, became "an essential part of mother work."[89] The same was true for the quiet revolutionaries. They maintained their identities—as wives, parents, sons, and daughters—through activism, which came to be a way of exhibiting and projecting familial love. But their actions were not only for their own families.

Preoccupations for the resurrection of one's own family diminished with inclusion into the movement for accountability. Members empathized with the plight of other Guatemalans because they were no longer "the other." They were "us." Caring was not limited to the "confines of a bounded family unit."[90] It was projected onto all group members, which helped create a Guatemalan identity among the quiet revolutionaries.

Their membership in the heterogeneous social movement helped form the quiet revolutionaries' identity as Guatemalans. They saw that their interests were the same as those of other members of the group, which were the same as the majority of Guatemalans. Only a small minority of the country had escaped the effects of the violence. Their desires—first for return of the disappeared and murdered (or for learning their fates), then for accountability or justice—led them to join organizations. They were predisposed to the calls from leaders of the groups and other quiet revolutionaries who urged collective protest, as Guatemalans, against state leaders as a means to achieve the goal of justice.[91]

The quiet revolutionaries had forged a national identity through protest. Their nationalism was used to legitimate their actions for themselves and their supporters. It was an ideology that helped mobilize political action against the ruling elites. It increased the solidarity of the group. Their nationalism required loyalty to the collective identity of nation and individual subjugation of personal interests such as individual culture and economic well-being in favor of broader goals.[92] But we would be remiss if we did not point out other factors that contributed to the quiet revolutionaries' collective identity as Guatemalans.

It is important to note that the quiet revolutionaries had always worked within the system. They had not turned to violent revolution when their loved ones were taken away from them. They turned to state institutions such as the police for help. They eschewed revolution. Certainly, their words indicate that at best they felt some sympathy for the rebels. But numerous factors suggest that they were predisposed against the existing revolutionary trail. Most of their number were Catholics, for example, and the Church had preached against communism. Moreover, many of the quiet revolutionaries recognized that it was the rebels' presence that resulted in their communities being targeted for elimination, particularly in northern Quiché, the hardest-hit province. In communities where state security forces used selective violence to eliminate potential opponents, some of their missing relatives had been members of Civil Defense Patrols, coerced into fighting the rebels.

At least some of the quiet revolutionaries, at a minimum, had a predisposition to seeing themselves as Guatemalan. Their activities as members of the social movement and the state security forces' efforts to repress them strengthened this identity and allowed the quiet revolutionaries to claim the moral high ground. They were not armed insurgents. Nor were they enemies of the people. They were Guatemalans, acting for the national community.

One of the last state actions that fueled the social movement and the collective identity as Guatemalan occurred in May 1993 when elected President Jorge Serrano attempted to seize total control of the government. Massive demonstrations, a lack of military support, and world opinion quickly led to Serrano's ouster.[93] This would be a high point for the quiet revolutionaries. Within the next few years, events undermined the movement and fractionalized its membership. We take up these matters in the next chapter.

CHAPTER SIX

The Movement Is Fragmented
by the Peace Accords

The social movement to end impunity and establish justice for the disappeared and murdered in Guatemala brought together a diverse group of people who likely would never have even met if not for the violence in the country. Through their shared experiences, they came to see themselves as Guatemalans and their efforts as designed to improve life for everyone in the country. During the same period, however, major players in the Guatemalan civil war were discussing an end to the hostilities. At the moment, it was unlikely that anyone in the movement would have foreseen that these discussions would result in an undermining of the movement to end impunity. But that is exactly what occurred. In this chapter we describe how the peace talks affected demobilization of the social movement. We also discuss the rise of vigilante justice as a public method to deal with impunity.

SOME GENERAL COMMENTS

Social movement demobilization during democratic transitions has occurred in several countries other than Guatemala, including Poland, Uruguay, Brazil, Russia, Chile, and Spain.[1] As democracy was restored, the grassroots movements began to decline and their former members began to seek institutionalized solutions to their countries' problems. In part, the turn toward the use of established mechanisms of political participation in newly democratizing countries was an attempt to prevent the return of authoritarian rule. The fear by social-movement members and leaders was that the use of protest tactics that worked under authoritarian rule might have the effect of resurrecting that which they had worked so hard to end.[2] Elites might, the argument went, define protest as dangerous and feel that authoritarian rule was preferable to anarchy.

In Guatemala and generally throughout the new democracies in Latin America, grassroots organizations that sought justice for the disappeared were unable to convince civilian governments to take up their cause. The newly elected democratic governments saw a need to remain friendly with the military.[3] Guatemalan history had clearly revealed the consequences of alienating the army. The CIA-sponsored coup in 1954 had succeeded in large part because President Arbenz had alienated the military.

In Guatemala and elsewhere in the world, pacts between opposition forces (such as the URNG), social-movement leaders (such as the heads of Guatemalan labor unions), and government elites undermined the movements to end impunity. The pacts were negotiated compromises in which each group agreed to forgo some self-interest in exchange for reducing the uncertainty inherent in the transition from authoritarian government to democracy. In general, such pact making reduced mobilization, which helped keep things calm during the initial periods of instability.[4]

THE PEACE PROCESS

The most influential pact making that undermined the social movement to end impunity in Guatemala was the agreement on the peace accords. Direct negotiations between the URNG and the Guatemalan government began in 1991 following the election of Jorge Serrano as president.[5] Both the army and the revolutionaries realized that a military solution was unlikely. There was pressure from the world audience to end the hostilities. The new president had asserted that the horrendous killings and related problems would cease when the war ended.[6] This was also the goal of major institutions and their members within Guatemala. The Catholic Church wanted an end to the slaughter, which had claimed the lives of far too many Catholic peasants and church workers. The business class also was tired of the killing. Businesspeople were not immune from kidnapping conducted by members of the revolutionary forces or business rivals. Wives complained that they lived in fear that their husbands would be disappeared. Revolutionary forces often made life difficult for plantation owners as well, targeting some and burning their holdings.[7] Ending the war seemed like a good solution to Guatemala's humanitarian, economic, and social problems.

The quiet revolutionaries also wanted peace. Leaders of the popular movement held negotiations with the URNG commanders in Mexico as a force apart from both the guerrillas and prior to the state's involvement; thus the movement was able, in the view of some Guatemalans, to somewhat shed the stigma that it was but a mouthpiece for the guerrillas. The groups that met with the rebel leaders eventually combined with other civil, non-governmental associations to form the Asamblea de Sociedad Civil (ASC, Assembly of Civil Society).

Although peace was desired by the quiet revolutionaries, it was not the unifying goal of their social movement. Ending impunity and establishing justice for the disappeared and murdered were their aims. "If there's to be real peace," concluded a *ladina*, "let there be justice."

The movement, although its members might not have foreseen it, was to become fractionalized by the peace process. As 1994 dawned, the peace process centered around a new accord between the state and the revolutionary forces. With the world now paying close attention to Guatemala, the two sides agreed that the United Nations should become their moderator. This placed the goal of peace in Guatemala at the front of the international stage.[8]

The Assembly of Civil Society, now representing a broad sector of society from both sides of the political spectrum, forged consensus proposals to put before the state and revolutionary negotiating parties. The various grassroots movements wanted a place in the peace process. For them and others, the negotiating table was where Guatemala's future was being decided; to be left out of the process was to be denied any power in Guatemala's future.[9] A member of the quiet revolutionaries commented that

> their meetings with the URNG and the army, they don't represent the entire Guatemalan population, the government and those others. So then, in this sense we are also asking, as civil society who are also the most affected by all this, that we be able to participate in the peace process. We've already done it. Requested our participation. Lamentably, the government hasn't answered us, but we believe that, if we are allowed to participate, that our country will get better and that the problem will be resolved. But this depends on the government, and on the army, whether they accept all the demands we have put forth. We, the civilian population, have put forth many demands regarding the Civil Patrols, military control, about the military detachments in the villages, about the "Model Villages," and the capturing of the civilian population. So then, I think that if they're to resolve all this, then we're going to construct a better Guatemala, bit by bit, and peace and tranquility.

CHANGING LEADERS

By the time the peace process reached the negotiating table in the mid-1990s, many of the most idealistic early leaders of various popular front organizations were dead. By then, there were not so many risk takers involved in the upper leadership. There was always the suspicion, held by many of the quiet revolutionaries, that those who were left in charge were not totally honest. Some group's leaders, *ladinos* from the capital city and Maya from the highlands, had access to fund-raising and consciousness-raising trips to Europe and America that also, on occasion, included visits to Disneyland and the Alps. Some quiet revolutionaries believed that on those journeys the leaders used monies (that were not necessarily accounted for when they received checks or cash donations) to buy gifts for their children. One union leader who proudly proclaimed himself a "big whore" used his position to obtain sexual favors from European and American women. Such union leaders sought their groups' own best interests during the peace process, undermining the social movement to end impunity.

It is, of course, easy to criticize these leaders from the safety of the twenty-first-century United States. Their actions may have been the result of simply knowing that from one day to the next one could be horribly tortured and killed. But questions remained about those who were left when all others around them had died or fled: Why were they still alive when all the others around them were not? Were they smarter, more careful, less drunk or brazen? Such questions were common among the quiet revolutionaries with whom Frank spoke.

Although the quiet revolutionaries for the most part clung to the collective identity of Guatemalan, they recognized that among them were those who sought their own best interests. A Mayan male commented, "We are not as united as we should be because many types of people have infiltrated and have achieved our division. It's that we never can be in agreement; some think one thing and others defend another thing. Such that we continue on suffering the same things."

As many of the new leaders positioned themselves to try and gain as much as possible at the negotiating table, old animosities and positions reemerged. The trade union movement, for example, remained male-dominated; women's rights and concerns were advocated, but arguably as a gesture. The trade union movement was primarily interested in salary increases or "proletarian politics." Moreover, the restoration of democracy and increased reliance on institutional mechanisms such as election politics and labor unions impeded women's participation, which had blossomed under authoritarian rule.[10]

Political parties in Latin America adopted women's issues to try and gain their support.[11] But the cooptation of gender issues by political parties fractured women's organizations in the direction of party lines and undermined the women's movements.[12]

The family movement had its own problems. Most of the quiet revolutionaries were Maya. But some organizations, such as GAM, were dominated by *ladinos*. There were few phones in the countryside and transportation was difficult, which decreased the likelihood of Mayan leadership and led to people in the capital city being the most able to lead the organizations. The Maya and other members of the quiet revolutionaries were suspicious of the *ladino* leadership. Many suspected that their leaders were spending donated monies on "drunken binges." A split occurred in GAM in 1992, in part around charges of such corruption, and a new group, the Association of Families of the Detained-Disappeared (FAMDEGUA), was born. GAM had split in 1989 when a majority of the Mayan leadership and a large sector of the base left to form CONAVIGUA, the National Coordinating Body of Guatemalan Widows.

Agriculturalists' demands likewise illustrate divisions among the quiet revolutionaries caused by differing goals. During fieldwork in 1992, a group of Mam Indians from the southwest coastal plain were involved in a land dispute and struggle that had gone on for several years. Through nonviolent direct action they were trying to regain control of a plantation. During the summer of 1992, after local authorities ignored their seventy-year-old land title, they decided, families and all, to march the more than two hundred kilometers to the capital city. They received some citizen support on the way but arrived in the capital city to spearhead their own march for their land. Other popular-movement groups such as trade unions and university students did not join the indigenous protestors. The protestors had legal permission for the demonstration and for presenting their land deeds at the presidential palace to ask for assistance. But before they could reach their destination, the march was disrupted and they were beaten and chased down the narrow cobblestone streets as if they were chickens being rounded up for market.

A few days later, popular movement members came out en masse in full view of international news media to protest the unjust beatings and dislocation from the city center. The lawless government actions against the protestors was an issue that brought the quiet revolutionaries together, while land reform was not. The distinction, however, may have not been noticed by the agriculturalists, and for them, the question remained as to why the numerous organizations had not joined the *cajoleños* before they were repressed.

Variations in the struggles taken up by popular movement organizations and leadership elites contributed to eventual divisiveness in the popular movement. While a large popular-movement response occurred and has continued to occur every June over the mass sequester of the CNT unionists in 1980, for example, a similar movement never developed for the almost two dozen unionists who were sequestered and disappeared from a Christian retreat center in Escuintla two months later. Certain struggles had their banners raised, often on "racial," ideological, or geographical lines. Fieldwork notes are replete with instances of persons supposedly in solidarity with others falling far short of those ideals.

The peace negotiations also had the unintended result of rekindling anti-Maya sentiments, which further fractionalized the social movement to end impunity. Accords signed in 1995 authorized potential constitutional changes that recognized the country's Mayan roots and intimated coming changes in Guatemalan institutions. Opponents argued that the proposed changes unfairly favored Maya at the expense of others.[13] Such claims fueled existing racism toward the Maya and divisions in the social movement.[14]

Most recently, hundred of thousands of former Civil Patrollers formed into organizations and coalitions and demanded that they be paid for their past services. They warned that they would shut down highways, airports, seaports, and electric plants if they were not fully compensated. Their demands further divided the quiet revolutionaries. Some of the former Civil Patrol members were poor farmers hoping to be compensated for years of free work that they did for the army at the risk of their own lives and the well-being of their families. But other ex-patrollers were among those who committed the slaughter and now threatened family members who sought to learn the fates of loved ones by attending or demanding exhumations from clandestine cemeteries. As it stands at the time of writing, though the Corte de Constitucionalidad (Constitutional Court) voted against any further compensation for former Civil Patrollers, Guatemala's president had announced a plan to compensate them by paying them to plant trees as part of a reforestation program.[15] Undoubtedly, such considerations are driven by elections; the former Civil Patrollers and their families have sizable ballot clout.

TRUTH COMMISSIONS

Foremost in undermining efforts to end impunity may have been the 1994 signing at the peace table of an accord to establish a truth commission to shed light on the killings but without identifying responsible individuals.

Truth commissions in general have become a popular means by which countries examine past human rights violations. Their use has been varied and controversial. They are seen as a compromise between prosecuting the perpetrators of the atrocities and forgiving them. The use of such commissions grew rapidly in fledgling democracies during the last two decades of the twentieth century. There was concern in such countries that prosecutions and punishments might initiate a return to authoritarian rule, as threatened elites might fight to reestablish the old order rather than accept their fates in court. But there was also recognition that completely ignoring former atrocities might lead to their resurrection.[16] Those who fail to learn the lessons of history, to paraphrase a famous quote, are doomed to repeat it. Forgetting the past allows individuals to eventually live as if the atrocities never occurred. The eventual outcome is that what one side argues is the truth, the other sees as lies. Without some official agreement between former enemies as to what happened and why, there is little chance for reconciliation.[17]

Most of the initial truth commissions were in Latin America, and the quiet revolutionaries had some knowledge of them.[18] One of the first was Argentina's 1984 National Commission on the Disappeared, which documented the disappearances of nearly 9,000 individuals during an authoritarian military regime. The commission's work is credited with leading to trials and convictions and contributing to the establishment of a reparations program.[19]

Chile's 1991 National Commission on Truth and Reconciliation, which accounted for nearly 3,000 disappearances and murders that took place under the rule of General Augusto Pinochet from 1973 to 1990, blamed Chile's armed forces for most of the violence but also placed some responsibility with the opposition forces. Most of the perpetrators, however, were shielded from prosecution by an amnesty granted to the military for many of their offenses.[20]

The year before the Guatemala accord was signed, neighboring El Salvador's Commission on the Truth reported on murders and disappearances committed during the country's dozen-year civil war. The report took the unprecedented step of naming Salvadoran military leaders and members of the revolutionary forces who were responsible for the atrocities.[21]

The Guatemalan agreement between the government and the URNG created a commission to investigate the human rights violations committed during Guatemala's lengthy civil war. The issue had been very sensitive. The rebels originally wanted a commission to establish "truth and justice." The majority of the quiet revolutionaries also favored such a body to establish accountability for the slaughter. "We don't want vengeance," one of their number explained. "Rather, what we want is justice."

The issue of a truth commission was not an easy one for all the quiet revolutionaries. They did not want to forget what had happened. To forget, in their view, was to preordain that matters would not improve. "If we leave everything to forgetting, well, there'd be no solution" was a common sentiment. But for some of the quiet revolutionaries, the continuing ambiguity of not knowing what had happened to their loved ones overshadowed all else and led them to consider trading a general pardon for knowledge about the missing, as this person did:

> What he [the president] wanted us to do was to forget the past, and to pardon them. Well, in my conceptualization, yes, I'm all for pardoning the past and for forgetting. But at least, you tell me as president, "Here are the whereabouts of your son; here they have him." I've seen orders where they have them, investigate where all the cadavers are. But not him.

The continuing ambiguity about the fates of the missing had started many of the quiet revolutionaries on the path to social activism. Now it continued to gnaw at some members' psyches and weakened their desires for legal accountability.

More powerful forces, however, were to derail the efforts for accountability. The army and its allied forces were unwilling to be held responsible for the more than 100,000 deaths. Eventually, the URNG and government agreed to remove the concept of justice from the commission's functions, perhaps because URNG leaders realized that this was the best they could get if peace was ever to be achieved.[22] But it is also likely that the rebels did not want to be held accountable for their share of the violence. At least, their position with respect to the establishment of the commission suggests that.

At the negotiating table, the URNG originally wanted the commission to be in operation only six months and to cover only atrocities committed after 1980.[23] Both of these caveats would have had the effect of limiting the accountability of the revolutionary movement for its share of the killing. The URNG had its greatest military effect prior to 1980, while the government's scorched-earth policy did not reach full fruition until later years. A brief period of operation by the commission could have resulted in it focusing its attention on the military's scorched-earth policy, which resulted in the most human rights violations, and ignoring, for the most part, the misdeeds of the URNG.

Other evidence also suggests that the URNG leaders may have feared a toothy truth commission. One of their number who was a member of the negotiating team reported in an interview that when the idea of a truth commission was first raised, members of the military negotiating team threatened that a URNG commander would be prosecuted for each member of the armed forces who was so treated. The military negotiators claimed that they had plenty of evidence to document atrocities by the guerrilla commanders and waved a folder at the URNG members, suggesting that they held the proof in their hands. The revolutionary leadership probably chose to go along with the military because the government was in a much better position to manipulate information and control the operation of the courts to work against the URNG leaders in the long run. The military negotiators must have concluded that a truthful telling of the overall violence would reveal that the government was the primary culprit, which would undercut military claims that the guerrillas were as much to blame for the killing as anyone.[24]

In the end, neither side wanted to see its members' names published as the responsible parties for killings, and the accord that established the Guatemalan commission had neither the words "truth" nor "justice" in the title. Rather, the Accord for the Establishment of a Commission for the Historical Clarification of Human Rights Violations and Other Acts of Violence That Have Caused the Suffering of the Guatemalan People explicitly prohibited commission reports from crediting specific individuals for human rights violations. "That is the function of the courts of law," according to the commission's final report.[25] There was a certain irony in the statement. The quiet revolutionaries had pushed for the justice system to hold the "deliverers of doom" accountable, but they rightly recognized that the courts were unlikely to accomplish the task.

RECOVERY OF HISTORICAL MEMORY PROJECT

There was another truth commission in Guatemala. The year after the accord was reached on the establishment of the Commission for Historical Clarification, the Catholic Church's Archbishop's Office on Human Rights in Guatemala began the Recovery of Historical Memory Project (REMHI). The Church long ago gave up its staunch anti-communist dogma,[26] and Monsignor Gerardi, who oversaw the project, was a leader in this regard primarily because he realized that rural Maya were the victims of the country's anti-communist fanaticism.

The Church-sponsored project tailored its objectives to the needs of the survivors of the disappeared and murdered, mostly poor rural Maya. The project set out to provide traditional burials for the victims of the slaughter, to provide moral and psychological assistance to their surviving loved ones and communities, and to provide legal help, particularly for establishing that someone was indeed dead.[27] These services met with favor by the quiet revolutionaries because they reflected an understanding of their experiences, including

> feelings of injustice, extreme hunger, and ill health . . . altered grieving processes for deceased family members, a sense of humiliation, and powerlessness and uncertainty about the future, all indications that the meaning of life has been totally altered.[28]

The method by which REMHI collected its information also met with approval from the quiet revolutionaries. The archbishop's office trained hundreds of interviewers, who collected testimony in rural areas from survivors and perpetrators; many quiet revolutionaries participated in the project as interviewers and as providers of evidence. When the project began, according to Juan Gerardi, it was the Church's aim "to be agents of reconciliation . . . and to try to place the victims and perpetrators within the framework of justice."[29] Reconciliation required that both victims and perpetrators be involved. In order to obtain reconciliation, there needed to be recognition of wrongdoing, a step that the official Commission on Historical Clarification was prohibited from taking. But reconciliation, according to Catholic teaching, requires an admission of guilt and contrition from perpetrators before there can be forgiveness from victims.[30] As a result, interviews, which were often performed by surviving victims, were conducted with the perpetrators of the violence as well as with those who suffered at their hands.

The REMHI project was most favored by the quiet revolutionaries because it threatened impunity. The authors of the report were in agreement with the quiet revolutionaries and wrote:

> The ability of government forces to operate without fear of punishment has been a central feature of the Guatemala conflict. The absolute power of military and police forces, their frequent clandestine activities, and the substitution of military power for civilian authority have contributed to what is widely referred to as a state of impunity.

Throughout the years, virtually no one has been investigated or prosecuted for committing crimes against humanity. To the contrary, many of those primarily responsible for the violence have retained their powerful posts and privileges. The ability of perpetrators to commit crimes with impunity has been a constant factor influencing the conduct of the army, police, military commissioners, and civilian patrol, and has contributed to further violence against the people. The inability to obtain justice frequently invokes a sense of powerlessness among victims and survivors. Long-lasting effects observed today include the lack of trust in the justice system, the reality that victims live next door to perpetrators in many communities, and the emergence of new forms of social violence, still protected by a mantle of impunity.[31]

The Church-sponsored report, based on more than six thousand interviews (the majority with indigenous people) and conducted by a reported eight hundred parish workers, illuminated the extent of the atrocities committed by the army. The report blames the Guatemalan military for the lion's share of the estimated 150,000 civilian murders and 50,000 disappearances that took place during the long civil war. The testimonies, some from the perpetrators, recount rapes, tortures, assassinations, disappearances, and planned massacres.[32] It is not light reading.

The release of the report on April 24, 1998, seemed to indicate change in Guatemala. An attendee described the ceremony at the cathedral in Guatemala City as "bold and moving."[33] Guatemala's bishops were on hand. The audience, mostly peasants, some in brightly colored indigenous clothing, filled the pews. Extra seats were needed to accommodate ambassadors and officials of the United Nations who had come to witness the historic event. The same attendee remembered thinking, as he left the ceremony, "how Guatemala had changed. Even a few years ago these truths could not have been spoken safely."[34]

It certainly seemed a different Guatemala, one in which democracy was catching on. The continuation of the negotiation process with the URNG, the signing of peace accords on December 29, 1996, and the importance given to the pursuit of development funds through the continual creation of an improved international image for the nation's government contributed to a lessening of the terror. All parties agreed that political violence in Guatemala had decreased dramatically.[35] But several incidents cast doubt about the transformation. Most notable at the time was the murder of Guatemalan Bishop Juan Gerardi, who had been the driving force behind the Church report.

A BISHOP IS DEAD

Just two days after the presentation of the Church-sponsored report, Gerardi's body was found in his garage by a Catholic priest, Mario Orantes, with whom the bishop shared living quarters at the Church of San Sebastian. His skull and face had been crushed beyond recognition by the force of his unknown attackers. Forensic reports indicated that he had suffered at least seventeen direct blows from a heavy cement block. The belief that the military was somehow involved quickly spread among the general population.

The investigation, however, did not focus on the military. Rather, almost immediately, a habitual drunk was arrested for the crime. Supposedly, he had tried to rob the bishop. This theory proved insupportable, and he was soon released. In his stead, the police arrested the parish cook and the priest who had found the body and took the priest's dog into custody as well. Supposedly, the prosecutors believed that the dog had attacked the bishop under the commands of his master, leaving, according to one forensic expert (who never actually saw the body), telltale bite marks. The motive for the crime, according to official sources, was one of passion. In some tellings, Orantes, the arrested priest, was Gerardi's homosexual lover. He killed the bishop because he was caught cheating with women. In another reincarnation of the tale, Orantes, still the homosexual, murdered Gerardi because the bishop, who in this tale is fiercely anti-homosexual, caught the priest "in the act." Neither tale sounds very plausible, but there were reports at the time that church leaders were fearful that Orantes may have played some role in the murder following threats from army agents that they would disclose his alleged homosexuality if he did not cooperate.[36]

Things did not go smoothly for the prosecution. An exhumation of the bishop's body failed to reveal any bite marks. About the same time, the Guatemalan Catholic Church released a report indicating that the military was probably responsible for Gerardi's murder, Orantes was innocent, and the Church had evidence to support its position. At an international meeting in Madrid, Spain, a leader of the Guatemalan Church said that the evidence included telephone records indicating that calls were made from the pay phone in front of the bishop's home to the headquarters of the national security forces and to a home occupied by army personnel. In addition, the Church leader reported that an army vehicle was seen near the murder scene on the night of the crime. Under mounting pressure from Church and human rights leaders, the government expanded its investigation to include an air force officer and one retired and four active army officers. The six voluntarily testified before members of the official investigation. They read prepared statements in which they denied any involvement in the bishop's death. In an unusual step, they were not questioned by any members of the prosecutor's office. Meanwhile, the parish cook was released, but Orantes was kept in jail.[37]

Orantes was released in February 1999 after spending seven months incarcerated. But his freedom did not last long. He and the parish cook were rearrested. In addition, the police arrested three military officers in connection with the killing. The three were charged with the "extrajudicial killing" of the bishop. Orantes was charged with murder, and the cook was charged with covering up evidence of the crime.[38] Under international political pressure, Guatemalan President Álvaro Arzú ordered an investigation on the bishop's murder, but the report was labeled "inadequate" by critics who believed the president knew more. However, if Arzú wanted to keep his job, he had "to keep his mouth shut."[39]

Before a decision was ever reached on the defendants, a judge's home was fire-bombed, and a half-dozen witnesses, a judge, and a prosecutor left the country, fearing for their lives. When one of the witnesses returned to testify, he was accompanied by five armed guards and wore a bulletproof vest. The brother of President Arzú was accused by a high-ranking Guatemalan church official of offering, during the trial, freedom for Father Orantes if the Church ceased its claims that the Guatemalan army was involved. And there were a number of suspicious incidents: six homeless individuals who stayed near the bishop's home and might have seen something on the night of the murder, suddenly died, and one of the prosecution's witnesses, while in prison, killed himself.[40]

Despite all the difficulties, three years after the murder, a three-judge panel found all but the cook guilty and sentenced the priest to twenty years in prison and each of the military men to thirty. The soldiers were convicted of Gerardi's "extrajudicial execution," which carried with it the implication that the government might be involved in the murder. That suggestion was supported by statements from the judges that the murder was politically motivated and that specific members of the presidential general staff were accessories.[41]

The 2001 verdict was celebrated as indicating a change in Guatemala. "All of Guatemala is happy because of this significant step toward eliminating impunity," a bishop was quoted as saying.[42] The Archbishop's Human Rights Office had been granted legal standing in the case, and an attorney for the office who had sat—along with two other Church attorneys—beside the public prosecutor during the trial, commented that "ten years ago it would be unheard of to see those guys sitting there, having to answer questions in an open court. We've taken a small step, but a step nonetheless in the struggle against impunity."[43] The executive director of the Americas Division of Human Rights Watch exclaimed that "the trial's outcome marks the end of an era in Guatemala" and added that "for the first time, a Guatemalan court has ruled that army officers cannot get away with murder."[44] Even the country's president, Alfonso Portillo, declared, "Today, for the first time in our history, law and justice have been applied to a political crime."[45]

It is doubtful, however, that the convictions in the Gerardi case indicated a transformation in Guatemalan society. Rather, the outcome seems more associated with idiosyncratic matters. For one, Gerardi was an international figure. His murder and the investigation and trial that followed were covered in the international press. Lacking such scrutiny, as would be the case for trials involving less celebrated victims, the Guatemalan judicial system might not have functioned in the same manner. In fact, very few individuals have been indicted, much less convicted, for crimes committed during the civil war.

Presidential politics also played a role in the convictions. The murder occurred while Arzú was president. Although he had signed the peace accords, he is blamed for effectively blocking the prosecution of military members. During the campaign for the presidency, Arzú's main opponent, Portillo, vowed, if elected, to solve the crime during the first months of his term in office. This was meaningful, as the party of Portillo was pro-immunity. The irony led some to speculate that the support of Portillo's party, the Frente Republicano Guatemalteco (FRG), for the prosecution of the military officers was personal. The leader of the FRG at the time was not Portillo but Guatemala's former dictator Efraín Ríos Montt, who was, until January 2004, president of Congress. He is usually fingered as the individual most responsible for the scorched-earth campaign, and it is not surprising that he sought a general amnesty for atrocities committed during the civil war. His party's support for the prosecutions was therefore surprising, but less so when one realizes that the highest-ranking military defendant, Colonel Lima Estrada, was formerly a close ally of the general who led the internal coup against Montt in 1983. From this perspective, Efraín Ríos Montt gains a bit of vengeance against his old enemies by the conviction of Estrada.[46]

THE AFTERMATH

Rather than undermining impunity, for many critics the Gerardi case strengthened it. The vicious murder was committed with purpose. The Recovery of Historical Memory Project (REMHI), the results of which Gerardi presented two days before his murder, was a threat to the military's impunity. His killers intended to notify the general society and reformers in the government that attacks on their impunity would be met with violence.[47] For some commentators, the implied threat had its intended outcome. As evidence, they offered their estimation that the human rights office previously headed by Gerardi was visibly less active following his death.[48]

Things got worse after Portillo was inaugurated as president in January 2000. The tactic of disappearance resurfaced; human rights activists were regularly followed, robbed, and threatened with death if they continued their activities; social-movement organization offices were burglarized, often several times each year, and evidence of atrocities was destroyed; activists were abducted and held for hours or tortured; and some individuals were simply murdered in the streets.[49] Journalists was also attacked and threatened.[50] Public officials were not immune from the terror. A United Nations report noted a tripling of violent attacks against judges, witnesses, and prosecutors following the peace accords. The chief prosecutor in the Gerardi murder fled the country after receiving death threats,[51] and a judge— the father of two social activists—was hacked to death by a mob under somewhat suspicious circumstances: the mob held him for more than ten hours, but the police made no attempt to rescue him. Guatemala's Supreme Court believed "paramilitary operatives" were to blame.[52] But the murder of the judge was probably more reflective of the disdain felt by rural people toward legal institutions.

VIGILANTE JUSTICE

Vigilante justice became more commonplace in Guatemala as a result of the pervasive view that legal officials would do nothing about criminal behavior. The U.N. Mission to Guatemala (MINUGUA) reported that more than three hundred "lynchings" occurred during the five years after the official end to the civil war. The lynchings did not involve hanging, as occurred in the "Wild West" of North America; these extrajudicial executions were often accomplished by setting the victims on fire fueled by gasoline or occasionally accomplished by stoning.[53] And although most lynchings were exacted against suspected criminals, the tactic was also used to settle old scores.[54] This occurred in July 2000 when a rural community lynched five family members who had all survived a 1993 massacre. Some of the family members had testified before one of the truth commissions against former local members of the Civil Patrol who had participated in the massacre. Their testimony helped send two of the former patrollers to two months in detention. Local residents who participated in the lynchings reported that it was ex-patrollers who "had organized the lynching, obligated villagers to attend, and further forced their participation in several meetings in its aftermath."[55] The suggestion is that the lynchings were motivated by vengeance.

It would be a mistake, however, to simply blame the vigilante justice on active or former military officials. To do so would be to ignore the extrajudicial acts as expressions of the failure in Guatemala to reinstate civil society and end impunity. Prior to the civil war, in rural communities, informal forms of social control such as family and community minimized the need for official law. When disputes occasionally arose, they were commonly settled by use of traditional Mayan law or "courts" similar to the common-law courts of Western tradition. A quiet revolutionary explained the traditional law:

> In many of the indigenous towns, they have their own system. When there is a problem, they look for those who represent the authority in that particular town. For example, in [name of village], there is not a presiding mayor, but there is a group of elderly women. When there are conflicts, the townspeople consult these women frequently, so that they can see what can be done. Or, at times, as well, there are men or families or women who have a lot of community respect and who are generally elderly persons who are consulted and who are those who frequently make decisions regarding community conflicts.

The scorched-earth policy and successive forms of violence severely undermined cohesion and trust in these communities, as well as their use of nonviolent dispute resolution. The military replaced the traditional methods of social control with military authority, which controlled almost all aspects of individuals' lives. When the war ended and the military loosened its hold on civil society, there were no mechanisms in place for limiting criminal behavior and punishing offenders. Victims were often without recourse to officials. Circumstances were worse in many of the indigenous communities, as a quiet revolutionary reported:

> The situation often arises that the workers [of the legal system] are *mestizos*, and they only speak Spanish. And very often, the indigenous people, especially the majority of women, don't speak in Spanish. Rather, they speak in a native language. So then, even though they make it to the tribunals, they often cannot get a [satisfactory] response.

At the turn of the twenty-first century, the Guatemalan criminal justice system lacked the ability and the motivation to do much about crime. The system was undermined during the civil war by the military in order to maintain impunity. One of the interviewees described the situation with respect to the judges during the civil war:

There are some good judges. They want to be good judges but they can't be. Because if they act like good judges, then they are sent to be killed. So then, under no circumstances can they be good, even though they would like to be. All of the judges have to be bad. They have to cover up many things, so many crimes, massacres. So then, even if you were to ask them to be conscientious, I imagine they wouldn't be able to be. Because there are bad judges that are like that. They are like that. And, like I told you, there are good judges that would like to be able to do something good, those who know very well how the real situation in the country is. But they are not able to do anything about it, if they don't want to see themselves in difficulties.

The lack of recourse to a just and effective criminal justice system led the quiet revolutionaries to conclude that "truthfully, the authorities do not protect you at all. So then, who? The only confidence is in the people."

The legal institutions were unable to establish themselves as effective units after the war ended. A result was rapidly escalating crime rates. The lynchings were an effort by individuals to control the increased crime.

A certain irony accompanies the use of vigilante justice. Some of its perpetrators almost certainly had at one time been quiet revolutionaries. They disdained the use of such punishments when employed against their relatives by the military and its allies. But mobs adopted punishments without trial as a means of restoring some order to their world. Drastic solutions were acceptable, from their perspective, since the legal institutions such as the police, courts, and prisons were unable to function as the law stated.

Some of the solutions that arose in Guatemala as a reaction to rising crime have favored resurrection of the old order. For one, the peace accords required that civil police would replace the military as the keepers of the peace. But the rising disorder in the country combined with the lack of trained officers led to the recycling of former military men into law enforcement, as well as the supposedly prohibited use of the military as crime control agents.[56] In addition, old leaders regained power. Efraín Ríos Montt, who is considered the individual most responsible for the scorched-earth policy, tried to regain the presidency following a decision by the Constitutional

Court, Guatemala's highest court, that he could seek the presidency. The court reached this decision shortly after mobs, apparently organized by Montt's party, rampaged through downtown communities in Guatemala City demanding that the former dictator be allowed to run.[57] His party, the FRG, won power in 1999 in large part because it promised to "get tough on crime." "The rats," Efraín Ríos Montt reportedly said of criminals, "we're going to kill them all!"[58]

CONCLUSION

The last decade of the twentieth century was a tumultuous period in Guatemala. During the early 1990s, members of the various social movements felt a camaraderie with each other. They had some differing goals, but efforts to end impunity was a unifying theme among them. They wanted to see an end to legal favoritism as well as the promotion of the rule of law. A highlight in this regard was the rejection by every segment of society in 1993 of President Serrano's attempt to oust all members of Congress. The president's failure to abide by the country's constitution left him without support. This success, combined with the continuation of the peace accord negotiations, gave the quiet revolutionaries hope that a transformed Guatemala might become reality.

The signing of the peace accords, however, did not lead to long-lasting changes. Many of its requirements were not implemented, some because they were rejected by voters and others because of a poor economic situation. These matters and others undermined the movement and fractionalized its membership.

As the twenty-first century began, Guatemala once again experienced extrajudicial executions. This time, however, common citizens were often the purveyors of doom. During the civil war, the government had at times turned its attention to common criminals, using its power to extrajudicially execute such individuals. But the reign of impunity that governed much of what went on in Guatemala transformed citizens in the new millennium into agents of the state. They lynched suspected criminals rather then leave justice in the hands of an impotent criminal justice system. Additionally, a new form of vigilante justice arose in Guatemala's capital city. Each month, some forty youngsters were murdered, summarily executed by unknown assailants, in acts that have been described as "a form of 'social cleansing' whereby vigilante groups and police regard the deaths as others might regard the removal of vermin."[59] The rights of citizens appeared buried, and human rights abuses continued, albeit at the hands of private citizens and not state agents.

The quiet revolutionaries' collective identity as Guatemalans had played a significant role in their active participation in the popular movement. Their nationalism was used to legitimize their demands for justice and accountability. It was an ideology that helped mobilize political action against the ruling elites. It increased the solidarity among the groups.

The peace accords undermined their collective identity as Guatemalan and played a determining factor in the exit of some members of the quiet revolutionaries from the movement.[60] Issues of "us versus them" became less important after the peace agreement. The civil war had been responsible for most of the killing. Once the war ended, fatalities continued to decline. One of the quiet revolutionaries, prior to the peace accords, explained:

> For me it's very painful to see Guatemala bleeding like this. I'm old now, but I don't want to see such killing. Some people have grown accustomed to everyone dying, and they're unmoved by it all. When we go to the demonstrations they say we're crazies, or lazies, or obscene phrases. But they don't know our pain. They don't know what we feel.

She separated herself from nonparticipants at demonstrations by referring to them as individuals who were nonplused by the slaughter. She identified with the protestors who had experienced emotional pain. After the war, though, activists were unable to mobilize protests by framing antagonists as individuals intent on slaughter.

Other collective identities arose among the quiet revolutionaries after the peace accords and undercut their collective identity as Guatemalan. Groups such as the Maya and unionists had sought their own best interests during the peace negotiations. These divisions were exacerbated following the end of the civil war and the relative normalization of politics. The quiet revolutionaries split over other matters as well. Some of their number were willing to trade legal accountability for the murders and disappearances in exchange for learning the whereabouts of their loved ones, dead or alive.

The failure of the criminal justice system and the rise of crime in Guatemala further undermined the collective identity of the quiet revolutionaries and diminished the likelihood that they would seek legal accountability for the murders and disappearances of their loved ones. Lynchings, in particular, rose in response to the ineffectiveness of criminal justice agents. The quiet revolutionaries had demonstrated in favor of the use of law, due process, and accountability. But lynchings stand outside the law and resulted in former members of the popular social movement turning away from calls for legal accountability. The failure to implement due process for offenders and victims in Guatemala resulted in a breakdown of citizens' use of law.

The lessons from Guatemala should not be lost on those attempting to implement democracy and its ideals in various corners of the world. Democracy is not necessarily about elections. It may have much more to do with the functioning of civil institutions. We discuss these matters in our concluding chapter.

CHAPTER SEVEN

Identity, Rule of Law, and Democracy

The saga of the quiet revolutionaries is a long one, and the ending is yet to be written. The specific events that sparked their political involvement and identity changes occurred more than twenty years ago, and the conditions that gave rise to the episodes, such as ethnic class differences, have existed for centuries.

Before the civil war, perhaps most people in the rural areas where much of the violence occurred perceived their own collective identities as members of the local communities or personal identities as gender-specific members of families. Outside assaults against neighbors were perceived as attacks against the community, and all who held the same collective identity might respond to it.

The widespread killings in Guatemala changed all that. The scorched-earth policy of the early 1980s resulted in the decimation of hundreds of communities. In some, the military slaughtered almost everyone and burned the homes and fields. In others, members fled to Mexico as refugees to escape the hell around them. Both scenarios resulted in the devastation of communities and undercut the identities of those remaining in the villages. The survivors must have wondered whether they still could be members of a community when the community no longer existed; were they mothers, wives, daughters, husbands, fathers, sons, nephews of a family group when their counterparts in those kinship ties no longer were present?

For many of the quiet revolutionaries, particularly the women, the ambiguous nature of their loved ones' disappearances or the inability to know what happened to the cadavers produced terrific anxiety. The hope of finding missing relatives alive drove them to try to learn their whereabouts.

To do otherwise would have meant surrendering the fragile identities to which they still clung. They looked for answers from culturally specific mechanisms such as dreams or from environmental cues. And they sought information from officials who they hoped could help them. But their efforts went unrewarded.

Those who endeavored to learn, through official channels, the whereabouts of missing loved ones were met with perceived injustices that further exhausted their psychological and economic resources. During chance encounters at morgues, police stations, and army barracks as they searched for the missing or while trying to establish responsibility for the murders of those found dead, they met other individuals in similar circumstances. There grew from these initial meetings a common sense of purpose among a diverse group of people.

Broadly put, the unifying goal of the quiet revolutionaries was to establish justice for the disappeared and murdered. For some members of the infant groups, this meant the return of living loved ones and the resurrection of families and personal identities. For most, it also meant the castigation of those responsible for the extrajudicial acts. During demonstrations, they called for an end to impunity in Guatemala and for implementation of the written law.

The diversity of the quiet revolutionaries created weak ties among a broad range of individuals who likely would never have even met except as a result of the violence that was everywhere. Outside attacks from official and quasi-official sources that were meant to destroy the growing popular movement only strengthened the solidarity of the groups and further assisted the formation of a collective identity as righteous Guatemalans. Offenses against any member of a group were seen as attacks against all, no matter whether the specific victim was Maya or *ladino,* student or teacher, man or woman, peasant or union organizer. The quiet revolutionaries had donned a pluralistic identity deemed necessary for the formation of democratic societies.

The peace accords undermined the quiet revolutionaries' pluralist, collective identity by fracturing the solidarity along the lines of homogeneous interests, as old animosities resurfaced. The establishment of a toothless official truth commission further undermined the unifying goal of ending impunity, although this was partially offset by the work of the Church-sponsored REMHI project. As anxiety about war-related incidents ebbed, it was replaced with concerns about more everyday matters such as fear of common crime. Vigilante justice arose in response and impeded implementation of the rule of law and democracy.

But it would likely be a mistake to dismiss the efforts of the quiet revolutionaries. The social movement to end impunity increased the chances for democracy to develop in Guatemala. The 2003 national elections were generally regarded by international observers to be free and fair. Broadened political participation of Maya and women seems to be one of the direct outcomes. There were 14 women, as of 2005, among the 158 members of the Congress of the Republic, including former quiet revolutionaries. Nationally, there were nearly 200 female judges, 2 women on the Supreme Court of Justice, and 1 on the Constitutional Court. Overall, women held positions as mayors, cabinet ministers, and presidential secretaries. Indigenous individuals also gained some political clout; there were 15 indigenous members of congress, and more than one-third of the nation's 331 mayors were indigenous people.[1]

The popular social movement also made it more difficult for the oligopoly to act in secret against its opponents; the Guatemalan congress, for example, instituted an oversight body for all intelligence agencies. The social movement attracted continuing worldwide attention, such as international allegations of genocide raised against Guatemalan political leaders. Democratic gains in Guatemala, however, may disappear without ongoing assistance and pressure from players outside of the country.

MINUGUA, the U.N. peacekeeping mission in Guatemala, sponsored several programs for translation of materials into indigenous "dialects" and for language interpreters to be available in several pilot programs in court systems. While the intentions of such a program were admirable and most certainly looked good on paper, the successes were never far-reaching, and the programs were cancelled after several years due to lack of funding and other concerns.

The United States has made some recent efforts to bolster democracy in Guatemala, most notably to improve the administration of justice and in particular the operation of the courts. These efforts, however, have focused on technical aspects such as case processing and have ignored broader issues.[2] What really is needed in Guatemala is a more "generic" reform of the criminal justice system that is aimed at ending impunity and implementing justice through rule of law.

RULE OF LAW AND DEMOCRACY

Rule of law is "a set of stable political rules and rights applied impartially to all citizens."[3] It is not a new idea. Socrates preached its tenets, and the

Magna Carta, often noted as a starting point for Western democracies, was a reflection of the ideal.

Rule of law is one of the foundational components of democracy because it suggests that people will be treated equally. Moreover, it places limits on government action. Officials may not do as they please but must constrain their behavior to what is acceptable to citizens:

> [S]uppose that on a particular issue a consensus exists about the legitimate boundaries of the state and that citizens are willing to withdraw their support from a sovereign who violates them. The sovereign will avoid violating these boundaries because doing so risks losing power. The sovereign's self-interest leads him to respect limits on his behavior; that is, these limits are self-enforcing. In contrast, if citizens hold different views about limits on the state or if they are unwilling to defend these limits, then the sovereign can violate these limits and retain sufficient support to survive.[4]

Democracy then requires that citizens protest arbitrary actions by government, even when those actions may be in their own best interests. The 1993 societal opposition to President Serrano's attempt to oust the Guatemalan congress is illustrative. Many people agreed with the president that many members of the congress were corrupt. But these critics were unwilling to support the president's unconstitutional "self-coup," as it has become known.[5] Rather, all segments of society joined in solidarity against the president, and it was he who was forced from office. Rule of law and democracy are intrinsically linked.

DEMOCRACY AND IDENTITY

Democracy requires individuals to sometimes forgo their own interests in favor of the interests of society. But this is not easy anywhere and perhaps especially not in more heterogeneous countries. A number of characteristics including race, religion, and social class may deeply divide a country such as Guatemala and prove the basis for individual decision making. This fragmentation is particularly evident if individual characteristics are at the core of identity. Rather then seeing issues through a frame that encompasses a diverse group of others, the individual perceives issues through a much narrower lens that allows only a parochial consideration of matters.[6] Such was the case in 1999 among Guatemalan voters, who were presented with constitutional revisions to protect the cultural rights of indigenous peoples, among other amendments. The 1985 constitution, which had established civilian rule, had done little to protect the rights of minorities. It was the peace accords that had required the constitutional reforms. First, however, they had to be approved by the Guatemalan congress (which happened in 1998) and then passed by the electorate. But the less than 19 percent of the population who voted—a mostly *ladino* group—rejected the reforms, reportedly because of racist attitudes against the Maya, although some are reported to have believed the reforms were divisive and threats to national unity.[7] A majority of the voters failed to recognize that protecting the rights of the indigenous population would in the long run facilitate the growth of democracy in Guatemala.

Democracy is not always about majority rule. Laws in democracies may be enacted to protect the rights of minorities. The Bill of Rights of the U.S. Constitution was meant to guarantee freedom from the tyranny of the majority. And the defeat of constitutional protections for the Maya in Guatemala likely means they will continue to be subservient to the wishes of *ladinos*.

The point we are making is that the majority of the electorate reached a decision about how to vote based on self-interest, or in this case, identity politics. They voted based on their collective identity as *ladinos*. Citizens, whether in the voting booth or in response to government action, make judgments as to whether the matters under consideration represent legitimate actions or fundamental transgressions. The decisions they make will be based on preferences and values.[8] These matters, however, will be considered in light of one's collective identity.

ELECTIONS DO NOT NECESSARILY EQUAL DEMOCRACY

We should not assume a country is democratic because it has elections, even if those elections are deemed nonfraudulent. The recent history of presidential elections in the United States illustrates the fallacy of equating democracy with elections. The United States arguably is one of the leading democratic countries in the world. The president, however, is never elected directly by the people. Rather, the president is elected by an electoral college. Also, not everyone who is eligible to vote in the United States bothers to register. And only a fraction of those who register to vote actually cast ballots. In addition, voting restrictions such as the elimination of those convicted of felonies from voting rolls remove from the electoral process sizable segments of poor people. Up until recently, presidential elections might more aptly be characterized as the selection of a leader from a list of two individuals who had been appointed by the elites of the two political parties. Some elections of the past fifty years have raised concerns about fraudulent behavior. The election of John Kennedy in 1960 is said to have been accomplished through illegal means orchestrated by Richard Daley, who was then mayor of Chicago. The election of Richard Nixon twelve years later was accomplished through the use of "dirty tricks" and payments of "hush money" to the Watergate burglars. The resultant scandal led to Nixon's resignation, but not before he appointed Gerald Ford his legal successor. And George W. Bush, president when this chapter was written, lost the popular general 2000 election to his opponent but was voted into office by the electoral college. The U.S. experience clearly indicates that a people can consider themselves democratic without necessarily having free general elections to select their leadership.

Guatemala has elected its head of state since 1986, but few individuals would argue that the country was a full-fledged democracy, even though the elections were considered fair.[9] The interviews with the quiet revolutionaries were replete with criticisms of elections and political parties; their relative disdain of electoral politics at the national level was for parties of the left as much as for centrist and rightist parties. For the quiet revolutionaries, elections provided only a "façade of democracy," in part because of the political posturing of candidates who promised reform during campaigns but delivered little after elections but also because they believed that elected officials did not represent them. "Here is the congress, and the judiciary, and there's the presidency," one noted. But "they are in the hands of the rich. So then, the poor and the indigenous have neither voice nor vote. We are nothing here. So then the law and all their quote, 'justice,' unquote, is for them." Such attitudes continue and could help explain the continuing low turnout for Guatemalan elections and the fact that its citizens do not evaluate democracy very positively as compared to the rest of Latin America.[10]

WHAT CAN WE SAY?

Democracy may be more about having one's interests considered than it is about other matters. In previous times, when societies were more homogeneous, this was not the problem it is today. Certainly there were socioeconomic and gender differences that shaped identities and divided societies, but these were probably tempered by cross-cutting ties. That is, individuals had ties to each other that helped make the interests of one the interests of all. In feudal times, for example, serf and noble were tied together. The serf provided the labor that fed the wealth of the lord. But the lord's military might protected the serf from attacks. Moreover, each might have weak ties to the other through servants or tradespeople. The point is that hardships to one class had some effect on the other. Their interests, although not necessarily the same, were linked.

Interests are not so readily intertwined in modern, heterogeneous societies. The Guatemalan *maquila* businessman of the 1990s, for example, was much less reliant on labor than plantation owners. If labor became a problem by demanding better working conditions or higher pay or better health benefits, the businessman could close the shop and move it elsewhere.[11] Ignoring the interests of workers and moving the place of business is a less practical solution for landowners.

Rule of law is the means by which people can come to see their interests considered. The law is a powerful thing. Laws can be used to establish rights and duties and to define differing social phenomena as legal or illegal. One perspective regarding the enactment of law sees the process as one involving all members of society. It is a consensual process in which the outcome reflects the needs and desires of all society members. Not all individuals or groups will be satisfied with the outcome, but because the process involved their input, they are considered more likely to view the new legislation as fair and to abide by it.[12] But law also can be seen as a political tool used by the powerful to support their own interests. From this perspective, law serves as an instrument of power in the process of competing group claims. Those who control it are able to get their way.[13]

In Guatemala the law was the tool of a powerful elite. Individual activities of everyday citizens were subordinate to the narrow concerns of a ruling clique. Individual freedom, prized and necessary in democratic societies, was absent from the world of individuals interviewed for this book. The law could be used in a discriminatory fashion to justify a wide variety of limitations on individual freedom. The labeling of activities such as union organizing or student protest as "terrorism" or "subversion," for example, allowed state-sanctioned forces to use violence against peaceful citizens.

When people see a system as unjust, it is because they do not see their interests reflected. Justice has been considered the central element in all law, practically the raison d'être of law itself, a foundation of social order.[14] The criminal justice system is of primary importance with respect to perceptions of justice. System actors are responsible for the application of the law and are the legal system's visible agents. How they are viewed by the citizenry will in large part determine the public's attitudes about system outcomes. The police have been widely studied in the United States and elsewhere because patrol officers are citizens' most constant contact with the legal system and its most conspicuous representatives.[15] Positive assessments of the police have repeatedly been found to be more prevalent among individuals who also report a strong sense of involvement and inclusion in the political system or general approval of the government.[16] Conversely, negative perceptions of the police have been associated with a lack of confidence in the state's legitimacy.[17] Moreover, police are the system's primary agents to detect and solve crimes, and people antagonistic to the police are unlikely to aid officers in curbing crime even when they themselves are the victims.[18] In general, police will encounter greater resistance to their authority when they are viewed poorly by the public.[19]

In Guatemala many police officers did little or nothing or actually hindered people's efforts to implement the written law. Rather than being perceived as belonging to an independent body that enforced the law without bias, police agents were seen as a tool of the military and oligopoly. No wonder the post–peace accord public seized suspected criminals from the police and dealt vigilante justice. They had no reason to believe the police would act in their interests.

Generally speaking, we can differentiate several types of justice or differing yet related areas of justice concerns. The first of these areas is that of substantive justice, or the justice resulting from processed outcomes.[20] In our daily lives, we might categorize getting hired for a job over other applicants, receiving a good grade in a class, or obtaining a sizable raise as substantive justice. Substantive justice, however, does not always have to be a positive result. It is the outcome of a process. An acquittal or finding of guilt are substantive outcomes of trials. They are tangible results of the processes in criminal justice proceedings.

Whether one accepts a substantive outcome as just or rails against it as an unfair imposition may largely depend on one's perceptions of procedural justice. When rules are followed, we are more satisfied with the results, whether we win or lose. Procedural justice, in fact, has been frequently examined in social psychological literature and defined as user satisfaction with the processing that produces outcomes.[21] In this sense, justice is conceptualized as a way of doing things.[22] The study of procedural justice may focus on the steps legal actors follow to arrive at substantive outcomes and on levels and elements of satisfaction by those persons involved in legal settings.[23] Selection of a jury is an element of procedure that may be viewed by participants and others as just or unjust.

The people interviewed for this book argued that procedural justice did not exist in Guatemala. Individuals were executed without charges being levied or trials being conducted. People were tortured in incomprehensible and myriad fashions, defying any modern code of law. From the view of the quiet revolutionaries, the courts were accessible only to people who had money. They believed that criminal justice officials acted only in favor of the ruling elite and against the interests of Maya, women, union members, activist students, and poor people. Justice was not served.

The lack of justice signaled to the quiet revolutionaries that they were not full-fledged members of the Guatemalan nation and that their interests were not to be served. Their demonstrations in favor of justice for the disappeared were also demands for the quiet revolutionaries to be treated as citizens of Guatemala and to receive the same benefits of the law as others. Eventually, they viewed the government as corrupt and denied that it represented Guatemalans. Rather, the government represented the military and financial elites. The quiet revolutionaries argued that they represented the Guatemalan people, and they demonstrated and demanded change on behalf of the people as well as the missing and murdered for whom they had commenced their organizational activities.

CONCLUSION

"No justice, no peace. No justice, no peace" has been a frequent and heated slogan of modern urban protest in the United States, and the sentiment has been expressed in numerous languages in other countries. The success or failure of postwar government efforts to implement democracy in Guatemala, Iraq, Palestine, and elsewhere may very well depend on citizens' perceptions of how well the respective governments provide justice. Without justice, individuals are unlikely to establish a pluralistic, collective identity as citizens of the nation. Rather, they will identify themselves as members of the disenfranchised groups, whether they be women, the Maya of Guatemala, or Sunni Muslims in Iraq. Under such circumstances, democracy is unlikely to flourish.

APPENDIX

DEVELOPMENT OF CONCEPTUAL FOCI

Once fieldwork was initiated in December 1990, participatory action and ethnographic foci, in addition to interview/survey data collection activities, led to a change in the principal research focus from a stress and coping framework to one reflecting a social psychology and social construction of victimization for family members of the disappeared and survivor-victims of state violence.[1]

Once in Guatemala, my interactions with respondents and informants led me to reconstruct my data collection approach and to eventually develop a new questionnaire to be used in the second period of fieldwork. The social construction framework transformed from one in which respondents were more or less mechanically shaped by their circumstances to a framework that took into account the place of social movement struggles by oppressed communities in Guatemalan history.

One key change in the research focus was the deindividualizing of respondents. Such deindividualization required a focus on the social roles of the respondents. Individual respondents were core activists in socially transformative ethnic, gender, and terror survivor-based movements, and simply viewing them as psychosocially traumatized persons was an unnecessary atomization of their social selves. They were more than victims of a particular extralegal human rights abuse. They were Mayans and agriculturalists and trade unionists and women and "the poor" who, yes, had lost loved ones to enforced disappearance or had themselves been detained and tortured. Respondents were nonetheless persons who possessed identities and social roles apart from family losses or episodes of bodily harm.

The second stage of data gathering occurred in 1992 and was guided by sociolegal themes. I was interested in learning the individual actions respondents had taken or in which they had participated in the pursuit of redress of government-sponsored extralegal actions. I also gathered data on the social ideology of respondents' worldviews regarding the state, social power relations, and the roles, function, and performance of the formal legal system.

MEASURES: INTERVIEW SCHEDULES A AND B
Questionnaire A: 1990 and 1992 (n = 61)

The two interviewed groups were not asked exactly the same questions. The initial interview schedule was developed with Thomas J. Crawford and Roxane C. Silver, both social psychologists at the University of California, Irvine, School of Social Ecology. Professor Crawford was responsible for initial suggestions and materials that led to the use of open-ended and scaled measures authored by Hadley Cantril.[2] The four open-ended questions by Cantril are the principal data collection items for the initial sixty-one subjects.

Professor Silver also contributed to the formation of research questions. She was instrumental in suggesting interview schedule items. Her research experience in studying various social psychological aspects of the lives of traumatic loss survivors in the United States and Canada was a key starting point for my work in Guatemala.[3]

Questionnaire A was designed to assess various components of theoretically derived social psychological constructs as well as to gather data related to respondents' memories and perceptions of traumatic incidents and situational elements of those incidents. The interview schedule was designed also to elicit qualitative, scaled, and survey data measuring frequencies and intensities of activities and ways of thinking that typified respondents' coping responses to their irrevocable losses. Some of those ideas and activities were oriented toward changing their individual and group social situations.

The interview schedule was based, too, on the anecdotal and therapeutical literature on the loss of family members through forced disappearance.[4] It covered respondents' sociodemographics and twelve major areas:

- world view and assumptive worlds;[5]
- ratings of quality of life and state of the nation;[6]
- intensity of somatic, anxious, and depressive symptoms in the week prior to interview;[7]

- details of the sequester of one family member (a number of respondents had more than one disappeared relative);[8]
- attributions of responsibility for the sequester and for the reasons motivating it;[9]
- anticipatory grief;[10]
- frequency of intrusive thoughts;[11]
- cognitive ideation regarding current physiological status and quality of life of the disappeared relative;[12]
- social support;[13]
- frequency of disclosure of trauma-related feelings;[14]
- frequency and types of behavioral strategies for coping with the sequester and subsequent disappearance;[15] and
- frequency of significant life changes since the disappearance.[16]

A final section of the interview emphasized a focus on self-capacitation. Six open-ended questions were adapted from Tait and Silver,[17] and these were designed to elicit information on what respondents had learned about themselves and the world around them since the sequester and the recommendations and advice that respondents could give to the people around them.

In order to develop an understanding of respondents' worldviews, they were initially asked four questions from Cantril's Self-Anchoring Striving Scale.[18] These were: (1) the best and (2) the worst possible lives for themselves, and (3) the best and (4) the worst possible national situation in a hypothetical ten-year future. To assess respondents' meanings associated with the sequester and subsequent disappearance of a loved one, respondents were asked: (1) why they thought their principal relative had been a victim of enforced disappearance, and (2) why they thought such things occurred in Guatemala.

Questionnaire B: 1992 (n = 19)

This interview schedule was developed with the assistance of Professors John Dombrink and Leo R. Chavez, both at the University of California, Irvine. Questionnaire B contained five principal data-gathering sections. The first section had open-ended questions that were guided by themes that had surfaced in the 1990 interviews regarding the law, social/political power, and human rights. Respondents were asked general questions and then extensively probed in Spanish about their conceptualizations and understandings of the law: What is the law? How does it work in your country? Are there times when it does not work in your country? Probing involved not only the elicitation of further explanatory dialogue but also of examples. Respondents were asked similar questions about definitions, personalities, and examples of power, the authorities, and human rights in Guatemala.

In a second section of the 1992 interviews, respondents were shown ten black-and-white cards. On nine cards were photos, and on one was a line drawing. Each card depicted a distinct Guatemalan social category, or persona. The ten personas depicted were those of an indigenous Mayan woman (identified as such by traditional clothing), a student (young man), a trade unionist (man), a teacher (woman), an army officer (man), a street vendor (woman), a businessman, a farmworker (young man), a housewife (in a drawing designed to obscure her socioeconomic class), and an orphaned child (pre-teenage boy with bag of glue for sniffing). Respondents were then told a story. In the scenario presented to respondents, each of the ten personas had a disappeared family member and had gone to the Supreme Court to demand action by the authorities and judicial system. The family member wanted to find the relative and evidence regarding the hypothetical sequester's circumstances and to find and punish the guilty parties. Respondents were then asked to sort the ten pictures from the one who would receive the most justice from the Supreme Court to the one who would receive the least or no justice. Respondents were then verbally probed for explanations of their rating or ordering.

The third section of the interview schedule was comprised of data that were evaluative (just/unjust) and explanatory (why/why not) commentary on three vignettes related to themes of investigating and prosecuting the enforced disappearance of a family member. In this section, respondents were presented with three vignettes that were taken from examples provided by the initial interviewees in 1990, the details of which, as it turned out, were known by many. Each of the three vignettes clearly described situations in which family members of the disappeared or extrajudicially executed had approached and petitioned legal authorities in the search for their missing loved ones. In each vignette, the claimant is frustrated in her legal petitions through the exercising of common elements of impunity in Guatemalan society.

In the first vignette, a young woman had lost her husband to sequester, brutal torture, and extrajudicial execution. It was deemed later in a Guatemalan court that a group of National Police officers had been involved in the sequester-murder episode. Through legal manipulations, the police officers were eventually released from custody and allowed to return to their jobs, and the president offered the young widow a job in the police station with the same officers guilty of her husband's murder in compensation for the loss of her husband. Respondents were asked if the happenings, as presented, were just or unjust and asked to justify their answers.

In the second of the three vignettes, a destitute and preliterate wife of a disappeared man is told by a court official to pay the sum of 300 *quetzales* to register her case and move it forward. Since the woman finds the amount prohibitive and her preliterate condition is an impediment to legal assistance, she abandons the case. Once again, respondents were asked whether these occurrences were just or unjust and asked to explain why or why not.

In the last vignette, a woman who has been involved for years in a human rights group in search of her disappeared husband is harassed by a local paramilitary institution in her village. The paramilitaries fire two shots at her shack, in her direction, and tell her that if she continues going to meetings she will end up where her husband ended up. She goes to the meeting anyway, though quite afraid. Respondents were then asked to evaluate and explain as above.

In the fourth section of the questionnaire, seven open-ended questions, adapted from Bumiller's study of the social construction of discrimination victims in the United States,[19] were presented to each of the nineteen respondents. Many of those interviewed had formally pursued legal avenues related to their complaints of having suffered varied human rights abuses, and they were first asked whether or not they had filed an official complaint. Regardless of their answers, they were then queried about (a) the costs or damages they had experienced due to the violations of their human rights; (b) whether they thought violations similar to those which they had reported happened to persons like themselves; (c) whether they believed people thought less of them for having been victimized; (d) whether or not the law is "on their side"; (e) whether or not some people get special treatment from the law; and (f) whether or not people in Guatemala get more or less "what they deserve."

The fifth questionnaire segment was designed as a self-capacitation section and was intended to assist respondents in validating their own opinions and actions. Here, respondents were asked what advice they would give to (a) all the judges of their country; (b) all the police of their country; (c) all the soldiers and officers of the army of their country; and (d) all the children of their country.

Questionnaire B had three additional sections.[20] Sociodemographic information collected on respondents included age, gender, schooling (dichotomous, whether or not a respondent had ever attended), schooling (continuous, the highest grade completed for each respondent), language(s) presently spoken in the home, language(s) spoken as a child, stated ethnic identity, presence of non-Spanish speakers in the home, presence of non-Spanish speakers in respondent's place of origin, number of persons living in the home, daily wage and the number of people supported by that wage, belief in a specific religious faith, geographical unit of the respondent's place of residence at the time of interview (a village, a town, a county seat, or a city), and the geographical unit of each respondent's place of birth (same four categories as place of residence).

One additional section of the interview requested respondents to indicate if they, someone in their family, someone in their community, or a friend, had ever been

> disappeared; sequestered and later found dead; died violently; had a home lost or destroyed; been captured or jailed without trial; suffered familial disintegration; been raped by the authorities; or been beaten or tortured by the authorities.

INTERVIEWING

In my introduction to the interviewees, before their consent, I explained respondents' rights as potential participants. I told them they could refuse to answer any questions and could terminate participation at any point in the interview. Respondents were also reminded of this at least one additional time during each interview.

Interviews lasted an average of one hour and were audio-recorded on ninety-minute cassette tapes. The interviews were, at times, tailored to the individual. Any idiosyncracies that may have been introduced by restating questions and/or by varying vocabulary is considered preferable to repeating identically worded sentences in noncolloquial Spanish like a prerecorded automaton.

Because of the delicate nature of the interview content as well as the sensitive nature of the data collection, respondents' names were never used in the interviews, typed or written onto the transcripts or field notes, or, to the extent possible, recorded on audio cassette. Audio-recorded verbal consents to be interviewed and tape-recorded were sought and received from all respondents. Specific places, names of family members (disappeared or otherwise), or other identifying information such as exact dates of sequesters unless commonly known were not used in the interview process, nor were they written in notes. No information is utilized in this study that would identify any individual respondent. This is true even if that respondent requested to be identified and gave her or his name and that of the disappeared or assassinated family member or members. All respondents were assigned numbers in sequence for data input and identification. With but a few exceptions, respondents and researcher had no further contact after the interviews.

SOME STRENGTHS OF THE RESEARCH
METHODOLOGIES EMPLOYED

One major and important strength of this study, in contrast to those that utilize only closed-category surveys, is that the interview process was made accessible to the literate and preliterate, schooled, unschooled, and under-schooled alike. With a comparatively low average national literacy rate (51.8 percent for those sixteen years and older),[21] especially among rural women (less than 40 percent),[22] the use of visual scaled and pile-sorting instruments with preliterate peoples was an important asset contributing to the representativity of the study sample and the validity of the research. Likert-style response categories were adapted by using drawings of either quetzal birds or ears of corn instead of written or memorized response formats. For example, for the category "Never," a blank page with the word *Nunca* was used. For the response category "Rarely," the word *Raramente* was written with two ears of corn on the page; for "Sometimes," the words *Algunas veces* were written on the response page with four ears of corn shown; for "Frequently," the word *Frecuentemente* was written on the page with eight ears of corn present; and, finally, for the response category "All the time," twenty ears of corn were depicted with the words *Todo el tiempo* written below them. These methodological strategies proved to be user-friendly with Mayan respondents who possessed limited Spanish abilities and with preliterates, particularly some rural women, who appeared to be quite comfortable with the five picture sheets simultaneously presented to them during the interviews.

Other strengths of this study center on the fact that little if any publicly disseminated research had been done with Guatemalan family members of the disappeared or personal survivors of state-sanctioned terrorism. While anecdotal clinical case studies and political science and broad sociological studies,[23] along with journalistic accounts, constitute the bulk of information gathered on state terror survivors, few focus on Guatemala apart from victim statistics and sequester descriptions.[24] Some recent anthropological work has involved reporting the transcriptions of intensive interviews with communities of Guatemalan survivors in a scientific context.[25] Only the Central American Association of Family Members of Detained-Disappeared

(ACAFADE) has published in-depth interviews in Spanish specifically with Guatemalan family members of the disappeared, accompanied by some type of analysis of those interviews in a theoretical context.[26] The ACAFADE publication is unique in that the victims are the chief data source and it examines victimization's relationships to political and cultural resistance, organizational behavior, and, ultimately, conceptualizations of justice and injustice.

Additional strengths of this study are the reliability and the validity of the results. The results are low in "quixotic reliability," which refers to the ability of one method of observation to produce an unvarying measurement.[27] Ideally, one wants variability in the answers to the questions as opposed to standard responses. The variability of answers reflected in the coding categories, the varied beliefs about the fates of disappeared loved ones, and the diverse reasons given for believing that human rights were violated in Guatemala are indications that this study has low quixotic reliability, as would be desirable.

Both instrumental (criterion) validity and theoretical (construct) validity were enhanced by a research methodology that actively involved respondent and informant participation throughout the phases of research and write-up. "Instrumental validity" refers to observations that are relatively consistent though reached through different measures. "Theoretical validity" is higher when theoretical constructs more accurately correspond to observations.[28] Because PAR methodology and participatory fieldwork were the guiding principles of this study, the inherent strengths in the validity of observations are multiple and robust.

NOTES

INTRODUCTION

1. Menchú 1984.
2. Harbury 1997.
3. Jonas 1996.
4. Afflitto 2000.
5. National Catholic Reporter 1998.
6. We are not suggesting that Native Americans in North America had things better. Many of the injustices we mention here also were perpetrated in the United States and Canada.
7. Brysk 2000.
8. Piero Gleijeses (1991:12) defines Indians in Guatemala as "the descendants of the vanquished Maya. Above the Indians were the Ladinos, an ambiguous category that encompassed all those who were not officially classed as Indians, blacks, or Chinese; it ranged from upper-class whites who boasted of their European lineage to landless Indians who had renounced the culture of their people."
9. Falla 1994; Jonas 2000b.
10. Durkheim 1933.
11. Janoff-Bulman 1992.
12. Kamenka 1980.
13. Royal 2000:32.
14. Afflitto 2000.
15. Beccaria 1983; Bonger 1969; Chambliss 1973, 1974; Marx and Engels 1964; Quinney 1974, 1977; Smith 1986; Taylor, Walton, and Young 1973.

CHAPTER ONE

1. Lovell and Lutz 1996.
2. Davis and Hodson 1982.

3. Tedeschi 1997.
4. Tennesen 1997.
5. Pan American Health Organization 2001.
6. Patrinos 1997.
7. Pan American Health Organization 2001.
8. Ashworth 1997; Casterline et al. 1997; de Onis et al. 1993; Rivera and Ruel 1997.
9. Curet et al. 2003.
10. Psacharopoulos and Patrinos 1994.
11. Heuveline and Goldman 2000; Pan American Health Organization 2001.
12. Pan American Health Organization 2001.
13. Freed 1991.
14. *Crónica* 1996.
15. Melville and Melville 1975.
16. Carlsen 1996.
17. Carmack 1988; Doyle 1997; Handy 1984, 1994; Jonas 2000b; Gleijeses 1991; Grieb 1979; Immerman 1982; McCreery 1983a,b, 1986; Schlesinger and Kinzer 1999; Smith 1990.
18. Carlsen 1996.
19. Smith 1984.
20. Kaimowitz 1996.
21. Falcoff 1999:42.
22. Kaimowitz 1996.
23. Handy 1990; REMHI 1999.
24. Lovell and Lutz 1996.
25. Carlsen 1996.
26. Gould 1994; McCreery 1994a.
27. Lovell and Lutz 1996; McCreery 1983a, 1986; REMHI 1999.
28. Smith 1986.
29. Kaimowitz 1996.
30. Commission for Historical Clarification 1998.
31. Falcoff 1999; Yashar 1997.
32. Dosal 1993.
33. Falcoff 1999.
34. Dosal 1993; Falcoff 1999; Yashar 1997.
35. Gleijeses 1991:10.
36. Gleijeses 1991; Grieb 1979.
37. Grieb 1979:282–283.
38. Handy 1984.
39. Handy 1984, 1994; Gleijeses 1991.
40. Dosal 1993; LaBarge 1960; Moberg 1996.
41. Dosal 1993; Yashar 1997.
42. Vidal 1995.
43. Moberg 1996.
44. Gillick 1994.
45. Dosal 1993:41.

46. Dosal 1993; LaBarge 1960; Schlesinger 1997; Schlesinger and Kinzer 1999.
47. Dosal 1993.
48. REMHI 1999.
49. Dosal 1993; Falcoff 1999; REMHI 1999; Vidal 1995.
50. Handy 1990.
51. REMHI 1999; Vidal 1995.
52. Dosal 1993:229.
53. Falcoff 1999; REMHI 1999.
54. Dosal 1993.
55. Doyle 1997.
56. Dosal 1993.
57. Falcoff 1999; *National Catholic Reporter* 1999.
58. REMHI 1999:187.
59. REMHI 1999:188.
60. REMHI 1999:188.
61. Doyle 1997.
62. Doyle 1997:35.
63. Kornbluh 1997.
64. Yashar 1997.
65. Doyle 1997; Yashar 1997.
66. Yashar 1997.
67. Vidal 1995; Yashar 1997.
68. Vidal 1995:793.
69. Doyle 1997; Kornbluh 1997.
70. Brett 2002.
71. Burt 1999; Doyle 1997; Falcoff 1999; Kornbluh 1997; Vidal 1995.
72. Kornbluh 1997.
73. Doyle 1997.
74. Ibid.
75. Burt 1999; Doyle 1997; Falcoff 1999; Kornbluh 1997; Vidal 1995.
76. Commission for Historical Clarification 1998; Yashar 1997.
77. Falcoff 1999; Yashar 1997.
78. Yashar 1997.
79. Commission for Historical Clarification 1998; Yashar 1997.
80. Doyle 1997.
81. Yashar 1997.
82. REMHI 1999; Yashar 1997.
83. REMHI 1999:191.
84. Ibid.
85. Perera 1993:41.
86. Ibid.
87. REMHI 1999.
88. Falcoff 1999; "Peace at Last" 1997; REMHI 1999.
89. Commission for Historical Clarification 1998.
90. Davis and Hodson 1982.
91. Ibarra 1991; Sloan 1984; Turk 1982.

92. Ibarra 1991; Peralta and Imery 1981.

93. Feldman 1991; Mitchell et al. 1986; Sluka 1995.

94. McClintock 1985.

95. We have determined these waves from a variety of sources that include historical and social science analyses in both Spanish and English. Twenty years of work with U.S.-based grassroots organizations supporting social change in Guatemala also informed the formation of these time lines. Finally, the periods were determined through interviews with numerous Guatemalans, including many of those who were formally interviewed or with whom Frank Afflitto associated during fieldwork. The stages are dependent on markers reflecting defining moments of mass violence against civilians, when tactics, targets, or intensities of the violence changed to reflect, create, or adapt to new social conditions. Guatemalan institutions that have studied the violence have also developed time lines. Some of this information is reflected in our own research as a base for our historical development. The authoritative Guatemalan temporal history of the violence would be that of the Commission for Historical Clarification. While it is highly informative and official, it does not provide us with all the information we need to set a sound framework for the context of the periods of violence reflected in our interviews. The time line produced by the commission was developed in a context of not naming names of the perpetrating forces or individuals of the violence and did not illuminate significant markers of who did what when. While we certainly defer to the Guatemalans in the creation of a time frame for their own lived realities, the descriptions we herein provide add to but do not supplant the Commission for Historical Clarification's time line. With that in mind, we are able to discern four major stages of the state terrorism over a thirty-two-year span.

96. Foucault 1979.

97. Ibid.

98. McClintock 1985.

99. Rarihokwats 1982.

100. McClintock 1985.

101. Freed 1991.

102. Ibid.

103. See Ibarra 1991 for related tables.

104. Smith 1990.

105. Nairn 1993; Roberts 2002.

106. Carmack 1988; REMHI 1999.

107. Carmack 1988; REMHI 1999.

108. Jonas 1998:47.

109. Jonas 1991.

110. Ciencia y Tecnología para Guatemala 1991.

111. Jonas 1998.

112. Ibid.

113. Ciencia y Tecnología para Guatemala 1991; Falla 1994; Ibarra 1991; McClintock 1985; Peralta and Imery 1981.

114. Ciencia y Tecnología para Guatemala 1991; McClintock 1985.

115. Guatemala News and Information Bureau 1986; REMHI 1999.
116. REMHI 1999.
117. Ibid.
118. McClintock 1985; REMHI 1999.
119. REMHI 1999.
120. Burt 1998:5.
121. REMHI 1999.

CHAPTER TWO

1. See, generally, Whyte 1991.
2. See Lee 1995 and Sluka 1990.
3. Turk 1982.
4. Warren (1998:95) reports that at the time, "it was dangerous to be carrying a Walkman or cassette tapes—favorite items for Maya youths—or the traditional black-and-white knit bag (*morral*) worn by the Maya men of a more politicized Chichicastenango."
5. Schutte 1991.
6. Schutte 1991; Sluka 1995.
7. Lancaster 1992; Sluka 1990, 1995.
8. Denzin 1989.
9. For an informative treatise on gossip and field research in Central America see Lancaster 1992.
10. For an extended discussion of related topic matter from fieldwork in Nicaragua see Lancaster 1992.
11. Clinical psychological literature has often referred to the therapist's role in taking on the pain of others as countertransference, and psychological literature from Latin America has addressed such issues with client populations of state-violence survivors. Bozzolo 1986; Lira et al. 1984; Nicoletti 1986; Weinstein 1984.
12. Lancaster 1992.
13. For a discussion of an awkward moment in fieldwork as the result of an accusation of being a CIA agent see Lancaster 1992.
14. *Boston Globe* 1996.
15. Researchers normally overcome such problems by studying a large number of individuals randomly selected from the population of interest. Gallup and other similar polls interview more than one thousand U.S. citizens to reach their conclusions. Included among the people they contact are many who know nothing about the topic of interest or are unwilling to express an opinion. Surveys are commonly used because the expense of hiring individuals and training them to do the interviews would be prohibitive. Such tactics, however, would not have worked in this study. The need to gain and maintain the trust of those with whom I spoke, combined with the nature of the research topic and the impossibility of obtaining or creating a random sample of the survivors of the disappeared, made such a strategy impossible. Rather, I chose to do what other qualitative researchers have

done: I conducted interviews with individuals who appeared to be particularly knowledgeable about the phenomenon under study.

16. Bumiller 1988.

17. ACAFADE 1988, 1990b; Berger 1992; Davis and Hodson 1982; McClintock 1985; Nelson et al. 1983; Painter 1987; Peralta and Edgardo 1971; Rarihokwats 1982.

18. ACAFADE 1988, 1990b; Peralta and Edgardo 1971; Peralta and Imery 1981.

CHAPTER THREE

1. REMHI 1999.

2. Personal correspondence with James Diego Vigil, who conducted fieldwork among the highland Maya in the mid-1970s; Gleijeses 1991; Wagley 1979.

3. REMHI 1999.

4. Bowlby 1979, 1980; Freud 2005; Parkes 1974; Sanders 1989.

5. Ufema 2002:22.

6. Bowlby 1980; Sanders 1989.

7. Green 1999; Sagan 2002.

8. Weinstein 1984; Weinstein, Maggi, and Gómez 1987.

9. Tarrow 1994:4.

10. Lord 1987.

11. McCubbin et al. 1976; McCubbin, Hunter, and Metres 1974.

12. Central to Tamotsu Shibutani's book *The Derelicts of Company K: A Sociological Study in Demoralization* (1978) is how important it is for humans to achieve clarity in ambiguous situations. His subjects—low-ranking military personnel—use gossip to work collectively to try to understand high-ranking military personnel's strategy. Their "collective effort" is connected to their development of a collective identity.

13. Stroebe et al. 1992.

14. Freud 1999, 2005; Sanders 1989.

15. Bowlby 1979, 1980; Parkes 1974; Sanders 1989.

16. Salimovich, Lira, and Weinstein 1992; Weinstein, Maggi, and Gómez 1987.

17. Snyder 1989.

18. Weinstein 1984; Weinstein, Maggi, and Gómez 1987.

19. Amnesty International 1988, 1989a,b; Association of Democratic Guatemalan Journalists 1986; Barry 1992; Bernstein, Lilly, and Patterson 1991; Galeano 1969; Sectores Surgidos por la Represión y la Impunidad 1992; McSherry 1989–1990; Menchú 1984; National Academy of Sciences 1992; National Lawyers Guild and La Raza Legal Alliance 1979; Painter 1987; Pérez 1990; Rarihokwats 1982; REMHI 1999; Webster 1990.

20. Bernstein, Lilly, and Patterson 1991; Galeano 1969; McClintock 1985.

21. Weinstein 1984; Weinstein, Maggi, and Gómez 1987.

22. Green 1999:77.

23. Ladd-Taylor 1994; Whittier 1995.
24. Leary, Wheeler, and Jenkins 1986.
25. Stryker and Serpe 1982.
26. Neuhouser 1998.
27. Becker 1960; Calhoun 1991.
28. Weber 1958.
29. Corradi 1982–1983; Martín-Baró 1988, 1989.
30. Green 1999:117.
31. Green 1999:124.
32. Brysk 1994b:40.
33. Brysk 1994b.

CHAPTER FOUR

1. A number of those interviewed from this group of relatives of disappeared union members had gone to psychiatric hospitals looking for their loved ones. A famous Guatemalan poet had been found tortured, imprisoned, and insane in the basement of the house of a chief of the security forces after an armed attack demolished the home, and thus the thought was that other "disappeared" persons also may have been tortured beyond sanity and "freed" to the custody of insane asylums.

2. Brysk 1994b:12.

3. Most Guatemalans relied on public transportation, and because there was no transfer system, had to purchase each bus ride separately. Workers in the poorest outlying areas at times had to take four to six bus rides a day to get to work and back. For those who earned little, bus fare represented a sizable portion of the family budget.

4. The *quetzal* was on par with the U.S. dollar at the time.

5. At the end of the torture session, this man was explicitly told that if he were to denounce the perpetrators publicly or tell anything of what had happened to him, he would be resequestered and disappeared.

6. Felstiner, Abel, and Sarat 1980–1981.

7. The use of "bad killing" was an allusion to torture. In formal, face-to-face interviewing, Guatemalans tend to tone down violent acts perpetrated on persons. This was particularly noticeable when rural women spoke. Words such as "chastisement" were used for torture, and "take advantage of" or "do damage" were used for rape.

CHAPTER FIVE

1. Blee 1998; Cerulo 1997.

2. Tarrow 1994:4.

3. On rational choice see Klandermans and Oegema 1987; Oberschall 1993; Oliver 1984; Olson 1965. On opportunity see McCarthy and Zald 1973.

4. Carden 1978; Fireman and Gamson 1979.

5. Oberschall 1993.

6. Oliver 1984.

7. Klandermans and Oegema 1987.

8. Meyer 2002.

9. McAdam and Paulsen 1993; Mueller 1980.

10. McAdam and Paulsen 1993.

11. Olson 1965.

12. Benford and Hunt 1992; Cohen 1985; Fantasia 1988; Gamson 1992; Johnston, Laraña, and Gusfield 1994; McAdam and Paulsen 1993; Snow and Benford 1992; Taylor and Whittier 1992.

13. Polletta and Jasper 2001:283.

14. Taylor 1989.

15. See generally Cerulo 1997; Johnston, Laraña, and Gusfield 1994; Hunt, Benford, and Snow 1994; Polletta and Jasper 2001; Snow and McAdam 2000.

16. Klandermans and Tarrow 1988.

17. McAdam 1982; McCarthy and Zald 1973, 1977.

18. De Tocqueville 1983:176.

19. Naples 2002a:210.

20. Klandermans 1997.

21. Jonas 1998.

22. Kurzman 1996.

23. Jonas 1998.

24. Brysk 1996; Warren 1998.

25. Lopez and Espiritu 1990:198.

26. Brysk 1996; Vigil 1973.

27. The work of Alison Brysk is most instructive on this matter, and much of what we have to say she has written before us (Brysk 1996, 2000).

28. Brysk 1996:46.

29. See generally Keck and Sikkink 1998.

30. Brysk 2000.

31. Ibid.

32. Warren 1998:29.

33. Commission for Historical Clarification 1998.

34. See Escobar and Alvarez 1992 for a description of Latin American social movements.

35. Brysk 1994; Buchanan 1987.

36. Arditti 1999; Fisher 1993.

37. Brysk 1994b; Fisher 1993.

38. Alvarez 1990; Bayard de Volo 2001; Chuchryk 1989; Fisher 1989, 1993; Friedman 1998; Jaquette 1991; Noonan 1995; Okeke-Ihejirika and Franceschet 2002; Stephen 1997; Waylen 1996.

39. Fisher 1993:2.

40. Alvarez 1990; Bustos 1980; Caldeira 1990; Fisher 1993; Hardin 1982; Jaquette 1991.

41. Hamilton 1924:5.

42. Parsons and Jesilow 2001.

43. Alvarez 1990; Bayard de Volo 2001; Blee 1998; Bookman and Morgen 1988; Brysk 1994b; Bystydzienski 1992; Bystydzienski and Sekhon 1999;

Chuchryk 1989; Fisher 1989, 1993; Friedman 1998; Hardy-Fanta 1993; Jaquette 1991; Jenness 1993; Kaplan 1997; Naples 1998, 2002a,b; Noonan 1995; Okeke-Ihejirika and Franceschet 2002; Parsons and Jesilow 2000; Prindeville 2003; Prindeville and Gomez 1999; Rocheleau, Thomas-Slayter, and Wangari 1996; Stephen 1997; Thomas-Slayter and Rocheleau 1994; Tilly and Gurin 1990; Twine and Blee 2001; Waylen 1996; Zinn and Dill 1994.

44. Krauss 1998; Parsons and Jesilow 2000.

45. Schele and Freidel 1990.

46. Restall 1995.

47. Dunn 1995:595.

48. Snow and Benford 1992:136.

49. Sociologist Randall Collins (1975:60) has highlighted this phenomenon as the "store of cultural devices" that movement members use "for invoking emotional solidarity."

50. Noonan 1995; Waylen 1996. For a general discussion of Marxism and feminism see Chinchilla 1991.

51. Waylen 1994:334.

52. Prindeville and Gomez 1999.

53. Berkovitch 1999.

54. Neuhouser 1998.

55. McAdam, McCarthy, and Zald 1966.

56. McAdam, Tarrow, and Tilly 2001.

57. Friedman 1998.

58. Naples 2002a:207.

59. Naples 2002a.

60. Naples 2002a:209.

61. Neuhouser 1998:349.

62. Alpert and Elliott 1995.

63. Urry 1990.

64. Nelson 1999.

65. Brysk 1996:46.

66. Little 2000.

67. Annis 1988.

68. Ibarra 1991; Corradi, Fagen, and Garreton 1992.

69. Opp and Roehl 1990.

70. Coser 1956:34.

71. Brysk (1994b) refers to a similar movement in Argentina as seeking accountability.

72. Rosenthal et al. 1985.

73. Granovetter 1973.

74. Ibid.

75. Ibid:1367.

76. Katz and Lazarsfeld 1955; Rogers 1962.

77. Korte and Milgram 1970.

78. Rosenthal et al. 1985.

79. Coser 1956:76.

80. American Friends Service Committee 1992; Gabriel 1994; Hale 1994; Lobo and Talbot 2001; Morris 1992; Resource Center for Nonviolence 1992.

81. Coser 1956:34.

82. Friedman and McAdam 1992; Opp and Roehl 1990; Polletta and Jasper 2001.

83. This is the case in most social movements. See DeNardo 1985; Opp and Roehl 1990; Taylor 1989.

84. Once again, these mechanisms are to be found in most social movements. See Opp and Roehl 1990; Zald and McCarthy 1980.

85. Krauss 1998:130.

86. Krauss 1998:134.

87. Parsons and Jesilow 2001.

88. Naples (2002a) has coined the term "activist mothering" to describe and document such a process.

89. Naples 2002b:233.

90. Naples 2002a:209.

91. It is not unusual for organizers to use a collective identity in this fashion. See Benford 1993; Gamson 1988; Gellner 1964; Jasper 1997; Snow et al. 1986; Tarrow 1994.

92. Edelman 1999; O'Leary 1997.

93. Jonas 1998.

CHAPTER SIX

1. Hipsher 1996, 1998.

2. Gunther and Higley 1992; Hipsher 1996.

3. Loveman 1991.

4. Gunther and Higley 1992; Hipsher 1996, 1998; Lievesley 1999; Weingast 1997.

5. Jonas 1998.

6. Freed 1991.

7. Wilkinson 1995.

8. Baranyi 1995; Jonas 2000b.

9. Jonas 2000b.

10. Chuchryk 1994; Foweraker 1995; Friedman 1998; Jaquette 1991, 1994a,b; Waylen 1994.

11. Waylen 1994.

12. Chuchryk 1994; Waylen 1994.

13. Jonas 1998; Warren 1998.

14. Nelson 1999.

15. Arrecis 2005.

16. Crocker 1999; Ensalaco 1994; Hayner 2001; Ratner 1998; Ross 1999; Schiff 1998.

17. Crocker 1999; Stanley 2002.

18. Hayner 1994, 2001; Ross 1999.

19. Hayner 1994, 2001.

20. Center for Civil and Human Rights 1993; Ensalaco 1994; Hayner 2001.

21. Ensalaco 1994; Hayner 1994, 2001.

22. Hayner 2001; Jonas 2000b; McSherry 1998; Ross 1999.

23. Ross 1999.

24. Ibid.

25. Commission for Historical Clarification 1998: prologue.

26. Brett 2002.

27. REMHI 1999; Ross 1999.

28. REMHI 1999:3.

29. REMHI 1999:xxiii; from the speech by Monsignor Juan Gerardi on the occasion of the presentation of the REMHI report.

30. Soyinka 1999; *National Catholic Reporter* 1998.

31. REMHI 1999:xxxiii.

32. REMHI 1999.

33. Cassel 1998:596.

34. Ibid.

35. Cassel 1998.

36. Cassel 1998; *Christian Century* 1998; *Economist* 1998a,b; *Time* 1998.

37. *Christian Century* 1998; *Economist* 1999; Kintner 1998; *NACLA Report on the Americas* 1999; REMHI 1999.

38. *America* 2000a,b; *Christian Century* 2000; Jeffrey 2000.

39. Jeffrey 2000.

40. Jeffrey 2001a,b,c; Mejia and McSherry 2001.

41. Jeffrey 2001a,b,c; Mejia and McSherry 2001.

42. Jeffrey 2001a:8.

43. Jeffrey 2001b:15.

44. Jeffrey 2001a:8.

45. Ibid.

46. Mejia and McSherry 2001.

47. Burt 1998; Cassel 1998; *Economist* 1998b.

48. Jeffrey 2000.

49. *Economist* 2002; Jeffrey 2002; Mejia 2002; Mejia and McSherry 2001; Roberts 2002; Seils 2002.

50. Erlick 2001.

51. McLaughlin 2002.

52. Gilbert 2002; Mejia and McSherry 2001.

53. Angelina Snodgrass Godoy (2002:661) defines *lynchings* "as incidents of physical violence committed by large numbers of private citizens against one or more individuals accused of having committed a 'criminal' offense, whether or not this violence resulted in the death of the victim(s)."

54. *Economist* 2001; Elton 2000; Erlick 2001; Feldman 2001; Gilbert 2002; Godoy 2002; Smith 2001.

55. Godoy 2002:651.

56. *Economist* 2001, 2002; Elton 2000; Erlick 2001; Feldman 2001; Gilbert 2002; Godoy 2002; Smith 2001.

57. Gonzalez 2003.
58. Godoy 2002:655.
59. Guardian Newspapers 2003.
60. In general see Edelman 1999; Polletta and Jasper 2001.

CHAPTER SEVEN

1. U.S. Department of State 2005. This document also supplies information on the criminal justice system and human rights practices in Guatemala.
2. Hammergren 2002.
3. Weingast 1997:245.
4. Weingast 1997:246.
5. Smyth 2000:4.
6. Bohman 2003.
7. Jonas 1998, 2000; Mejia 1999.
8. Weingast 1997:246.
9. Lehoucq 2002.
10. Lagos 1997.
11. Alpert and Elliott 1995.
12. Allen 1980; Chambliss 1974; Durkheim 1933; Taylor, Walton, and Young 1973; Weber 1998.
13. Beccaria 1983; Bonger 1969; Chambliss 1973, 1974; Marx and Engels 1964; Quinney 1974, 1977; Smith 1986; Taylor, Walton, and Young 1973.
14. Kamenka 1980.
15. Benson 1981; Hahn 1971; Sarat 1977; Walker and Richardson 1974.
16. On involvement and inclusion see Albrecht and Green 1977; Benson 1981; Sampson and Bartusch 1998. On approval see Brown and Coulter 1983; Chackerian and Barrett 1973.
17. Paternoster et al. 1997; Tyler 1990, 1997, 2001.
18. Bayley and Mendelsohn 1969; Decker 1981; Gallagher et al. 2001; Hahn 1971; President's Commission on Law Enforcement and Administration of Justice 1967; Scaglion and Condon 1980; Stephens 1996; Thurman and Reisig 1996; Tyler 2004, 2005; Wycoff 1988.
19. Chevigny 1969; Mastrofski, Snipes, and Supina 1996; White, Cox, and Basehart 1991.
20. Kamenka 1980.
21. Thibaut and Walker 1975; Tyler 1988.
22. Engel 2005; Kamenka 1980.
23. Tyler 1990.

APPENDIX

1. Afflitto 1993.
2. Cantril 1965.

3. Downey, Silver, and Wortman 1990; Silver, Boone, and Stones 1983; Silver and Wortman 1980; Tait and Silver 1989; Wortman and Silver 1987, 1989.

4. Abad Gómez 1986; ACAFADE 1988; Guarino and Liwski 1983; Maggi and Domínguez 1984; Weinstein 1984; Weinstein et al. 1987.

5. Cantril 1965; Janoff-Bulman 1989a, 1989b.

6. Cantril 1965; Schwab et al. 1979.

7. Cervantes et al. 1989; Derogatis 1983; Padilla et al. 1988.

8. Armenian 1986; Breslau and Davis 1987; Hobfoll et al. 1991; Hourani et al. 1986; Solomon et al. 1990.

9. Tait and Silver 1989; Taylor 1983.

10. Mancini 1986.

11. Downey, Silver, and Wortman 1990; Tait and Silver 1989.

12. Abad Gómez 1986; Maggi and Domínguez 1984; Weinstein 1984; Weinstein et al. 1987.

13. O'Reilly 1988; Thoits 1986; Vachon and Stylianos 1988.

14. Pennebaker and Susman 1988; Pennebaker et al. 1990.

15. McCubbin et al. 1976.

16. Tait and Silver 1989.

17. Ibid.

18. Cantril 1965.

19. Bumiller 1988.

20. The opening section of the interview schedule, which came after the researcher's introduction and explanation of respondent rights and elicitation of verbal consent, concerned psychoemotional symptoms. These data were elicited with the same measures utilized for these items in Questionnaire A (Cervantes, Salgado de Snyder, and Padilla 1989; Derogatis 1983; Padilla, Cervantes, Maldonado, and García 1988) and are not analyzed in this study.

21. *Crónica* 1996:17.

22. Guatemala Human Rights Commission/USA 1995.

23. See for example Abad Gómez 1986; Corradi 1982–1983, 1985; Maggi and Domínguez 1984; Pelento and Braun de Dunayevich 1990; Ricón 1990; Weinstein 1984; Weinstein et al. 1987.

24. ACAFADE 1989, 1990a; Americas Watch 1985; Amnesty International 1981; Peralta and Edgardo 1971; Peralta and Imery 1981; Simon 1987.

25. Carmack 1988; Falla 1994; Manz 1988.

26. ACAFADE 1988, 1990b.

27. Kirk and Miller 1986.

28. Ibid.

REFERENCES

ACAFADE. See Central American Association of Family Members of Detained-Disappeared.

Afflitto, F. M. 1993. *A Qualitative Social Ecological Analysis of Living as a Family Member of Disappeared Persons in Guatemala, 1990–1992*. Master's thesis, Program in Social Ecology, University of California, Irvine.

———. 2000. "The Homogenizing Effects of State-Sponsored Terrorism: The Case of Guatemala." In *Death Squad: The Anthropology of State Terror*, edited by J. A. Sluka and A. Jeffrey, 114–126. University of Pennsylvania Press.

Albrecht, S. L., and Green, M. 1977. "Attitudes Toward the Police and the Larger Attitude Complex: Implications for Police-community Relationships." *Criminology* 15:67–86.

Allen, R. E. 1980. *Socrates and Legal Obligation*. Minneapolis: University of Minnesota Press.

Alpert, A., and J. Elliott. 1995. "Maquila Menace: Guatemalan Women Defy Their Brutal Bosses." *Dollars and Sense* 202:28–31.

Alvarez, S. 1990. *Engendering Democracy in Brazil: Women's Movements in Transition Politics*. Princeton, NJ: Princeton University Press.

America. 2000a. "Guatemalan Judge Commits Three Army Officers to Trial." America 182 (20): 4.

———. 2000b. "Guatemalan Police Arrest Four, Issue Warrant for Priest." *America* 182 (4): 4.

American Friends Service Committee. 1992. *Indigenous Land Rights Reader: 500 Years of Resistance*. Philadelphia, PA: American Friends Service Committee.

Americas Watch. 1985. *Guatemala: The Group for Mutual Support, 1984–1985*. New York: Americas Watch.

Amnesty International. 1981. *"Disappearances," A Workbook*. New York: Amnesty International USA.

———. 1988. "Unionists Targeted at Bottling Plant." *Amnesty International Newsletter*, April, 4, 8.

———. 1989a. "Again, the Death Squads." *Amnesty Action*, March/April, 1, 3.

———. 1989b. *Guatemala violaciones de los derechos humanos durante el gobierno civil* [Guatemala human rights violations during civilian rule]. London: Amnesty International.

Annis, S. 1988. "Story from a Peaceful Town: San Antonio Aguas Calientes." In *Harvest of Violence: The Maya Indians and the Guatemalan Crisis*, edited by R. Carmack, 155–173. Norman: University of Oklahoma Press.

Arditti, R. 1999. *Searching for Life: The Grandmothers of the Plaza de Mayo and the Disappeared Children of Argentina*. Berkeley: University of California Press.

Argentine National Commission on the Disappeared. 1986. *Nunca Más: The Report*. New York: Farrar, Straus, Giroux.

Armenian, H. K. 1986. "In Wartime: Options for Epidemiology." *American Journal of Epidemiology* 124:28–32.

Arrecis, F. G. 2005. "Ex PAC esperan pago." *Prensa Libre* (Guatemala City), October 9. www.prensalibre.com/pl/2005/octubre/09/125155.html.

Ashworth, A. 1997. "Community-Based Longitudinal Nutrition and Health Studies: Classical Examples from Guatemala, Haiti and Mexico." *European Journal of Clinical Nutrition* 51:126.

Association of Democratic Guatemalan Journalists. 1986. "The Disappeared: A Survivor's Story." *Guatemala* 6 (1): 3.

Baranyi, S. 1995. *The Challenge in Guatemala: Verifying Human Rights, Strengthening National Institutions, and Enhancing an Integrated U.N. Approach to Peace*. London: Centre for the Study of Global Governance, London School of Economics.

Barry, T. 1992. *Inside Guatemala*. Albuquerque, NM: Inter-Hemispheric Education Resources Center.

Bayard de Volo, L. 2001. *Mothers of Heroes and Martyrs*. Baltimore, MD: John Hopkins University Press.

Bayley, D. H., and H. Mendelsohn. 1969. *Minorities and the Police: Confrontation in America*. New York, NY: Free Press.

Beccaria, C. 1983. *An Essay on Crimes and Punishments*. Brookline Village, MA: Branden Press.

Becker, H. S. 1960. "Notes on the Concept of Commitment." *American Journal of Sociology* 66:32–40.

Benford R. D. 1993. " 'You Could Be the Hundredth Monkey': Collective Action Frames and Vocabularies of Motive Within the Nuclear Disarmament Movement." *Sociological Quarterly* 34:195–216.

Benford, R. D., and S. A. Hunt. 1992. "Dramaturgy and Social Movements: the Social Construction and Communication of Power." *Sociological Inquiry* 62:36–55.

Benson, P. R. 1981. "Political Alienation and Public Satisfaction with Police Services." *Pacific Sociological Review* 24:45–64.

Berger, S. A. 1992. *Political and Agrarian Development in Guatemala*. Boulder, CO: Westview Press.

Berkovitch, N. 1999. *From Motherhood to Citizenship: Women's Rights and International Organizations*. Baltimore, MD: Johns Hopkins University Press.

Bernstein, D., M. Lilly, and W. Patterson. 1991. "Gramajo Faces Two Suits for Human Rights Abuses." *Report on Guatemala* 12 (3): 4–5, 13.

Blee, K. M., ed. 1998. *No Middle Ground: Women and Radical Protest*. New York: New York University Press.

Bohman, J. 2003. "Reflexive Public Deliberation: Democracy and the Limits Of Pluralism." *Philosophy and Social Criticism* 29:85–105.

Bonger, W. A. 1969. *Criminality and Economic Conditions*. Bloomington: Indiana University Press.

Bookman, A., and S. Morgen, eds. 1988. *Women and the Politics of Empowerment*. Philadelphia: Temple University Press.

Boston Globe. 1996. "The CIA Link to Torture Hailed in Guatemala," June 30.

Bowlby, J. 1979. *The Making and Breaking of Affectional Bonds*. London: Tavistock.

———. 1980. *Attachment and Loss*, vol. 3: *Loss, Sadness, and Depression*. New York: Basic Books.

Bozzolo, R. C. 1986. "Counter-Transferential Aspects in the Assistance to the Relatives of Missing People." In *Efectos psicológicos de la represión política* [Psychological effects of political repression], edited by D. R. Kordon, L. I. Edelman, D. M. Lagos, E. Nicoletti, R. C. Bozzolo, D. Siaky, M. L'Hoste, O. Bonano, and D. Kersner. Buenos Aires: Sudamericana/Planeta.

Breslau, N., and G. C. Davis. 1987. "Posttraumatic Stress Disorder: the Etiologic Specificity of Wartime Stressors." *American Journal of Psychiatry* 144:578–583.

Brett, E. T. 2002. "The U.S. Catholic Press on Guatemala." *Journal of Church and State* 44:115–134.

Brown, K., and P. B. Coulter. 1983. "Subjective and Objective Measures of Police Service Delivery." *Public Administration Review* 43:50–8.

Brysk, A. 1994a. "Acting Globally: The Indian Rights and International Politics in Latin America." In *Indigenous Peoples and Democracy in Latin America*, edited by D. L. Van Cott, 29–54. Washington, DC: St. Martin's Press and Inter-American Dialogue.

———. 1994b. *The Politics of Human Rights in Argentina*. Stanford, CA: Stanford University Press.

———. 1996. "Turning Weakness into Strength: the Internationalization of Indian Rights." *Latin American Perspectives* 23 (2): 38–57.

———. 2000. *From Tribal Village to Global Village: Indian Rights and International Relations in Latin America*. Stanford, CA: Stanford University Press.

Buchanan, P. G. 1987. "The Varied Faces of Domination: State Terror, Economic Policy, and Social Rupture During the Argentine 'Proceso,' 1976–81." *American Journal of Political Science* 31:336–382.

Bumiller, K. 1988. *The Civil Rights Society*. Baltimore, MD: Johns Hopkins University Press.

Burt, J-M. 1998. "Impunity and the Murder of Monsignor Gerardi." *NACLA Report on the Americas* 31 (6): 5.

———. 1999. "Time for a U.S. Truth Commission." *NACLA Report on the Americas* 32 (6): 5.

Bustos, J. G. 1980. "Mythology About Women, with Special Reference to Chile." In *Sex and Class in Latin America*, edited by J. Nash and H. I. Safa, 30–45. Brooklyn, NY: J. F. Bergin.

Bystydzienski, J. M., ed. 1992. *Women Transforming Politics: Worldwide Strategies for Empowerment*. Bloomington: Indiana University Press.

Bystydzienski, J. M., and J. Sekhon, eds. 1999. *Democratization and Women's Grassroots Movements*. Bloomington: Indiana University Press.

Caldeira, T. P. de Rio. 1990. "Women, Daily Life and Politics." In *Women and Social Change in Latin America*, edited by E. Jelin, 47–78. London: Zed Books.

Calhoun, C. 1991. "The Problem of Identity in Collective Action." In *Macro-Micro Linkages in Sociology*, edited by Joan Huber, 51–75. Newbury Park, CA: Sage.

Cantril, H. 1965. *The Pattern of Human Concerns*. New Brunswick, NJ: Rutgers University Press.

Carden, M. L. 1978. "The Proliferation of a Social Movement: Ideology and Individual Incentives in the Contemporary Feminist Movement." In *Research in Social Movements, Conflict, and Change*, vol. 1, edited by L. Kriesberg, 179–196. Greenwich, CT: JAI.

Carlsen, R. S. 1996. "Social Organization and Disorganization in Santiago Atitlan, Guatemala." *Ethnology* 35:141–160.

Carmack, R. M., ed. 1988. *Harvest of Violence: The Maya Indians and the Guatemalan Crisis*. Norman: University of Oklahoma Press.

Cassel, D. W. Jr. 1998. "Murder with Impunity." *Christian Century* 115 (18): 596–597.

Casterline, J. E., L. H. Allen, and M. T. Ruel. 1997. "Vitamin B-12 Deficiency Is Very Prevalent in Lactating Guatemalan Women and Their Infants at Three Months Postpartum." *Journal of Nutrition* 127:1966–1975.

Castillo, O. R. 1989. *Para que no cayera la esperanza* [So that hope would not fail]. Tegucigalpa, Honduras: Editorial Guaymuras.

Center for Civil and Human Rights. 1993. *Report of the Chilean National Commission on Truth and Reconciliation*, vol. 1. Notre Dame, IN: Center for Civil and Human Rights, Notre Dame Law School.

Central American Association of Family Members of Detained-Disappeared (ACAFADE). 1988. *La práctica de la desaparición forzada de personas en Guatemala* [The practice of the forced disappearance of persons in Guatemala]. San José, Costa Rica: ACAFADE.

———. 1989. *Desaparecidos en Centroamérica* [Disappeared persons in Central America]. San José: ACAFADE.

———. 1990a. *Desaparecidos en Centroamérica 1990* [*Disappeared persons in Central America 1990*]. San José: ACAFADE.

———. 1990b. *Florecerás Guatemala* [You will flower, Guatemala]. San José: ACAFADE.

Cerulo, K. A. 1997. "Identity Construction: New Issues, New Directions." *Annual Review of Sociology* 23:385–409.

Cervantes, R. C., V. N. Salgado de Snyder, and A. M. Padilla. 1989. "Post-traumatic Stress in Immigrants from Central America and Mexico." *Hospital and Community Psychiatry* 40:615–619.

Chackerian, R., and R. E. Barrett. 1973. "Police Professionalism and Citizen Evaluation." *Urban Affairs Quarterly* 8:345–349.

Chambliss, W. J. 1973. *The Law of Vagrancy*. Andover, MA: Warner Modular Publications.

———. 1974. *Functional and Conflict Theories of Crime*. New York: MSS Modular Publications.

Chevigny, P. 1969. *Police Power: Police Abuses in New York City*. New York: Pantheon.

Chinchilla, N. S. 1991. "Marxism, Feminism, and the Struggle for Democracy in Latin America." *Gender and Society* 5:291–310.

Christian Century. 1998. "Bishop's Murder Remains Unsolved," 115 (November 11): 1050.

———. 2000. "Priest Charged Again in Bishop's Death," 117 (April 12): 420.

Chuchryk, P. 1989. "Subversive Mothers: The Women's Opposition to the Military Regime in Chile." In *Women, the State, and Development*, edited by S. E. Charlton, J. Everett, and K. Staudt, 130–151. Albany, NY: SUNY Press.

———. 1994. "Feminist Anti-Authoritarian Politics: The Role of Women's Organizations in the Chilean Transition to Democracy." In *The Women's Movement in Latin America: Participation and Democracy*, edited by J. S. Jaquette, 65–108. Boulder, CO: Westview Press.

Ciencia y Tecnología para Guatemala. 1991. *El estado de seguridad nacional* [The national security state]. 1991. Mexico City: Ciencia y Tecnología para Guatemala.

Cohen J. 1985. "Strategy or Identity: New Theoretical Paradigms and Contemporary Social Movements." *Social Research* 52: 663–716.

Collins, R. 1975. *Conflict Sociology: Toward an Explanatory Science*. New York: Academic Press.

Commission for Historical Clarification (CEH). 1998. *Guatemala, Memory of Silence = Tz'inil Na'tab'al*. Report. Guatemala City: CEH.

Continental Operative Secretariat. 1992. *Continental Campaign: 500 Years of Indigenous, Black, and Grassroots Resistance*. Managua, Nicaragua: Continental Operative Secretariat.

Corradi, J. 1982–1983. "The Mode of Destruction: Terror in Argentina." *Telos* 54 (Winter): 61–76.

Corradi, J. E., P. W. Fagen, and M. A. Garreton, eds. 1992. *Fear at the Edge: State Terror and Resistance in Latin America*. Berkeley: University of California Press.

Coser, L. 1956. *Functions of Social Conflict*. New York: Free Press.

Crocker, D. A. 1999. "Reckoning with Past Wrongs: A Normative Framework." *Ethics and International Affairs* 13:43–64.

Curet, L. B., A. Foster-Rosales, R. Hale, E. Kestler, C. Medina, L. Altamirano,

C. Reyes, and D. Jarquin. 2003. "FIGO Save the Mothers Initiative: the Central America and USA Collaboration." *International Journal of Gynecology and Obstetrics* 80:213–221.

Davis, S. H., and J. Hodson. 1982. *Witnesses to Political Violence in Guatemala: The Suppression of a Rural Development Movement*. Boston: Oxfam America.

de Onis, M., C. Monteiro, J. Akre, and G. Glugstone. 1993. "The Worldwide Magnitude of Protein-energy Malnutrition: An Overview from the WHO Global Database on Child Growth." *Bulletin of the World Health Organization* 71:703–712.

Decker, S. H. 1981. "Citizen Attitudes Toward the Police: A Review of Past Findings and Suggestions for Future Policy." *Journal of Police Science and Administration* 9:80–87.

DeNardo, J. 1985. *Power in Numbers: The Political Strategy of Protest and Rebellion*. Princeton, NJ: Princeton University Press.

Denzin, N. 1989. *The Research Act: A Theoretical Introduction to Sociological Methods*. 3d ed. Englewood Cliffs, NJ: Prentice-Hall.

Derogatis, L. R. 1983. *The Brief Symptom Inventory: Administration, Scoring, and Procedures Manual-II*. Towson, MD: Clinical Psychometric Research.

Dosal, P. J. 1993. *Doing Business with the Dictators: A Political History of United Fruit in Guatemala, 1899–1944*. Wilmington, DE: SR Books.

Downey, G., R. C. Silver, and C. B. Wortman. 1990. "Reconsidering the Attribution-Adjustment Relation Following a Major Negative Event: Coping with the Loss of a Child." *Journal of Personality and Social Psychology* 59:925–940.

Doyle, K. 1997. "The Art of the Coup: A Paper Trail of Covert Actions in Guatemala." *NACLA Report on the Americas* 31 (2): 34–39.

Dunn, A. E. 1995. "A Cry at Daybreak: Death, Disease, and Defence of Community in a Highland Ixil-Mayan Village." *Ethnohistory* 42:595–606.

Durkheim, E. 1933. *The Division of Labor in Society*. New York: Free Press.

Economist. 1998a. "Baloodunnit? Guatemala." September 12, 37.

———. 1998b. "A Bishop Dead." May 2, 33–34.

———. 1999. "Guatemala: Pending Justice." March 13, 46.

———. 2001. " 'Be Careful, Very Careful'; Justice in Guatemala." June 23, 4.

———. 2002. "Law, or Force; Human Rights in Guatemala." May 11, 36.

Edelman, M. 1999. *Peasants Against Globalization: Rural Social Movements in Costa Rica*. Stanford, CA: Stanford University Press.

Elton, C. 2000. "Guatemala's Lynch-Mob Justice." *Christian Science Monitor*, December 1.

Engel, R. S. 2005. "Citizens' Perceptions of Distributive and Procedural Injustice During Traffic Stops with Police." *Journal of Research in Crime and Delinquency* 42:445–481.

Ensalaco, M. 1994. "Truth Commissions for Chile and El Salvador: A Report and Assessment." *Human Rights Quarterly* 16:656–675.

Erlick, J. C. 2001. "The Sorrows of Peace in Guatemala." *World Policy Journal* 18 (2): 65–70.

Escobar, A., and S. E. Alvarez. 1992. *The Making of Social Movements in Latin America: Identity, Strategy, and Democracy.* Boulder, CO: Westview Press.

Falcoff, M. 1999. "Why We Were in Central America." *Commentary* 107 (5): 42.

Falla, R. 1994. *Massacres in the Jungle: Ixcán, Guatemala, 1975–1982.* Boulder, CO: Westview Press.

Fantasia, R. 1988. *Cultures of Solidarity.* Berkeley: University of California Press.

Feldman, A. 1991. *Formations of Violence: The Narrative of the Body and Political Terror in Northern Ireland.* Chicago: University of Chicago Press.

Feldman, M. 2001. "Mob Justice in Guatemala." *NACLA Report on the Americas* 34 (5): 1.

Felstiner, W. L. F., R. L. Abel, and A. Sarat. 1980–1981. "The Emergence and Transformation of Dispute: Naming, Blaming, and Claiming." *Law and Society Review* 15, no. 3/4:631–654.

Fireman, B., and W. A. Gamson. 1979. "Utilitarian Logic in the Resource Mobilization Perspective." In *The Dynamics of Social Movements*, edited by M. N. Zald and J. D. McCarthy, 8–45. Cambridge, MA: Winthrop.

Fisher, J. 1989. *Mothers of the Disappeared.* Boston, MA: South End Press.

———. 1993. *Out of the Shadows: Women, Resistance, and Politics in South America.* London: Latin American Bureau.

Foucault, M. 1979. *Discipline and Punish: The Birth of the Prison.* New York: Vintage Books.

Foweraker, J. 1995. *Theorizing Social Movements.* London: Pluto Press.

Freed, K. 1991. "Cracking the 'Culture of Death.'" *Los Angeles Times*, September 19.

Freud, S. 1999. *The Interpretation of Dreams.* Translated by Joyce Crick, with introduction and notes by Ritchie Robertson. New York: Oxford University Press.

———. 2005. *On Murder, Mourning, and Melancholia.* Translated by Shaun Whiteside, with introduction by Maud Ellmann. London: Penguin Books.

Friedman, D., and D. McAdam. 1992. "Collective Identity and Activism: Networks, Choices and the Life of a Social Movement." In *Frontiers in Social Movement Theory*, edited by A. Morris and C. M. Mueller, 156–173. New Haven, CT: Yale University Press.

Friedman, E. J. 1998. "Paradoxes of Gendered Political Opportunity in the Venezuelan Transition to Democracy." *Latin American Research Review* 33 (3): 87–135.

Gabriel, J. 1994. "Initiating a Movement: Indigenous, Black, and Grassroots Struggles in the Americas." *Race and Class* 35 (3): 1–17.

Galeano, E. 1969. *Guatemala: Occupied Country.* New York: Monthly Review Press.

Gallagher, C., E. Maguire, S. Mastrofski, and R. Reisig. 2001. *The Public Image of the Police.* Alexandria, VA: International Association of Chiefs of Police.

Gamson, W. A. 1988. "Political Discourse and Collective Action." *International Social Movement Research* 1:219–244.

———. 1992. *Talking Politics.* New York: Cambridge University Press.

Gellner, E. 1964. *Thought and Change.* London: Weidenfeld and Nicolson.

Gilbert, R. B. 2002. "Guatemala's Violent Peace." *America* 186 (10): 7.

Gillick, S. S. 1994. "Life and Labor in a Banana Enclave: Bananeros, the United Fruit Company, and the Limits of Trade Unionism in Guatemala, 1906 to 1931." Ph.D. dissertation, Tulane University.

Gleijeses, P. 1991. *Shattered Hope: The Guatemalan Revolution and the United States, 1944–1954.* Princeton, NJ: Princeton University Press.

Godoy, A. S. 2002. "Lynchings and the Democratization of Terror in Postwar Guatemala: Implications for Human Rights." *Human Rights Quarterly* 24:640–661.

Gonzalez, D. 2003. "Former Dictator to Seek Guatemalan Presidency." *New York Times,* August 1.

Gould, J. 1994. "El café, el trabajo, y la comunidad indígena de Matagalpa, 1880–1925." In *Tierra, café y sociedad: Ensayos sobre la historia agraria centroamericana* [Land, coffee, and society: Essays on Central American agrarian history], edited by H. Pérez Brignoli and M. Samper, 279–376. San José, Costa Rica: Programa Costa Rica, FLACSO.

Granovetter, M. S. 1973. "The Strength of Weak Ties." *American Journal of Sociology* 78:1360–1380.

Green, L. 1999. *Fear as a Way of Life: Mayan Widows in Rural Guatemala.* New York: Columbia University Press.

Grieb, K. J. 1979. *Guatemalan Caudillo, The Regime of Jorge Ubico: Guatemala, 1931–1944.* Athens, OH: Ohio University Press.

Guardian Newspapers. 2003. "Murdered with Impunity, the Street Children Who Live and Die Like Vermin." May 28. At http://www.buzzle.com/editorials/5-28-2003-40914.asp.

Guarino, M., and N. Liwski. 1983. *Hijos de desaparecidos: Secuelas del abandono forzado* [Children of the disappeared: Sequelae of forced abandonment]. Buenos Aires: Ediciones del Movimiento Ecuménico por los Derechos Humanos.

Guatemala Human Rights Commission, USA. 1995. Bulletin 13, no. 3–4. Washington, DC: Guatemala Human Rights Commission.

Guatemala News and Information Bureau. 1986. *¡Guatemala! Última Hora* 7 (5). Berkeley, CA.

Gunther, R., and J. Higley, eds. 1992. *Elites and Democratic Consolidation in Latin America and Southern Europe.* Cambridge, England: Cambridge University Press.

Hahn, H. 1971. "Ghetto Assessments of Police Protection and Authority." *Law and Society Review* 6:183–194.

Hale, C. R. 1994. "Between Che Guevara and the Pachamama: Mestizos, Indians and Identity Politics in the Anti-Quicentenary Campaign." *Critical Anthropology* 14 (1): 9–39.

Hamilton, M. E. 1924. *The Policewoman: Her Service and Ideals*. New York: F. A. Stokes.

Hammergren, L. 2002. "Do Judicial Councils Further Judicial Reform? Lessons from Latin America." Carnegie Paper No. 28, June. Rule of Law Series, Democracy and Rule of Law Project. Washington, DC: Carnegie Endowment for International Peace. http://www.carnegieendowment .org/publications/index.cfm?fa=view&id=1015&proj=zdrl.

Handy, J. 1984. *Gift of the Devil: A History of Guatemala*. Toronto: Between the Lines.

———. 1990. "The Corporate Community, Campesino Organizations, and Agrarian Reform: 1950–1954." In *Guatemalan Indians and the State: 1540–1988*, edited by C. A. Smith, 163–182. Austin: University of Texas Press.

———. 1994. *Revolution in the Countryside: Rural Conflict and Agrarian Reform in Guatemala, 1944–1954*. Chapel Hill: University of North Carolina Press.

Harbury, J. 1997. *Searching for Everardo: A Story of Love, War, and the CIA in Guatemala*. New York: Warner Books.

Hardin, R. 1982. *Collective Action*. Baltimore: Johns Hopkins University Press.

Hardy-Fanta, C. 1993. *Latina Politics, Latino Politics: Gender, Culture, and Political Participation in Boston*. Philadelphia: Temple University Press.

Harris, J., and P. Jesilow. 2000. "It's Not the Old Ball Game: Three Strikes and the Courtroom Workgroup." *Justice Quarterly* 17:185–203.

Hayner, P. B. 1994. "Fifteen Truth Commissions—1974 to 1994: A Comparative Study." *Human Rights Quarterly* 16:597–655.

———. 2001. *Unspeakable Truths: Confronting State Terror and Atrocity*. New York: Routledge.

Heuveline, P., and N. Goldman. 2000. "A Description of Child Illness and Treatment Behavior in Guatemala." *Social Science and Medicine* 50: 345–364.

Hipsher, P. L. 1996. "Democratization and the Decline of Urban Social Movements in Chile and Spain." *Comparative Politics* 28:273–297.

———. 1998. "Democratic Transitions and Social Movement Outcomes: The Chilean Shantytown Dwellers' Movement in Comparative Perspective." In *From Contention to Democracy*, edited by M. G. Giugni, D. McAdam, and C. Tilly, 149–168. Oxford, England: Rowman and Littlefield.

Hobfoll, S. E., C. D. Spielberger, S. Breznitz, C. Figley, S. Folkman, B. Lepper-Green, D. Meichenbaum, N. A. Milgram, I. Sandler, I. Sarason, and B. van der Kolk. 1991. "War-Related Stress: Addressing the Stress of War and Other Traumatic Events." *American Psychologist* 46:848–855.

Hourani, L. L., H. Armenian, H. Zurayk, and L. Afifi. 1986. "A Population-Based Survey of Loss and Psychological Stress During War." *Social Science and Medicine* 23:269–275.

Hunt, S. A., R. D. Benford, and D. A. Snow. 1994. "Identity Fields: Framing Processes and the Social Construction of Movement Identities." In *New Social Movements: From Ideology to Identity*, edited by E. Laraña, H. Johnston, and J. R. Gusfield. Philadelphia: Temple University Press.

Ibarra, F. C. 1991. *El recurso del miedo: Ensayo sobre estado y terror en Guatemala* [The recourse of fear: Essay on the state and terror in Guatemala]. San José, Costa Rica: Editorial Universitaria Centroamericana (EDUCA), Serie Investigaciones.

Immerman, R. H. 1982. *The CIA in Guatemala: The Foreign Policy of Intervention.* Austin: University of Texas Press.

InterPress Service/Weekly News Update. 1999. "Guatemalan Church Faults Government Inquiry." *NACLA Report on the Americas* 32 (4): 1. http://www.nacla.org/art_display.php?art=556.

Janoff-Bulman, R. 1989a. "Assumptive Worlds and the Stress of Traumatic Events: Applications of the Schema Construct." *Social Cognition* 7: 113–136.

———. 1989b. "The Benefits of Illusions, the Threat of Disillusionment, and the Limitations of Inaccuracy." *Journal of Social and Clinical Psychology* 8:158–175.

———. 1992. *Shattered Assumptions: Towards a New Psychology of Trauma.* New York: Free Press.

Jaquette, J. S., ed. 1991. *The Women's Movement in Latin America: Feminism and the Transition to Democracy.* Boulder, CO: Westview Press.

———, ed. 1994a. *The Women's Movement in Latin America: Participation and Democracy.* 2d ed. Boulder, CO: Westview Press.

———. 1994b. "Women's Movements and the Challenge of Democratic Politics in Latin America." *Social Politics* 1:335–340.

———. 2001. "Regional Differences and Contrasting Views." *Journal of Democracy* 12 (3): 111–125.

Jasper, J. M. 1997. *The Art of Moral Protest.* Chicago: University of Chicago Press.

Jeffrey, P. 2000. "New Gerardi Report Termed Inadequate." *National Catholic Reporter* 37 (3).

———. 2001a. "Justice in Guatemala." *Christian Century* 118 (19): 8.

———. 2001b. "Observers at Bishop's Murder Trial See Assault on Military." *National Catholic Reporter* 37 (28): 15.

———. 2001c. "Testimony Implicates Military in Bishop's Murder." *National Catholic Reporter* 37 (2): 12.

———. 2002. "Five Years Later, No Peace in Guatemala." *Christian Century* 119 (9): 14.

Jenness, V. 1993. *Making It Work: The Prostitute's Rights Movement in Perspective.* New York: Aldine de Gruyter.

Johnston H., E. Laraña, and J. R. Gusfield. 1994. "Identities, Grievances, and the New Social Movements." In *New Social Movements: From Ideology to Identity,* edited by E. Laraña, H. Johnston, and J. R. Gusfield, 185–208. Philadelphia: Temple University Press.

Jonas, S. 1991. *The Battle for Guatemala: Rebels, Death Squads, and U.S. Power.* Boulder, CO: Westview Press.

———. 1996. "Dangerous Liaisons: The U.S. in Guatemala." *Foreign Policy* 103:144–160.

———. 1998. "Can Peace Bring Democracy or Social Justice? The Case of Guatemala." *Social Justice* 25 (4): 40–74.

———. 2000a. "Democratization Through Peace: The Difficult Case of Guatemala." *Journal of Interamerican Studies and World Affairs* 42 (4): 9–38.

———. 2000b. *Of Centaurs and Doves: Guatemala's Peace Process.* Boulder, CO: Westview Press.

Kaimowitz, D. 1996. "Guatemala: Linaje y Racismo." *Latin American Research Review* 31:201–210.

Kamenka, E. 1980. "What Is Justice?" In *Justice,* edited by E. Kamenka and A. E. Tay, 1–24. New York: St. Martin's Press.

Kaplan, T. 1997. *Crazy for Democracy: Women in Grassroots Movements.* New York: Routledge.

Katz, E., and P. Lazarsfeld. 1955. *Personal Influence.* New York: Free Press.

Keck, M. E., and K. Sikkink. 1998. *Activists Beyond Borders: Advocacy Networks in International Politics.* Ithaca, NY: Cornell University Press.

Kintner, M. W. 1998. "Bishop's Death Probe Broadens, Entangles Military, Fellow Priest." *National Catholic Reporter* 34 (37): 10.

Kirk, J., and M. Miller. 1986. *Reliability and Validity in Qualitative Research.* Newbury Park, CA: Sage.

Klandermans, B. 1997. *The Social Psychology of Protest.* Cambridge, MA: Blackwell.

Klandermans, B., and D. Oegema. 1987. "Potentials, Networks, Motivations and Barriers: Steps Towards Participation in Social Movements." *American Sociological Review* 52:519–531.

Klandermans, B., and S. Tarrow. 1988. "Mobilization into Social Movements: Synthesizing European and American Approaches." In *International Social Movement Research,* edited by B. Klandermans, H. Kriesi, and S. Tarrow, 1–38. Greenwich, CT: JAI Press.

Kordon, D. R., L. I. Edelman, D. M. Lagos, E. Nicoletti, R. C. Bozzolo, D. Siaky, M. L'Hoste, O. Bonano, and D. Kersner, eds. 1986. *Efectos psicológicos de la represión política* [Psychological effects of political repression]. Buenos Aires: Sudamericana/Planeta.

Kornbluh, P. 1997. "Licensed to Kill." *Nation,* June 16, 5.

Korte, C., and S. Milgram. 1970. "Acquaintance Networks between Racial Groups." *Journal of Personality and Social Psychology* 15:101–108.

Krauss, C. 1998. "Toxic Waste Protests and the Politicization of White, Working-Class Women." In *Community Activism and Feminist Politics: Organizing Across Race, Class, and Gender,* edited by N. A. Naples. London: Routledge.

Kurzman, C. 1996. "Structural Opportunity and Perceived Opportunity in Social-Movement Theory: The Iranian Revolution of 1979." *American Sociological Review* 61:153–170.

LaBarge, R. A. 1960. *Impact of the United Fruit Company on the Economic Development of Guatemala: 1946–1954.* New Orleans: Middle American Research Institute, Tulane University.

Ladd-Taylor, M. 1994. *Mother-Work: Women, Child Welfare, and the State, 1890–1930*. Urbana: University of Illinois Press.

Lagos, M. 1997. "Latin America's Smiling Mask." *Journal of Democracy* 8 (3): 125–138.

Lancaster, R. N. 1992. *Life Is Hard: Machismo, Danger, and the Intimacy of Power in Nicaragua*. Berkeley: University of California Press.

Leary, M. R., D. S. Wheeler, and T. B. Jenkins. 1986. "Aspects of Identity and Behavioral Preference: Studies of Occupational and Recreational Choice." *Social Psychology Quarterly* 49:11–18.

Lee, R. M. 1995. *Dangerous Fieldwork*. Beverly Hills: Sage.

Lehoucq, F. 2002. "The 1999 Elections in Guatemala." *Electoral Studies* 21:107–114.

Lievesley, G. 1999. *Democracy in Latin America: Mobilization, Power, and the Search for a New Politics*. Manchester, England: Manchester University Press.

Lira, E., E. Weinstein, R. Domínguez, J. Kovalskys, A. Maggi, A. Morales, and F. Pollarolo, eds. 1984. *Psicoterapia y represión política* [Psychotherapy and political repression]. Mexico City: Siglo Veintiuno.

Little, W. E. 2000. "Home as a Place of Exhibition and Performance: Mayan Household Transformations in Guatemala." *Ethnology* 39 (2): 163–164.

Lobo, S., and S. Talbot, compilers. 2001. *Native American Voices: A Reader*. Upper Saddle River, NJ: Prentice Hall.

Lopez, D., and Y. Espiritu. 1990. "Panethnicity in the United States: A Theoretical Framework." *Ethnic and Racial Studies* 13:198–224.

Lord, J. H. 1987. "Survivor Grief Following a Drunk-Driving Crash." *Death Studies* 11:413–435.

Lovell, W. G., and C. H. Lutz. 1996. " 'A Dark Obverse': Maya Survival in Guatemala, 1520–1994." *Geographical Review* 86:398–407.

Loveman, B. 1991. "Mision Cumplida? Civil Military Relations and the Chilean Political Transition." *Journal of Interamerican Studies and World Affairs* 33 (3): 35–74.

Maggi, A., and R. Domínguez. 1984. "Reflexiones sobre psicoterapia con hijos de detenidos-desaparecidos" [Reflections on psychotherapy with children of the detained-disappeared]. In *Psicoterapia y represión política*, edited by E. Lira et al. Mexico City: Siglo Veintiuno.

Mancini, M. E. 1986. "Creating and Therapeutically Utilizing Anticipatory Grief in Survivors of Sudden Death." In *Loss and Anticipatory Grief*, edited by T. A. Rando. Lexington, MA: D. C. Heath.

Manz, B. 1988. *Refugees of a Hidden War: The Aftermath of Counterinsurgency in Guatemala*. Albany, NY: State University of New York Press.

Martín-Baró, I. 1988. *Acción e ideología: Psicología social desde Centroamérica* [Action and ideology: Social psychology from Central America]. San Salvador, El Salvador: UCA Editores.

———. 1989. "Political Violence and War as Causes of Psychosocial Trauma in El Salvador." *International Journal of Mental Health* 18 (1): 3–20.

Marx, K., and F. Engels. 1964. *The Communist Manifesto*. New York: Washington Square Press.

Mastrofski, S. D., J. B. Snipes, and A. E. Supina. 1996. "Compliance on Demand: the Public's Response to Specific Police Requests." *Journal of Research in Crime and Delinquency* 33:269–305.

McAdam, D. 1982. *Political Process and the Development of Black Insurgency, 1930–1970.* Chicago: University of Chicago Press.

McAdam, D., J. D. McCarthy, and M. N. Zald, eds. 1966. *Comparative Perspectives on Social Movements: Political Opportunities, Mobilizing Structures, and Cultural Framings.* Cambridge, England: Cambridge University Press.

McAdam, D., and R. Paulsen. 1993. "Specifying the Relationship Between Social Ties and Activism." *American Journal of Sociology* 99: 640–667.

McAdam, D., S. Tarrow, and C. Tilly. 2001. *Dynamics of Contention.* Cambridge, England: Cambridge University Press.

McCarthy, J. D., and M. N. Zald. 1973. *The Trend of Social Movements in America: Professionalization and Resource Mobilization.* Morristown, NJ: General Learning Press.

———. 1977. "Resource Mobilization and Social Movements: A Partial Theory." *American Journal of Sociology* 82:1212–1241.

McClintock, M. 1985. *The American Connection.* Vol. 2: *State Terror and Popular Resistance in Guatemala.* London: Zed Books.

McCreery, D. 1983a. "Debt Servitude in Rural Guatemala, 1876–1936." *Hispanic American Historical Review* 6: 735–759.

———. 1983b. *Development and the State in Reforma Guatemala, 1871–1885.* Athens, OH: Ohio University, Center for International Studies.

———. 1986. " 'An Odious Feudalism:' Mandamiento Labor and Commercial Agriculture in Guatemala, 1858–1920." *Latin American Perspectives* 13:99–117.

———. 1994a. "El impacto del café en las tierras de las comunidades indígenas: Guatemala, 1870–1930." In *Tierra, café y sociedad: Ensayos sobre la historia agraria centroamericana,* edited by H. Pérez Brignoli and M. Samper, 227–278. San José, Costa Rica: Programa Costa Rica, FLACSO.

———. 1994b. *Rural Guatemala, 1760–1940.* Stanford, CA: Stanford University Press.

McCubbin, H. I., B. B. Dahl, G. R. Lester, D. Benson, and M. L. Robertson. 1976. "Coping Repertoires of Families Adapting to Prolonged War-Induced Separations." *Journal of Marriage and the Family* 38:461–471.

McCubbin, H. I., B. B. Dahl, P. J. Metres, E. J. Hunter, and J. A. Plag, eds. 1974. *Family Separation and Reunion: Families of Prisoners of War and Servicemen Missing in Action.* San Diego, CA: Center for Prisoner of War Studies, Naval Health Research Center.

McLaughlin, C. 2002. "Guatemala: Never Again." *Race and Class* 44 (1): 135–137.

McSherry, J. P. 1989–1990. "Nun's Torture in Guatemala Shows Spiraling Violence." *In These Times* 14 (7): 16.

———. 1998. "The Emergence of 'Guardian Democracy.'" *NACLA Report on the Americas* 32 (3): 16–25.

Mejia, R. M. 1999. "Guatemala's Tenuous Peace." *NACLA Report on the Americas* 33 (1): 4–5.

———. 2002. "Another Human Rights Worker Murdered in Guatemala." *NACLA Report on the Americas* 36 (1): 2–3.

Mejia, R. M., and J. P. McSherry. 2001. "Justice in the Gerardi Case: But Terror Continues." *NACLA Report on the Americas* 35 (1): 8.

Melville, T., and M. Melville. 1975. *Tierra y poder en Guatemala* [Land and power in Guatemala]. San José, Costa Rica: Editorial Universitaria Centroamericana (EDUCA).

Menchú, R. 1984. *Me llamo Rigoberta Menchú y así me nació la conciencia* [I, Rigoberta Menchú: An Indian Woman in Guatemala]. Edited by Elisabeth Burgos-Debray, and translated by Ann Wright. London: Verso.

Meyer, D. S. 2002. "Opportunities and Identities: Bridge-Building in the Study of Social Movements." In *Social Movements: Identity, Culture and the State*, edited by D. S. Meyer, N. Whittier, and B. Robnett. New York: Oxford University Press.

Mitchell, C., M. Stohl, D. Carleton, and G. A. Lopez. 1986. "State Terrorism: Issues of Concept and Measurement." In *Government Violence and Repression: An Agenda for Research*, edited by M. Stohl and G. A. Lopez, 1–26. New York: Greenwood Press.

Moberg, M. 1996. "Crown Colony as Banana Republic: The United Fruit Company in British Honduras, 1900–1920." *Journal of Latin American Studies* 28:357–381.

Morris, K. 1992. *International Directory and Resource Guide: 500 Years of Resistance*. Oakland, CA: South and Meso-American Indian Information Center.

Mueller, E. N. 1980. "The Psychology of Political Protest and Violence." In *Handbook of Political Conflict*, edited by T. R. Gurr. New York: Free Press.

Nairn, A. 1993. "The Roots of Torture: U.S. Complicity and the Need for Change." In *Confronting the Heart of Darkness: An International Symposium on Torture in Guatemala*, edited by Shari Turitz, 4–10. Washington, DC: Guatemala Human Rights Commission, USA.

Naples, N. A., ed. 1998. *Community Activism and Feminist Politics: Organizing Across Race, Class, and Gender*. New York: Routledge.

———. 2002a. "Activist Mothering and Community Work: Fighting Oppression in Low-Income Neighborhoods." In *Child Care and Inequality: Rethinking Carework for Children and Youth*, edited by F. M. Cancian, D. Kurz, A. S. London, R. Reviere, and M. C. Touminen. London: Routledge.

———. 2002b. "Materialist Feminist Discourse Analysis and Social Movement Research: Mapping the Changing Context for 'Community Control.'" In *Social Movements: Identity, Culture, and the State*, edited by D. S. Meyer, N. Whittier, and B. Robnett. New York: Oxford University Press.

National Academy of Sciences, Committee on Human Rights, and Institute of Medicine, Committee on Health and Human Rights. 1992. *Scientists and Human Rights in Guatemala: Report of a Delegation.* Washington, DC: National Academy Press.

National Catholic Reporter. 1998. "U.S. Must Face Its Role in Guatemala's Tragic Past." 34 (15): 28.

———. 1999. "U.S. Presence Began with CIA Overthrow of Arbenz." 35 (19): 15.

National Lawyers Guild and La Raza Legal Alliance. 1979. *Guatemala: Repression and Resistance.* New York: National Lawyers Guild.

Nelson, C. W., and K. I. Taylor, with J. Kruger. 1983. *Witness to Genocide: The Present Situation of Indians in Guatemala.* London: Survival International.

Nelson, D. M. 1999. *A Finger in the Wound: Body Politics in Quincentennial Guatemala.* Berkeley: University of California Press.

Neuhouser, K. 1998. " 'If I Had Abandoned My Children': Community Mobilization and Commitment to the Identity of Mother in Northeast Brazil." *Social Forces* 77:331–358.

Nicoletti, E. 1986. "Some Reflexions [*sic*] on Clinical Work with Relatives of Missing People. A Particular Elaboration of Loss." In *Efectos psicológicos de la represión política,* edited by Kordon, et al.

Noonan, R. K. 1995. "Women Against the State: Political Opportunities and Collective Action Frames in Chile's Transition to Democracy." *Sociological Forum* 10:81–111.

Oberschall, A. 1993. *Social Movements: Ideologies, Interests, and Identities.* New Brunswick, NJ: Transaction.

Okeke-Ihejirika, P. E., and S. Franceschet. 2002. "Democratization and State Feminism: Gender Politics in Africa and Latin America." *Development and Change* 33:439–466.

O'Leary, B. 1997. "On the Nature of Nationalism: An Appraisal of Ernest Gellner's Writings on Nationalism." *British Journal of Political Science* 27:191–222.

Oliver, P. 1984. "If You Don't Do It, Nobody Else Will: Active and Token Contributions to Local Collective Action." *American Sociological Review* 49:601–610.

Olson, M. Jr. 1965. *The Logic of Collective Action: Public Goods and the Theory of Groups.* Cambridge, MA: Harvard University Press.

Opp, K.-D., and W. Roehl. 1990. "Regression, Micromobilization, and Political Protest." *Social Forces* 69:521–547.

O'Reilly, P. 1988. "Methodological Issues in Social Support and Social Network Research." *Social Science and Medicine* 26: 863–873.

Padilla, A. M., R. C. Cervantes, M. Maldonado, and R. E. García. 1988. "Coping Responses to Psychosocial Stressors among Mexican and Central American Immigrants." *Journal of Community Psychology* 16:418–427.

Painter, J. 1987. *Guatemala, False Hope, False Freedom: The Rich, the Poor, and the Christian Democrats.* London: Catholic Institute for International Relations and Latin America Bureau.

Pan American Health Organization. 2001. *Country Health Profile. Guatemala.* Washington, DC: Pan American Health Organization. http://www.paho.org/english/sha/prflgut.htm#poblacion. Accessed October 8, 2006.

Parkes, C. M. 1974. " 'Seeking' and 'Finding' a Lost Object: Evidence from Recent Studies of the Reaction to Bereavement." In *Normal and Pathological Responses to Bereavement*, by J. Ellard, V. Volkan, and N. L. Paul. New York: MSS Information Corp.

Parsons, D., and P. Jesilow. 2000. "Women in Policing: A Tale of Cultural Conformity." In *Contemporary Issues in Crime and Criminal Justice*, edited by H. Pontell and D. Schicor, 287–306. Upper Saddle River, NJ: Prentice Hall.

————. 2001. *In the Same Voice: Women and Men in Law Enforcement*. Santa Ana, CA: Seven Locks Press.

Paternoster, R., R. Bachman, R. Brame, and L. Sherman. 1997. "Do Fair Procedures Matter? The Effect of Procedural Justice on Spouse Assault." *Law and Society Review* 31:163–204.

Patrinos, H. A. 1997. "Differences in Education and Earnings Across Ethnic Groups in Guatemala." *Quarterly Review of Economics and Finance* 37:809–821.

"Peace at Last." 1997. *Maclean's*, January 13, 35.

Pennebaker, J., and J. R. Susman. 1988. "Disclosure of Traumas and Psychosomatic Processes." *Social Science and Medicine* 26:327–332.

Pennebaker, J. W., M. Colder, and L. K. Sharp. 1990. "Accelerating the Coping Process." *Journal of Personality and Social Psychology* 58:528–537.

Peralta, A., and G. Edgardo. 1971. *La violencia en Guatemala como fenómeno político* [Violence in Guatemala as a political phenomenon]. Cuaderno No. 61. Cuernavaca, Mexico: Centro Intercultural de Documentación (CIDOC).

Peralta, A. G., and R. J. Imery. 1981. *Dialéctica del terror en Guatemala* [Dialectic of terror in Guatemala]. San José, Costa Rica: EDUCA.

Perera, V. 1993. *Unfinished Conquest: The Guatemalan Tragedy*. Berkeley: University of California Press.

Pérez, M. 1990. "En Las Cárceles Clandestinas De Rios Montt" [In the clandestine jails of Rios Montt]. *Otra Guatemala* 3 (12): 32–33.

Polletta, F., and J. M. Jasper. 2001. "Collective Identity and Social Movements." *Annual Review of Sociology* 27:283–305.

President's Commission on Law Enforcement and Administration of Justice. 1967. *Task Force Report: The Police*. Washington, DC: Government Printing Office.

Prindeville, D-M. 2003. *On the Streets and in the State House: American Indian and Hispanic Women and Environmental Policymaking in New Mexico*. New York: Routledge.

Prindeville, D-M., and T. B. Gomez. 1999. "American Indian Women Leaders, Public Policy, and the Importance of Gender and Ethnic Identity." *Women and Politics* 20 (2): 17–32.

Psacharopoulos, G., and H. A. Patrinos, eds. 1994. *Indigenous People and Poverty in Latin America: An Empirical Analysis*. Washington, DC: World Bank.

Quinney, R. 1974. *Critique of Legal Order: Crime Control in Capitalist Society*. Boston: Little, Brown.

———. 1977. *Class, State, and Crime: On the Theory and Practice of Criminal Justice.* New York: D. McKay.

Rarihokwats, ed. 1982. *Guatemala! The Horror and the Hope.* York, PA: Four Arrows.

Ratner, S. R. 1998. "International Law: The Trials of Global Norms." *Foreign Policy* 110:65–80.

Recovery of Historical Memory Project (REMHI). 1999. *Guatemala: Never Again!* Maryknoll, NY: Orbis Books.

Resource Center for Nonviolence. 1992. *1492–1992: Commemorating 500 Years of Indigenous Resistance. A Community Reader.* Santa Cruz, CA: Resource Center for Nonviolence.

Restall, M. 1995. " 'He Wished It in Vain': Subordination and Resistance Among Maya Women in Post-Conquest Yucatan." *Ethnohistory* 42: 577–594.

Rivera, J. and M. T. Ruel. 1997. "Growth Retardation Starts in the First Three Months of Life among Rural Guatemalan Children." *European Journal of Clinical Nutrition* 51:92–96.

Roberts, H. 2002. "Mental Health, Truth, and Justice in Guatemala." *Lancet* 359:953.

Rocheleau, D., B. Thomas-Slayter, and E. Wangari, eds. 1996. *Feminist Political Ecology: Global Issues and Local Experiences.* London: Routledge.

Rogers, E. 1962. *Diffusion of Innovations.* New York: Free Press.

Rosenthal, N., M. Fingrutd, M. Ethier, R. Karant, and D. McDonald. 1985. "Social Movements and Network Analysis: A Case Study of Nineteenth-Century Women's Reform in New York State." *American Journal of Sociology* 90:1022–1054.

Ross, A. J. 1999. "The Body of the Truth: Truth Commissions in Guatemala and South Africa." Ph.D. dissertation, Department of Geography, University of California, Berkeley.

Royal, R. 2000. "Does Religion Hinder Heroism?" *American Enterprise* 11:32.

Sagan, C. F. 2002. "Personal Testimonies of Fourteen Indigenous Guatemalan Women." Ph.D. dissertation, Learning and Change in Human Systems, California Institute of Integral Studies.

Salimovich, S., E. Lira, and E. Weinstein. 1992. "Victims of Fear: The Social Psychology of Repression." In *Fear at the Edge: State Terror and Resistance in Latin America,* edited by J. E. Corradi, P. W. Fagen, and M. A. Garreton. Berkeley: University of California Press.

Sampson, R., and D. Bartusch. 1998. "Legal Cynicism and (Subcultural?) Tolerance of Deviance: the Neighborhood Context of Racial Differences." *Law and Society Review* 32:777–804.

Sanders, C. M. 1989. *Grief: The Mourning After Dealing with Adult Bereavement.* New York: John Wiley and Sons.

Sarat, A. 1977. "Studying American Legal Culture: an Assessment of Survey Evidence." *Law and Society Review* 11:427–488.

Scaglion, R., and R. G. Condon. 1980. "Determinants of Attitudes Toward City Police." *Criminology* 17:485–494.

Schele, L., and D. Freidel. 1990. *A Forest of Kings: The Untold Story of the Ancient Maya*. New York: Morrow.

Schiff, B. 1998. "War Crimes and Truth Commissions: Constructing International Morality and Constraining the State." Paper presented at the annual meeting of the International Studies Association, Minneapolis, MN, March.

Schlesinger, S. 1997. "The C.I.A. Censors History." *Nation*, July 14, 20–22.

Schlesinger, S., and S. Kinzer. 1999. *Bitter Fruit: the Story of the American Coup in Guatemala*. Cambridge, MA: Harvard University Press.

Schutte, G. 1991. "Racial Oppression and Social Research: Field Work Under Racial Conflict in South Africa." *Qualitative Sociology* 14 (2): 127–146.

Schwab, J. J., R. A. Bell, G. J. Warheit, and R. B. Schwab. 1979. *Social Order and Mental Health: The Florida Health Study*. New York: Brunner/ Mazel.

Seils, P. F. 2002. "Reconciliation in Guatemala: the Role of Intelligent Justice." *Race and Class* 44 (1): 33–59.

Shibutani, T. 1978. *The Derelicts of Company K: A Sociological Study of Demoralization*. Berkeley: University of California Press.

Silver, R. L., C. Boon, and M. H. Stones. 1983. "Searching for Meaning in Misfortune: Making Sense of Incest." *Journal of Social Issues* 39 (2): 81–102.

Silver, R. L., and C. Wortman. 1980. "Coping with Undesirable Life Events." In *Human Helplessness*, edited by J. Garber and M. E. P. Seligman. New York: Academic Press.

Simon, J.-M. 1987. *Guatemala: Eternal Spring—Eternal Tyranny*. New York: W. W. Norton.

Sloan, J. W. 1984. "State Repression and Enforcement Terrorism in Latin America." In *The State as Terrorist: The Dynamics of Governmental Violence and Repression*, edited by M. Stohl and G. A. Lopez, 83–98. Westport, CT: Greenwood Press.

Sluka, J. A. 1990. "Participant Observation in Violent Social Contexts." *Human Organization* 49 (2): 114–126.

———. 1995. "Domination, Resistance and Political Culture in Northern Ireland's Catholic-Nationalist Ghettoes." *Critique of Anthropology* 15: 71–102.

Smith, A. 1986. *Inquiry into the Nature and Causes of the Wealth of Nations*. Books 1–3. New York: Penguin Books.

Smith, C. A. 1984. "Local History in a Global Context: Social and Economic Transitions in Western Guatemala." *Comparative Studies in Society and History* 26: 193–228.

Smith, C. A. (with M. M. Moors), ed. 1990. *Guatemalan Indians and the State: 1540–1988*. Austin: University of Texas Press.

Smith, P. 2001. "Memory Without History: Who Owns Guatemala's Past?" *Washington Quarterly* 24 (2): 59–72.

Smyth, F. 2000. "U.S. Turns Blind Eye to Guatemala's Narco-Military." *NACLA Report on the Americas* 33 (4): 4.

Snow, D. A., and R. Benford. 1992. "Master Frames and Cycles of Protest." In *Frontiers in Social Movement Theory*, edited by A. D. Morris and C. M. Mueller, 133–155. New Haven, CT: Yale University Press.

Snow, D. A., and D. McAdam. 2000. "Identity Work Processes in the Context of Social Movements." In *Self, Identity, and Social Movements*, edited by S. Stryker, T. J. Owens, and R. White. Minneapolis: University of Minnesota Press.

Snow, D. A., E. B. Rochford Jr., S. K. Worden, and R. D. Benford. 1986. "Frame Alignment Processes, Micromobilization, and Movement Participation." *American Sociological Review* 51:464–481.

Snyder, C. R. 1989. "Reality Negotiation: From Excuses to Hope and Beyond." *Journal of Social and Clinical Psychology* 8:130–157.

Solomon, Z., M. Mikulincer, and N. Habershaim. 1990. "Life-Events, Coping Strategies, Social Resources, and Somatic Complaints Among Combat Stress Reaction Casualties." *British Journal of Medical Psychology* 63:137–148.

Soyinka, W. 1999. *The Burden of Memory, the Muse of Forgiveness*. NY: Oxford University Press.

Stanley, E. 2002. "What Next? The Aftermath of Organised Truth Telling." *Race and Class* 44 (1): 1–15.

Stephen, L. 1997. *Women and Social Movements in Latin America: Power from Below*. Austin: University of Texas Press.

Stephens, D. W. 1996. "Community Problem-oriented Policing: Measuring Impact." In *Quantifying Quality in Policing*, edited by L. T. Hoover, 95–129. Washington, DC: Police Executive Research Forum.

Stevens, E. 1973. "Machismo and Marianismo." *Science* 10:57–63.

Stroebe, M., M. M. Gergen, K. J. Gergen, and W. Stroebe. 1992. "Broken Hearts or Broken Bonds: Love and Death in Historical Perspective." *American Psychologist* 47:1205–1212.

Stryker, S., and R. T. Serpe. 1982. "Commitment, Identity Salience, and Role Behavior: Theory and Research Example." In *Personality, Roles, and Social Behavior*, edited by W. J. Ickes and E. S. Knowles. New York: Springer-Verlag.

Tait, R., and R. C. Silver. 1989. "Coming to Terms with Major Negative Life Events." In *Unintended Thought*, edited by J. S. Uleman and J. A. Bargh. New York: Guilford.

Tarrow, S. 1994. *Power in Movement. Social Movements, Collective Action, and Mass Politics in the Modern State*. Cambridge, England: Cambridge University Press.

Taylor, C. 1989. *Sources of the Self: The Making of the Modern Identity*. Cambridge, MA: Harvard University Press.

Taylor, I., P. Walton, and J. Young. 1973. *The New Criminology: for a Social Theory of Deviance*. London: Routledge and Kegan Paul.

Taylor, S. E. 1983. "Adjustment to Threatening Events Theory of Cognitive Adaptation." *American Psychologist* 38:1161–1173.

Taylor, V., and N. E. Whittier. 1992. "Collective Identity in Social Movement Communities: Lesbian Feminist Mobilization." In *Frontiers in Social Movement Theory*, edited by A. D. Morris and C. M. Mueller, 104–129. New Haven, CT: Yale University Press.

Tedeschi, T. 1997. "Natural Attractions of the Caribbean, Central America, and South America." *Audubon* 99 (6):121–133.

Tennesen, M. 1997. "Tikal Is for the Birds." *Wildlife Conservation* 100 (3): 58–60.

Thibaut, J., and L. Walker. 1975. *Procedural Justice: A Psychological Analysis.* Hillsdale, NJ: Lawrence Erlbaum Associates.

Thoits, P. 1986. "Social Support as Coping Assistance." *Journal of Consulting and Clinical Psychology* 54:416–423.

Thomas-Slayter, B. P., and D. E. Rocheleau. 1994. *Essential Connections: Linking Gender to Effective Natural Resource Management and Sustainable Development.* East Lansing, MI: Women in International Development, Michigan State University.

Thurman, Q. C., and M. D. Reisig. 1996. "Community-Oriented Research in an Era of Community Policing." *American Behavioral Scientist* 39:570–586.

Tilly, L. A., and P. Gurin, eds. 1990. *Women, Politics, and Change.* New York: Russell Sage Foundation.

Tocqueville, A. 1983. *The Old Regime and the French Revolution.* Translated by S. Gilbert. Garden City, NY: Anchor Books.

Turk, A. T. 1982. *Political Criminality: The Defiance and Defense of Authority.* Beverly Hills, CA: Sage.

Twine, F. W., and K. M. Blee. 2001. *Feminism and Antiracism: International Struggles for Justice.* New York: New York University Press.

Tyler, T. 1988. "What Is Procedural Justice?: Criteria Used by Citizens to Assess the Fairness of Legal Procedures." *Law and Society Review* 22:103–135.

———. 1990. *Why People Obey the Law.* New Haven, CT: Yale University Press.

———. 1997. "Procedural Fairness and Compliance with the Law." *Swiss Journal of Economics and Statistics* 133:219–240.

———. 2001. "Public Trust and Confidence in Legal Authorities: What Do Majority and Minority Group Members Want from Law and Legal Institutions?" *Behavioral Sciences and the Law* 19:215–235.

———. 2004. "Enhancing Police Legitimacy." *Annals of the American Academy of Political and Social Science* 593 (May): 84–99.

———. 2005. "Policing in Black and White: Ethnic Group Differences in Trust and Confidence in the Police." *Police Quarterly* 8:322–342.

Ufema, J. 2002. "Puppy Love." *Nursing* 32 (1): 22.

Urry, J. 1990. *The Tourist Gaze: Leisure and Travel in Contemporary Societies.* Newbury Park, CA: Sage.

U.S. Department of State. 1999. *Guatemala Country Report on Human Rights Practices for 1998.* Washington, DC: U.S. Department of State, Bureau of Democracy, Human Rights, and Labor. At http://www.state gov/www/global/human_rights/1998_hrp_report/guatemal.html.

———. 2005. "Country Reports on Human Rights Practices, Guatemala." http://www.state.gov/g/drl/rls/hrrpt/2005/61729.htm.

Vachon, M. L. S., and S. K. Stylianos. 1988. "The Role of Social Support in Bereavement." *Journal of Social Issues* 44:175–190.

Vidal, G. 1995. "In the Lair of the Octopus." *Nation,* June 5, 792–794.

Vigil, J. D. 1973. "Legacy of Hispanic Colonial Past: Race and Ethnic Relations in the Western Highlands of Guatemala." Master's thesis, University of California, Los Angeles.

Wagley, C. 1979. Foreword to *In Revolt Against the Dead,* by Douglass Brintnall. New York: Gordon and Breach.

Walker, N. D., and R. J. Richardson. 1974. *Public Attitudes Toward the Police.* Chapel Hill, NC: Institute for Research in Social Science.

Warren, K. B. 1998. *Indigenous Movements and Their Critics: Pan-Maya Activism in Guatemala.* Princeton, NJ: Princeton University Press.

Waylen, G. 1994. "Women and Democratization: Conceptualizing Gender Relations in Transition Politics." *World Politics* 46:327–354.

———. 1996. *Gender in Third World Politics.* Buckingham, England: Open University Press.

Weber, E. P. 1998. *Pluralism by the Rules: Conflict and Cooperation in Environmental Regulation.* Washington, DC: Georgetown University Press.

Weber, M. 1958. *The Protestant Ethic and the Spirit of Capitalism.* Translated by Talcott Parsons. New York: Scribner.

Webster, K. 1990. "Deception in Guatemala: How the U.S. Media Bought a Cover-Up." *Progressive,* February, 26–32.

Weingast, B. R. 1997. "The Political Foundations of Democracy and the Rule of Law." *American Political Science Review* 91:245–263.

Weinstein, E. 1984. "Notas acerca del tratamiento psicoterapéutico de familiares de detenidos-desaparecidos: Una propuesta alternativa" [Notes in reference to the psychotherapeutic treatment of families of the detained-disappeared: An alternative proposal]. In *Psicoterapia y represión política* [Psychotherapy and Political Repression], edited by E. Lira, E. Weinstein, R. Domínguez, J. Kovalskys, A. Maggi, E. Morales, and F. Pollarolo. Mexico City: Siglo Ventiuno.

Weinstein, E., E. Lira, M. E. Rojas, D. Becker, M. I. Castillo, A. Maggi, E. Gómez, R. Domínguez, S. Salamovich, F. Pollarolo, E. Neumann and A. Monreal, eds. 1987. *Trauma, duelo y reparación una experiencia de trabajo psicosocial en Chile.* Santiago, Chile: Fundación de Ayuda Social de las Iglesias Cristianas (FASIC), Editorial Interamericana.

Weinstein, E., A. Maggi, and E. Gómez (with R. Domínguez, E. Lira, A. Monreal, and F. Pollarolo). 1987. "El desaparecimiento como forma de represión política [Disappearance as a Form of Political Repression]." In *Una experiencia de trabajo psicosocial en Chile,* edited by E. Weinstein, E. Lira, M. E. Rojas, D. Becker, M. I. Castillo, A. Maggi, E. Gómez, R. Domínguez, S. Salamovich, F. Pollarolo, E. Neumann, and A. Monreal. Santiago, Chile: FASIC, Editorial Interamericana.

White, M. F., T. C. Cox, and J. Basehart. 1991. "Theoretical Considerations of Officer Profanity and Obscenity." In *Police Deviance,* edited by T. Barker and D. L. Carter. Cincinnati, OH: Anderson.

Whittier, Nancy. 1995. *Feminist Generations: The Persistence of the Radical Women's Movement.* Philadelphia: Temple University Press.

Whyte, W. F., ed. 1991. *Participatory Action Research.* Newbury Park, CA: Sage.

Wilkinson, D. 1995. " 'Democracy' Comes to Guatemala." *World Policy Journal* 12 (4): 71–81.

Wortman, C. B., and R. C. Silver. 1987. "Coping with Irrevocable Loss." In *Cataclysms, Crises, and Catastrophes: Psychology in Action,* edited by G. R. VandenBos and B. K. Bryant, 189–235. Washington, DC: American Psychological Association.

———. 1989. "The Myths of Coping with Loss." *Journal of Consulting and Clinical Psychology* 57:349–357.

Wycoff, M. 1988. "The Benefits of Community Policing: Evidence and Conjecture." In *Community Policing: Rhetoric or Reality,* edited by J. Green and S. Mastrofski, 103–120. New York: Praeger.

Yashar, D. J. 1997. *Demanding Democracy: Reform and Reaction in Costa Rica and Guatemala, 1870s–1950s.* Stanford, CA: Stanford University Press.

Zald, M., and J. McCarthy. 1980. "Social Movement Industries: Cooperation and Conflict Amongst Social Movement Organizations." *Research in Social Movements, Conflicts and Change* 3:1–20.

Zinn, M. B. and B. T. Dill, eds. 1994. *Women of Color in U.S. Society.* Philadelphia: Temple University Press.

INDEX